IMAGES
of America

COLLINGDALE BOROUGH

On the Cover: Members of the junior class of 1930 pose for a picture outside the Collingdale Junior High building. Automobiles were the main attraction, and rumors of drag races became common on some of the roads in Collingdale. The Collingdale Junior High building served seventh through ninth grades until the school was closed in 1982. (Courtesy of Collingdale High School Alumni Association—Ann Speer collection.)

IMAGES
of America

COLLINGDALE BOROUGH

Elizabeth MacGuire

ARCADIA
PUBLISHING

ISBN 978-0-7385-9767-6

Published by Arcadia Publishing
Charleston, South Carolina

Printed in the United States of America

Library of Congress Control Number: 2012940977

For all general information, please contact Arcadia Publishing:
Telephone 843-853-2070
Fax 843-853-0044
E-mail sales@arcadiapublishing.com
For customer service and orders:
Toll-Free 1-888-313-2665

Visit us on the Internet at www.arcadiapublishing.com

To my family and my best friend, Vicky Tuttle,
who stood by me when things got rough.

Contents

ACKNOWLEDGMENTS

A project like this requires many hands. Some hands have been unseen, but nevertheless have created an impact. Other hands are visible and have also helped bring this project to light. It is the many hands that have supported this endeavor that made this book possible. From the beginning, I've appreciated all the support given to help me bring the rich history of Collingdale to light so that others may learn from it. I truly believe that local history needs to be recorded before it is lost forever.

So it is with a humble heart that I wish to thank Tom Morse, president of the Collingdale High School Alumni Association, for opening up the alumni room for me and sharing its treasure trove of pictures and information. I also wish to especially thank David Fingerle, who introduced me to Fran McCoy, Chuck Meehan, and Frank Basil after the Memorial Day ceremony on May 30, 2011.

Local history, by its very nature, is often forgotten unless some earth-shattering event happens that puts the town in the spotlight. Like most small towns, Collingdale does have its bad moments, and times when it seems as if nothing will ever be right again. I prefer to look for positive aspects and not the negative ones. This being said, I also want to acknowledge that I could not possibly put all the information I received from various sources into this book.

I definitely wish to thank Helen Dick Deyo Moyer for her extensive information about her family, Keith Lockhart for loaning me his extensive collection of photographs, Stynor Carter, president of Collingdale Fire Company No. 1, and Fred Howell Sr. for photographs of the fire company and borough, and Donald Bird for allowing me to search through his father's collection of negatives—Joe Bird was a true historian.

Finally, I wish to thank my editors at Arcadia Publishing for being so understanding and supportive.

Introduction

Every small town has its beginning. For Collingdale, Pennsylvania, the time came on December 23, 1891, when a small group of individuals came together to incorporate the town. The story of Collingdale, however, does not begin there. It actually starts in 1699, when a baby came into the world on a farmstead near Springfield Road—that baby's name was John Bartram. Growing up on that beautiful family farm, Bartram developed a special interest in botany cultivated by the beauty he encountered. His interest in plants and flowers led him to study horticulture and discover dozens of new species.

Known as the father of American botany, Bartram's work was widely distributed around the world. When he died in September 1777, his legacy spread and influenced many future horticulturists. Among those influenced by Bartram was Maximilian LaRoche.

LaRoche was a florist by trade, having learned it from his father. He studied Bartram's papers, and knowing that some of his relatives lived in Darby, LaRoche cultivated a relationship with them. He decided, along with two of his friends, to acquire land in the area in 1882. At that time, he acquired 30 acres near John Bartram's birthplace from the Bunting and Hibberd families. In 1884, LaRoche formed the Collingdale Land Improvement Company with his friends Dr. Jacob Boon and William McCausland. The company cleared the 30 acres for sale to prospective buyers. Nine families had farms in the tiny village they decided to name Collingdale after a railroad official. Conflicting sources, however, say that the village got its name from a town in New Jersey called Collingswood; they could not name it Collingswood because it would be too confusing.

The three petitioned to annex their land from Darby when two factors made it possible to do so. The first factor was an 1890 Pennsylvania Supreme Court ruling that allowed new boroughs and townships to form from existing boroughs and townships. The second factor was the redirection of the Baltimore & Ohio (B&O) Railroad, which played a significant role in the decision. Developers saw this as a great opportunity to expand businesses in the area and began eagerly acquiring land near the railroad's path. LaRoche wanted to preserve at least one-third of his land for the cultivation of his flowers and built two greenhouses in the area. He set up his florist shop near the railroad so he could ship fresh flowers to Philadelphia and other areas using the railway post offices. At that time, having a post office showed that a community had established itself; the Collingdale post office was established in 1888.

With this information, LaRoche and the other townspeople decided to secede from Darby Borough and form their own community: Collingdale. One of the first businesses was LaRoche's florist shop. He specialized in roses and chrysanthemums.

Considered the "Father of Collingdale," LaRoche took an active part in the establishment of the new borough's government and was its first burgess. Part of his ongoing efforts ensured that the community continued its legacy of being family-friendly and responsive to its citizens' needs. For example, he built and supervised work at the Collingdale Manufacturing Company, which provided the wood for 60 houses in the borough.

The first Borough Council, established on January 10, 1892, included the usual civil organizations such as fire, police, and sanitation departments. These departments formed a basis for the growth of the community, but it was churches that sustained it. From the beginning, Collingdale churches provided spiritual, economic, and social support. This, along with the need of a good education for the community's youth, drove the community forward.

Many credit Margaret Brisbane Harris for this growth. Her undying devotion to her students showed itself daily. Starting in 1890, before the community was incorporated, Harris devoted her time and efforts to the youth of the borough. It was not easy. The first school was on the second floor of Pop Eliskey's store on the corner of Clifton and Hibberd Avenues. Classes were also held at Floral Hall on Sharon and Pusey Avenues until a schoolhouse could be built in 1894.

Many others had a hand in helping the community grow, including Harris's brother Enon M. Harris Jr., who laid out the streets of Collingdale, and Isaac "Ike" Diehl, who laid out the first sewer system. Once the new sewer system was in place, the borough was primed to grow. Electric lighting became important for the growing community, so an agreement was signed in January 1893 with Clifton Electric Light Co., making electric street lamps possible. Before the lamps were in place, most people carried lanterns and lit candles in their windows to facilitate travel during the evening hours. White painted stumps along the road reflected the light of the lanterns.

With sanitation and lighting in place, Collingdale welcomed more families. Some reasons people cited for choosing Collingdale as their new home included the established churches, rural setting, and friendly people. Others cited reasons such as the establishment of a school, ease of transportation from Darby to Philadelphia and beyond, and other community amenities.

Aside from the comforts of modern civilization, Collingdale encountered new problems such as horse thievery and robbery. The first police chief, William Fitzpatrick, took the oath of office in January 1928. Before then, the police department—like the oldest suburban enforcement agencies— ran with only one police officer. Volunteers helped to keep the peace and to ensure the laws on loose cattle and swine were enforced. Ike Diehl served as a police officer from January 8, 1912, until March 16, 1914, when he was appointed as the highway and sewer inspector. During his term in office, Diehl supervised the formation of roads and set up operations for the new sewer system.

Fire proved to be a great issue for the tiny borough, as the first church building, Collingdale Baptist Church, established on May 6, 1889, burned to the ground on October 31, 1898. It was rebuilt two years later through fundraising efforts that netted over $3,000. The fire, however, proved the need for an established fire company in the borough. Thus, a charter for the first fire company was established on October 6, 1906, which allowed the company to request volunteers and equipment for fighting fires in the borough. A second fire company was established in 1916.

Collingdale did not remain rural for long. As new families settled in and new houses were built on what was once farmland, some lamented the loss of the "country feel," while others welcomed the changes. With these changes, however, new issues arose. More children needed a place to learn.

There were also racial tensions that came about with the growth of the borough. Some of the older citizens—those who still held onto land that they acquired or inherited from the nine founding families—got upset at the changes taking place in Collingdale. Newspapers of the time noted that racial tensions were high and the sight of a white mask or cap sent ominous signals to the flourishing community. This tension is clearly seen through a set of injunctions made by the borough in July 1902. One of the injunctions concerned a "colored camp meeting" being held on land owned by Thomas Bartram on Springfield Road. The other concerned a proposal to create an African-American cemetery on the same property. Both injunctions battled for the community's attention. In the case Collingdale Borough v. The Eden Cemetery, Judge Isaac Johnson first ruled in favor of the borough, but the case was overturned in December 1902. Some citizens rejected the second court's decision and vowed to back the earlier decision favoring the borough.

It is interesting to note that two locals who had streets in Collingdale named in their honor were ardent abolitionists. John Bartram's family, for instance, helped escaped slaves to freedom as part of the Underground Railroad. Bartram Avenue is the oldest street in Collingdale, having once extended all the way to Springfield Road. The Bartram family barn, where John was born, was located on the land in question for the cemetery, which was near Springfield Road. John Blunston and John Bartram were Quakers, a group that denounced slavery. Their position developed in part because of Quaker protests in 1688 (the Germantown Protest) and 1715; Blunston participated in the latter protest.

A census taken in 1900, about nine years after the incorporation of Collingdale, showed how quickly the borough grew. According to the census, 603 people resided in homes that were built along with the growing businesses. By 1909, the community took on an almost suburban aspect with its network of rails and jitney routes. Most of the borough remained wooded areas, such as Boon Forest, named for Dr. Jacob Boon, which extended from Clifton Avenue to Chester Pike. It would not be long, however, before the community would need to grow again.

Three of the four cemeteries in Collingdale were established during the early years of the 20th century. This growth limited the amount of space available for residential and business needs. Mount Zion Methodist Meeting Cemetery, the oldest cemetery in Collingdale, was incorporated in 1808. The site of one of the first Methodist churches in America, it is now owned and being restored by the Friends of Darby Methodist Meeting Cemetery, a nonprofit corporation.

The most important thing to remember is that the tiny borough of Collingdale remained much as it was in the beginning: a family-friendly community. That meant that whenever a community member was in trouble, someone was always available to help. It is this sense of community that makes Collingdale unique.

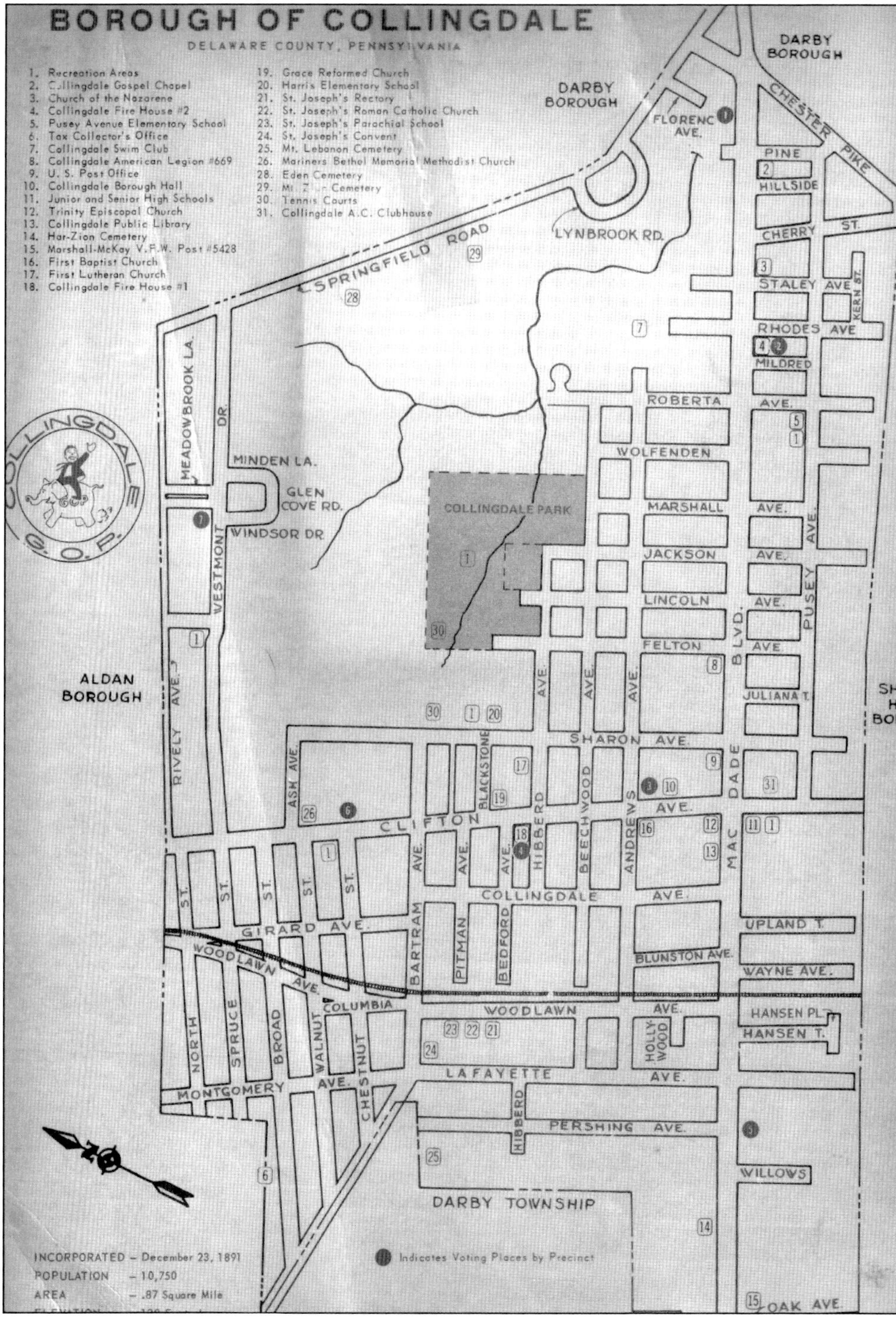

This map of Collingdale with the proposed site of Collingdale Park marked in the center was handed out by the Republican Party of Collingdale in 1972. (Courtesy of Frank Hansen Printing.)

One

Growth of a Community

Growth Spurts

Collingdale's growth did not happen overnight. A number of factors contributed to the borough's expansion, and accessibility to transportation proved to be the primary one. From the beginning, the boundaries of the borough were set by the most accessible transportation routes. Many people settled their families in Collingdale because of its convenience to major centers of industry. Its original boundaries were set in the May 1891 petition sent to the Quarter Session Court of Delaware County. The southern boundary was alongside the train route established a few years earlier by the Baltimore & Ohio (B&O) Railroad.

The original boundaries were set as Springfield Avenue and Chester Pike to the northeast, the B&O Railroad tracks to the southeast, Clifton Avenue to the southwest, and Rively Avenue to the northwest. This allocation of space proved to be too small for the growing population, so three years after Collingdale became its own entity, it annexed some adjacent land, which nearly doubled the size of the borough. With this new land purchase, the southwestern boundary moved from Clifton Avenue to Lafayette Avenue. The petition for the land purchase was drawn and an ordinance was written and approved in 1894. Two other annexations occurred, adding additional land and moving the southwestern boundary to Oak Avenue. The last ordinance was issued in 1922, adding the last .93 square mile to Collingdale's total area.

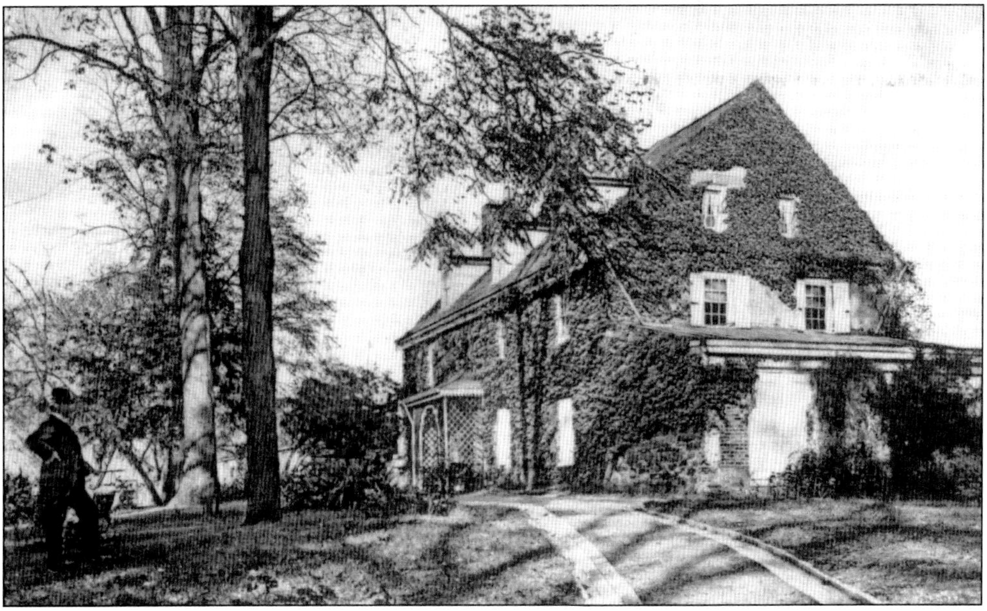

Early settlers held land grants from William Penn. Among them was John Bartram, grandfather of the famous botanist. This is the house John Bartram built in 1731 in the Kingsessing area of Philadelphia. (Courtesy of Keith Lockhart.)

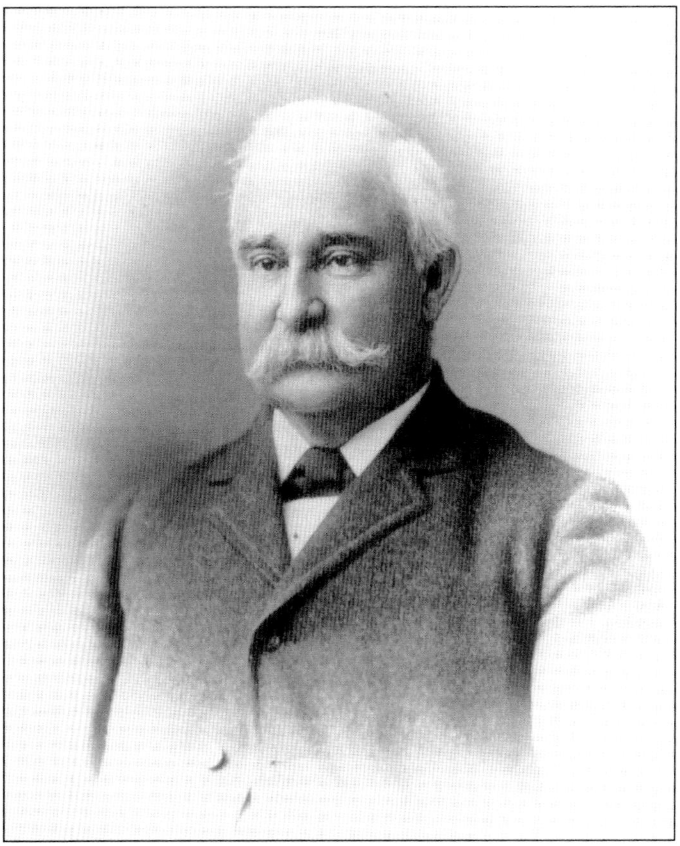

Dr. Jacob Boon, one of three partners in the Collingdale Land Improvement Company, was a prominent physician in the area who owned much of the real estate in the county. In 1885, he purchased land from Clifton Avenue east to Springfield Road from the Bunting and Hibberd families. He had a railway station named after him on the Pennsylvania Railroad, and his land was known as Boon Forest until it was developed in the early 1920s. (Courtesy of James Powers.)

Enon M. Harris Jr., pictured here in 1886 as a young man, was a surveyor by trade. He arrived in Darby in 1885 with his sister, Margaret B. Harris. He purchased land from Maximilian LaRoche for a farm on Felton Avenue. Known for his successful process for developing potash, Enon Harris was also instrumental in surveying and mapping the tiny borough's streets. Margaret B. Harris also helped with the layout. (Photograph by P.B. DeMorat; courtesy of Helen Dick Deyo Moyer.)

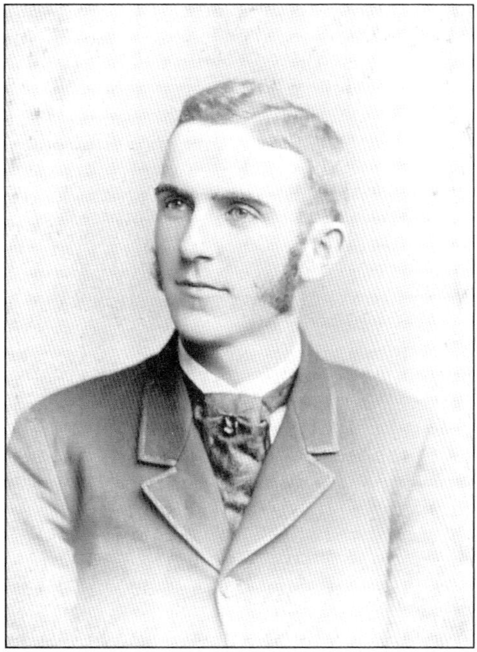

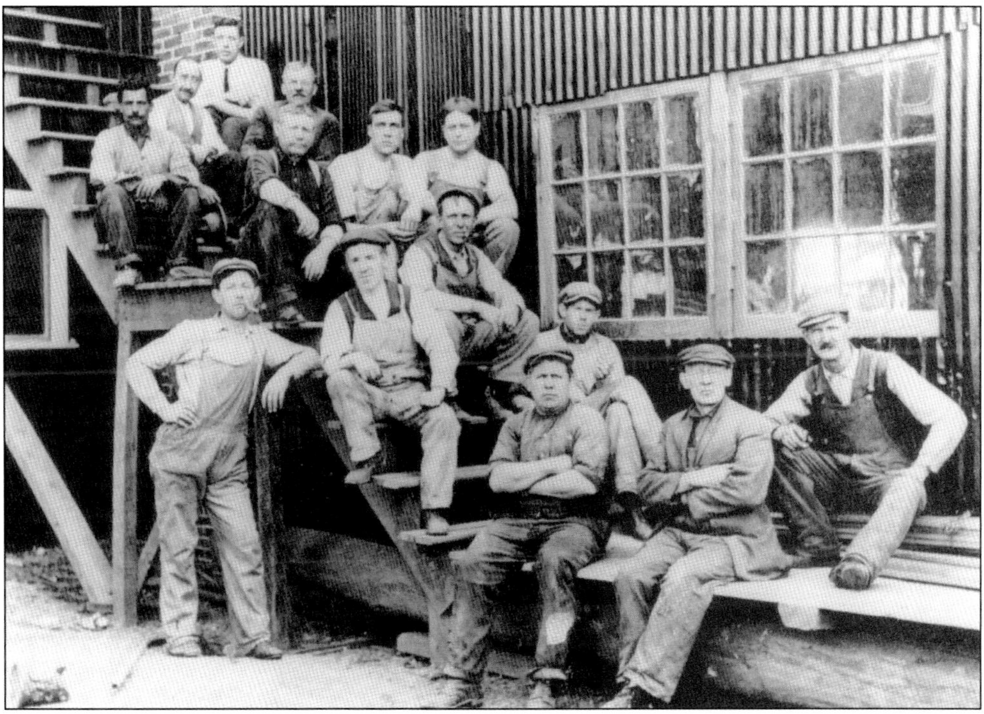

As the borough grew in size, more businesses began to line the main thoroughfare of Parker Avenue. Boon Forest soon gave rise to houses and businesses such as Collingdale Manufacturing Company, established in 1893 by Maximilian LaRoche. Soon afterward, LaRoche transferred ownership to his brother-in-law, Otto Wand. Wand ran the business until 1910, when he sold it; it was renamed Collingdale Millwork Company. In this 1910 photograph, workers take a break as they wait for an order to come in for processing. (Courtesy of Jim Powers.)

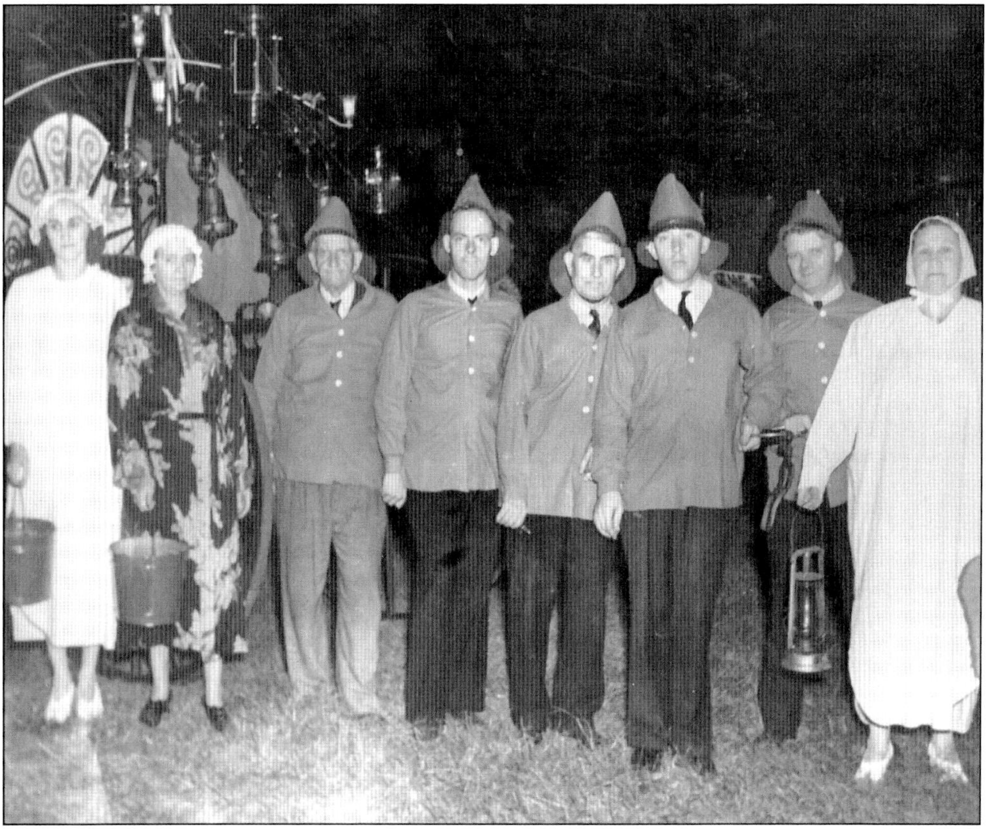

Entertainment, in the form of plays and reenactments, brought the small community together. Collingdale Fire Company No. 1 often put on shows for fundraising purposes. One such play, *The Fire Brigade*, was made into a film in 1927, which was shown in the Darby Theater. Collingdale Fire Company No. 1, along with Darby Fire Companies No. 1 and No. 2, sold tickets and realized a profit of $46.66. Reenactments, such as the one seen here, were popular during the 1920s. (Courtesy of Stynor Carter and Fred Howell Sr.)

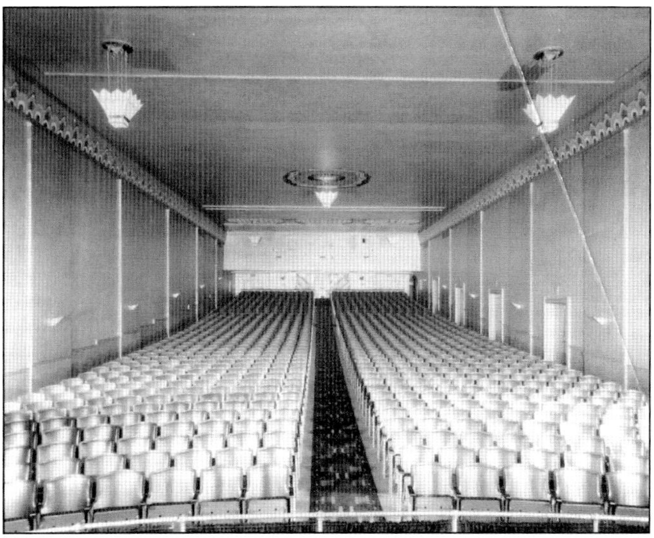

Bijou movie houses, such as the Villa Theater, provided entertainment and a place to perform. Opened in 1927, the Villa Theater sponsored many talent shows and contests. Joe Bird, Collingdale High School alumnus (1941) and historian, recalls singing with his older brother Warren on the Villa Theater stage and winning first prize in a contest there. (Courtesy of Collingdale High School Alumni Association—Irvin R. Glazer collection; photograph by William M. Rittase.)

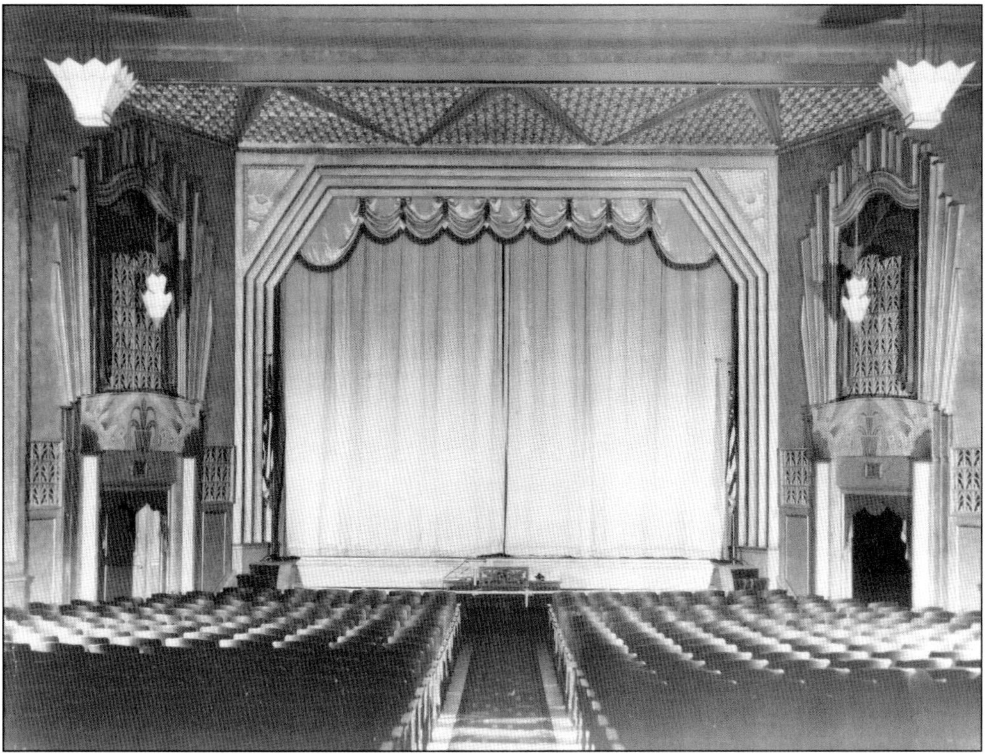

Another view of the Villa Theater shows the stage where many of the contests and talent shows occurred. For a small town like Collingdale, the Villa's rich tapestry and velour drapes made a person feel like royalty. The screen was state of the art, showing many popular movies. The Villa closed in 1930 due to debts and a badly damaged basement, but the building reopened for Collingdale High School graduations from 1930 to 1933. (Courtesy of Collingdale High School Alumni Association—Irvin R. Glazer collection; photograph by William M. Rittase.)

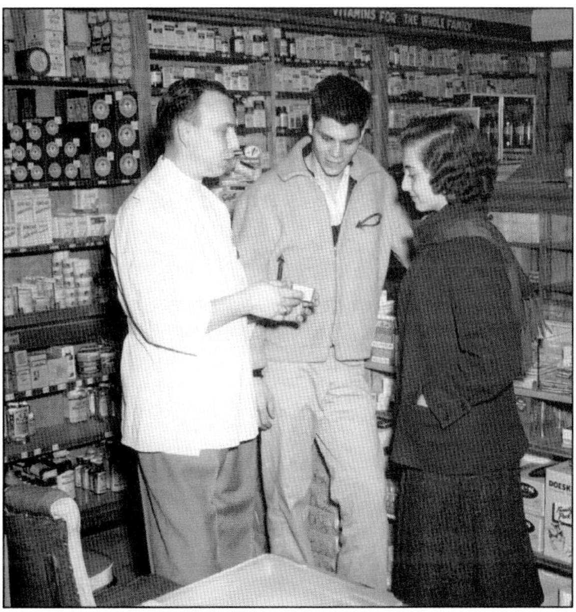

Drugstores and family markets dominated the borough's landscape in the 1910s and 1920s, before the advent of home refrigeration. Fond memories of sipping sodas at the corner drugstore, where one could get a sundae for 5¢, were too soon replaced by other remembrances. Bycer's drugstore was a popular hangout for young people. In this 1953 photograph, Phillip Bycer helps two young people decide what to purchase. (Courtesy of Collingdale High School Alumni Association—Ann Speer collection.)

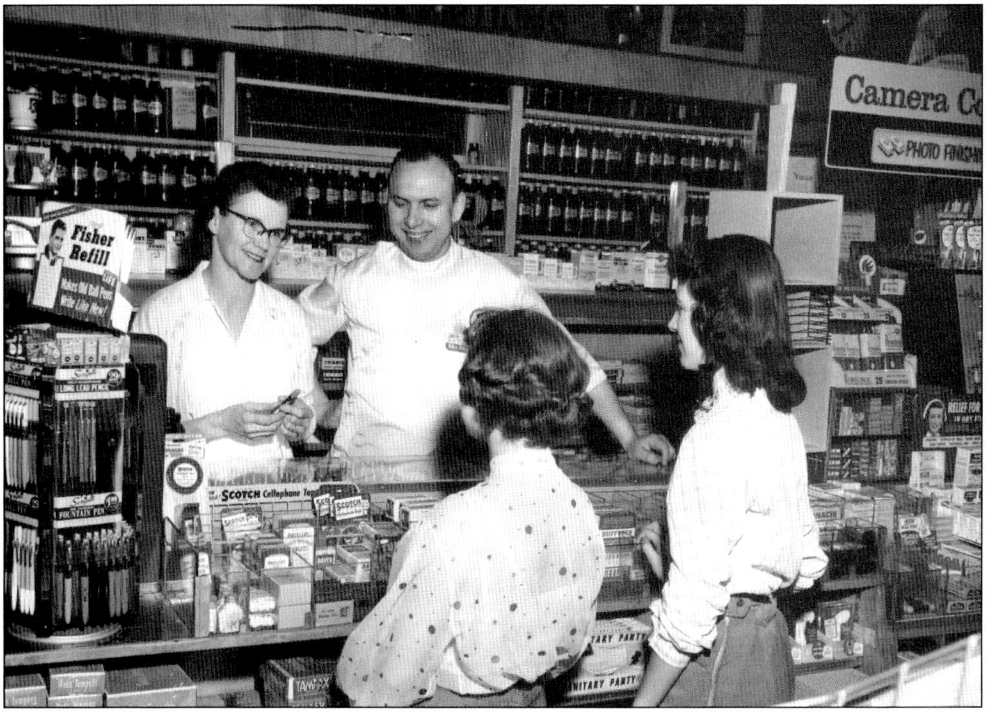

Another view of a typical drugstore in the 1950s demonstrates that drugstores carried more than just prescriptions. Gone are the marble countertops that graced the old stores, as most of them stopped preparing foods. Instead, cramped counters stuffed with odds and ends lined every space imaginable. Here, Phillip and Evelyn Bycer help two young women with their purchases. (Courtesy of Collingdale High School Alumni Association—Ann Speer collection.)

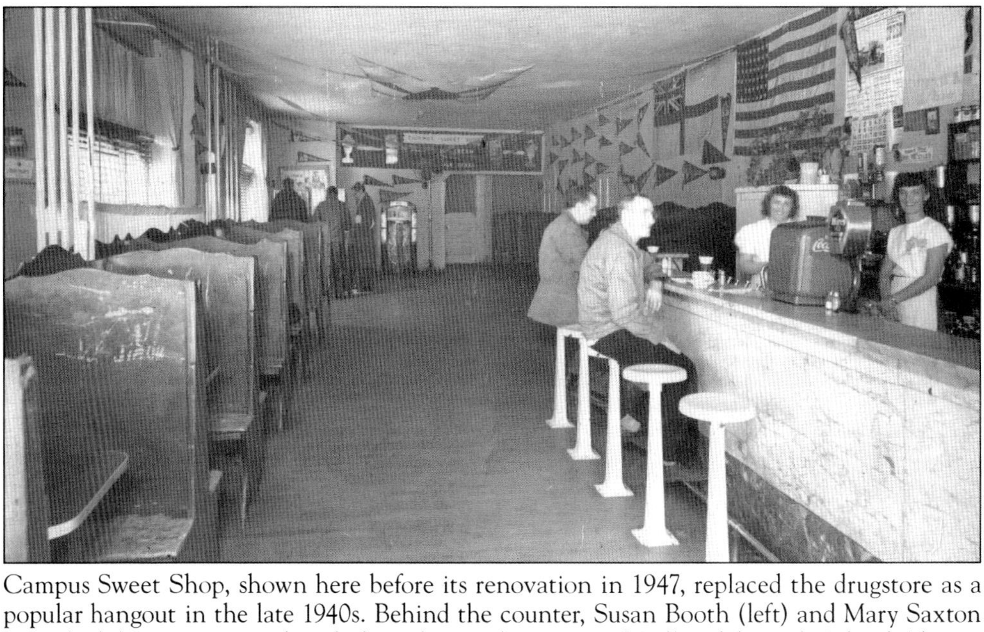

Campus Sweet Shop, shown here before its renovation in 1947, replaced the drugstore as a popular hangout in the late 1940s. Behind the counter, Susan Booth (left) and Mary Saxton West (right) serve two unidentified gentlemen. (Courtesy of Collingdale High School Alumni Association—Irvin B. Glazer collection; photograph by Jacob Stelman.)

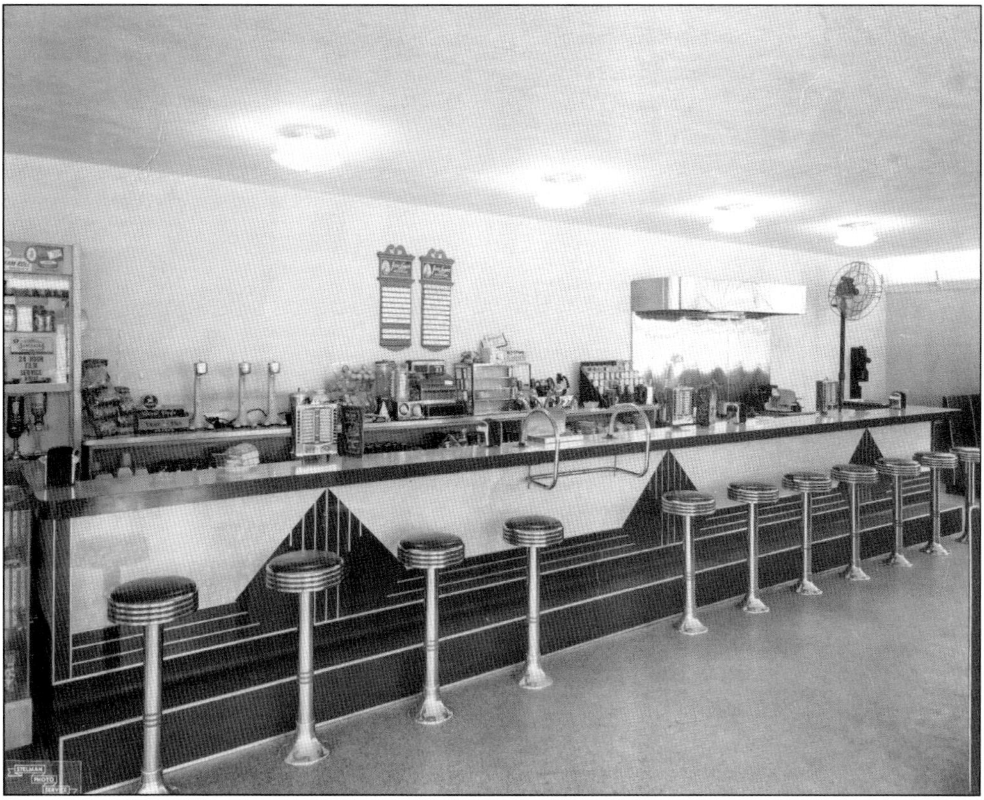

Campus Sweet Shop reopened in 1948 after an intensive renovation that improved the interior with chrome countertops and saucer-like chairs. It was renamed Sue's Sweet Shop. Delighted kids from the high school swarmed the shop after school, and it remained popular until it officially closed on June 6, 1975. (Courtesy of Collingdale High School Alumni Association—Irvin B. Glazer collection; photograph by Jacob Stelman.)

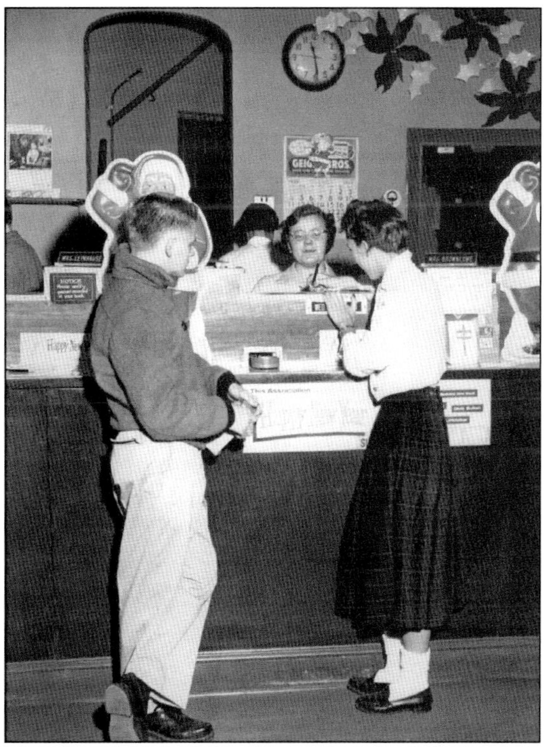

Banks and savings and loan organizations had branches in Collingdale during the 1940s and 1950s, providing another measure for growth. This December 1955 photograph shows Mrs. Brownlowe helping a young woman cash in her Christmas Club savings book; at the time, starting a Christmas Club savings book was very trendy. (Courtesy of Collingdale High School Alumni Association—Ann Speer collection.)

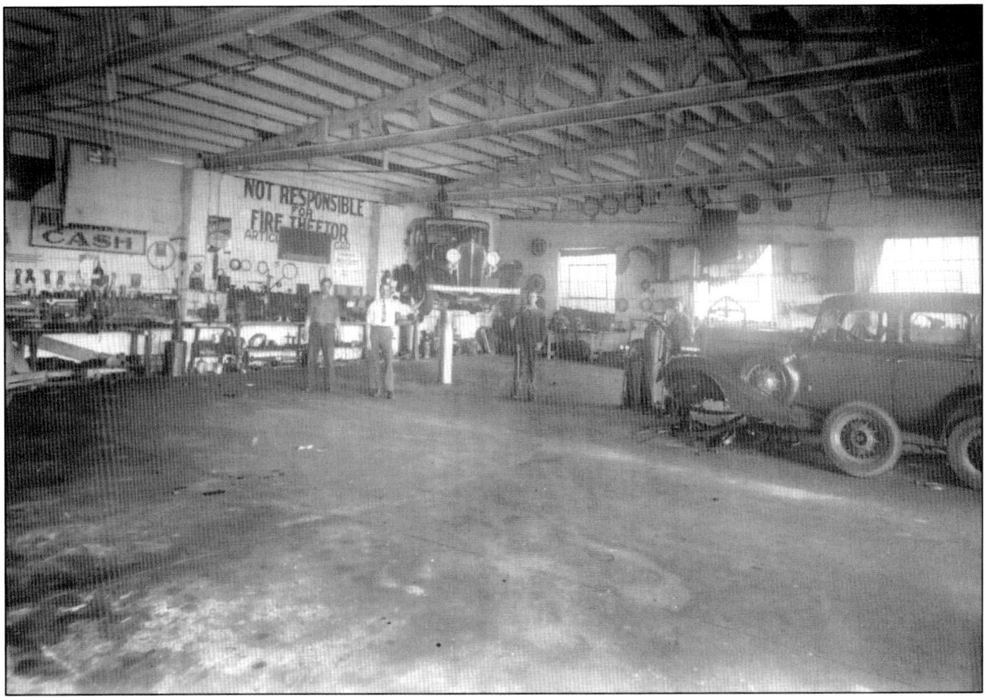

Graf Brothers automobile dealership opened its doors in the fall of 1925. This is the huge auto bay, where cars would be repaired either for sale or as part of a maintenance contract. The dealership contained three bays for auto repair and a big lot to hold used cars for sale. The corner of Rhodes and MacDade Boulevards is still home to an auto repair shop. (Courtesy of Collingdale High School Alumni Association—Joe Dinmore collection.)

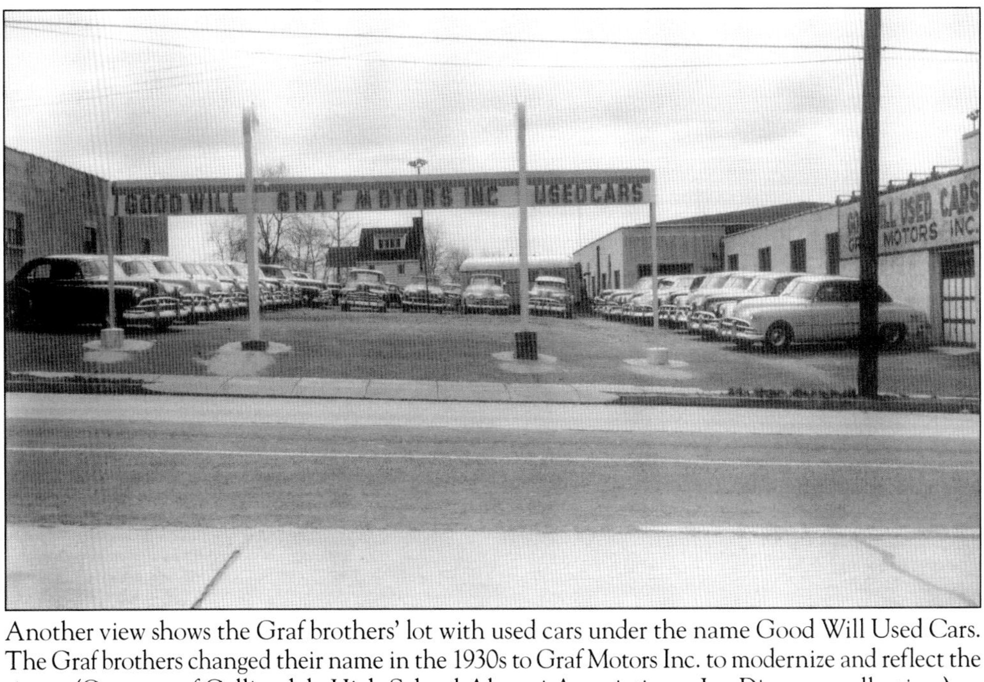

Another view shows the Graf brothers' lot with used cars under the name Good Will Used Cars. The Graf brothers changed their name in the 1930s to Graf Motors Inc. to modernize and reflect the times. (Courtesy of Collingdale High School Alumni Association—Joe Dinmore collection.)

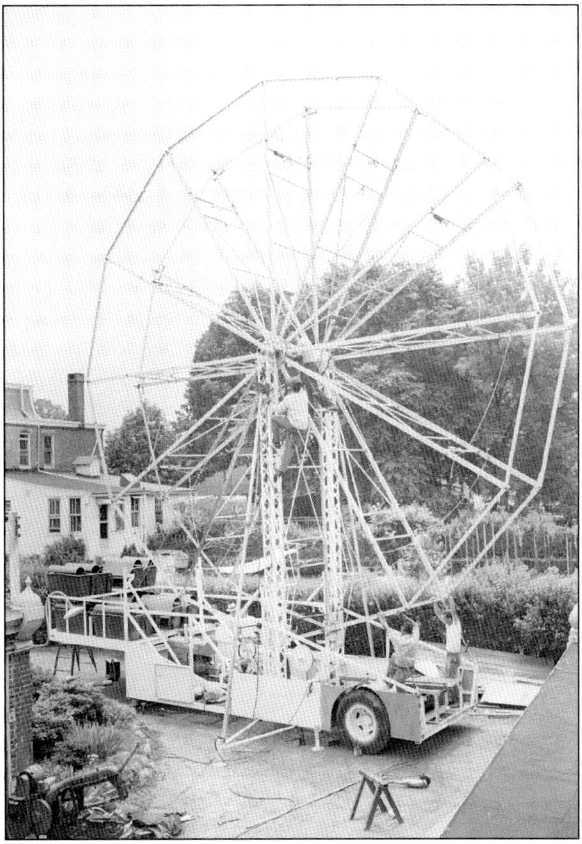

In the 1960s, Collingdale Fire Company No. 2 often held carnivals in the parking lot and field adjacent to Shaffer's auto shop. The most popular ride was the Ferris wheel, which towered over the pavement and allowed riders to see for miles around. The carnivals benefited the fire company in many ways, but by the 1990s, they became unprofitable due to a number of factors. (Courtesy of Donald Bird—Joe Bird collection.)

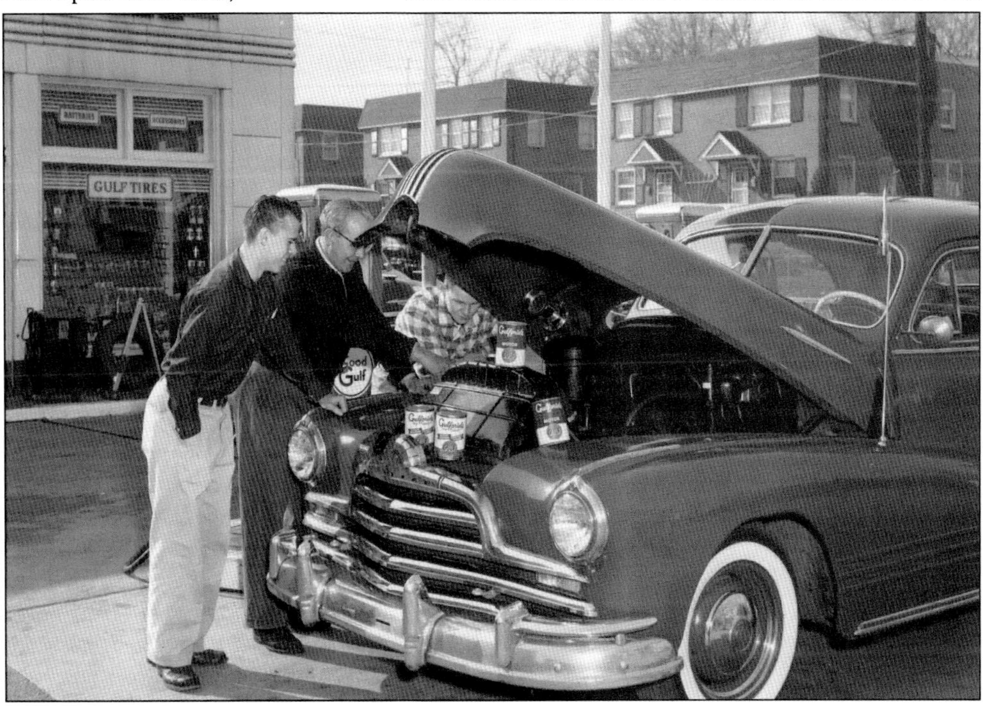

Gas stations, such as Sinclair, provided a much-needed commodity. Some became full-service stations, such as the Gulf station in this 1950s photograph. Along with automobile repair shops and dealerships, gas stations created an incentive for growth, as having those commodities available made it easier for Collingdale to remain a family-friendly community. (Courtesy of Collingdale High School Alumni Association—Ann Speer collection.)

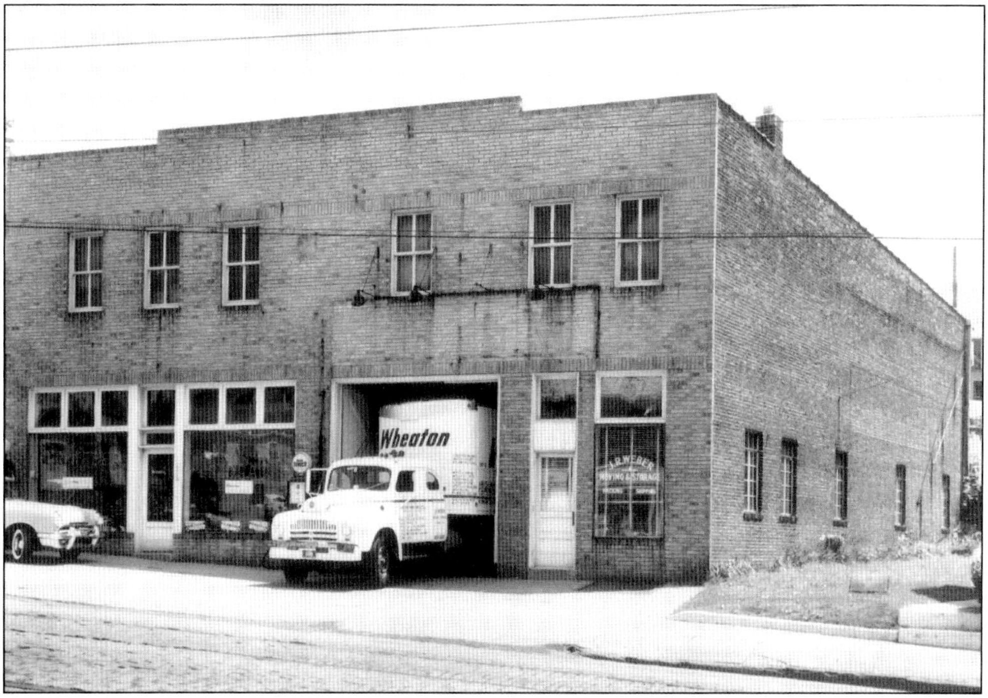

As with most small towns, Collingdale found itself in need of moving and storage companies. J.R. Weber Moving and Storage served the community for over 100 years before closing its doors forever in the early 1970s. In this 1955 photograph of its location on the corner of MacDade Boulevard and Roberta Avenue, it is evident that the company did brisk business during its heyday. (Courtesy of Collingdale High School Alumni Association—Joe Dinmore collection.)

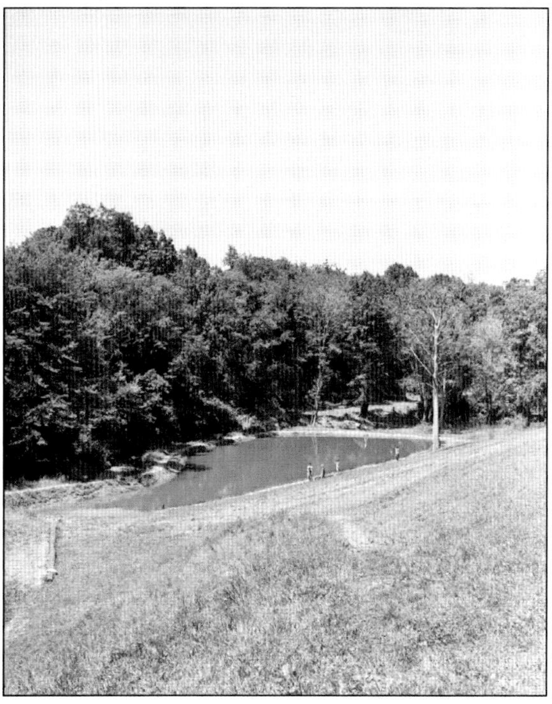

Parks and recreation areas provide families with green spaces and places to play. Maximilian LaRoche, the "Father of Collingdale," was a horticulturist and enjoyed cultivating planted things. Other burgesses also considered the need to have some open space, but it was not until the US Army moved its anti-aircraft base out in 1961 that the idea of having a large park came into being. This picture from 1970 shows Collingdale Pond. (Courtesy of Donald Bird—Joe Bird collection.)

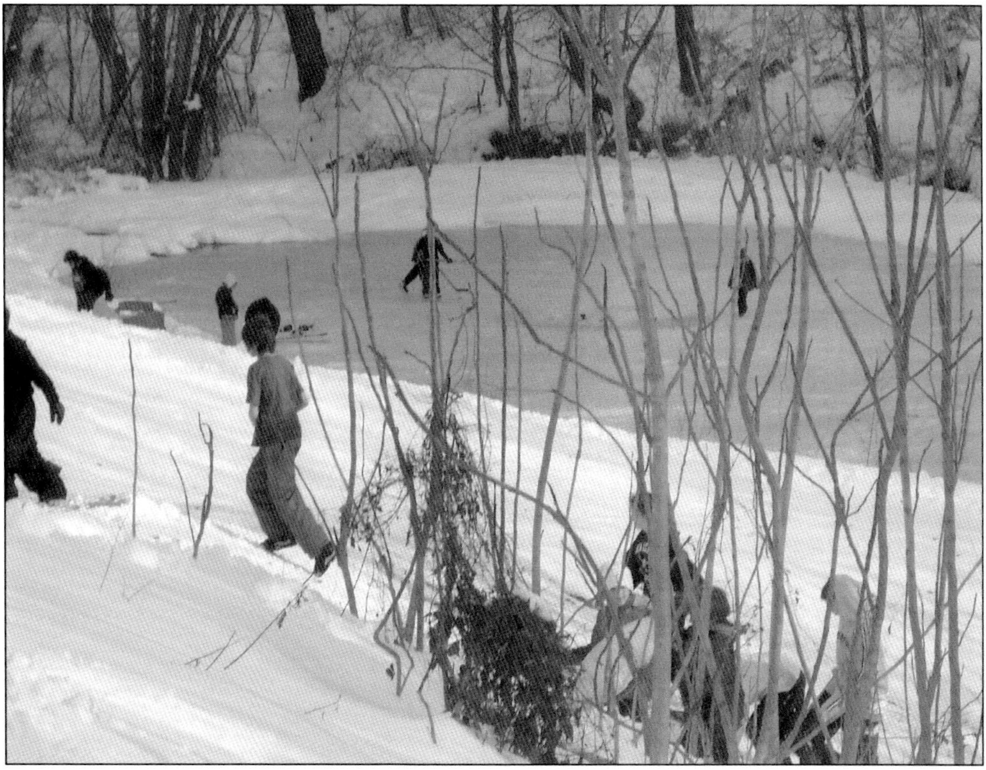

Collingdale Park was dedicated on September 3, 1973. One of the activities mentioned during the dedication was ice-skating. In this image, taken on December 21, 2009, after one of the worst snowstorms in the history of Collingdale, children skate on the frozen lake. The steep hill behind the pavilion is a perfect spot for sledding. (Photograph by Elizabeth MacGuire.)

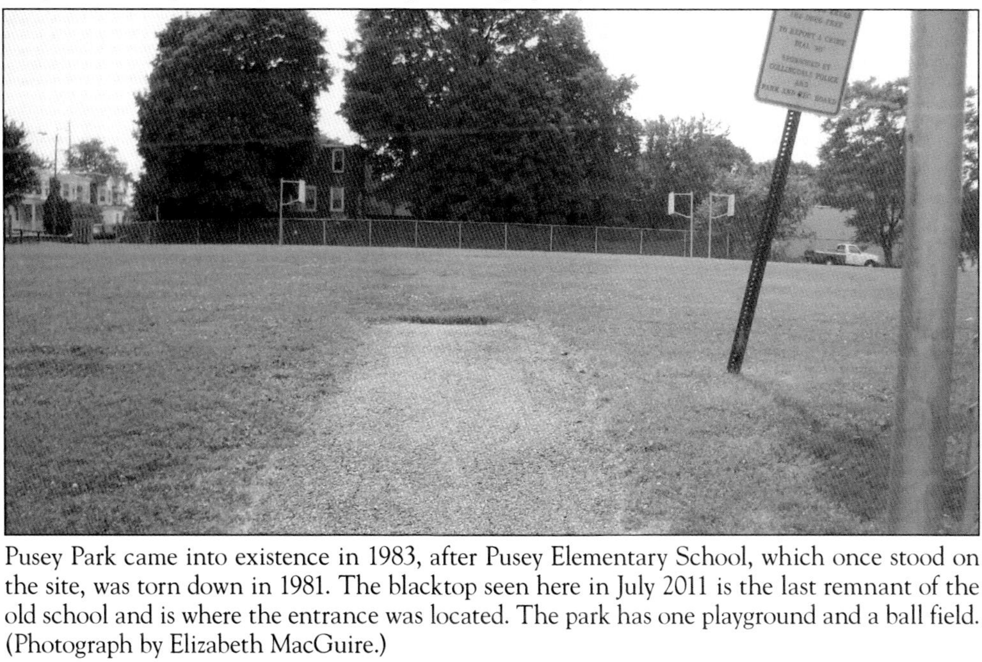

Pusey Park came into existence in 1983, after Pusey Elementary School, which once stood on the site, was torn down in 1981. The blacktop seen here in July 2011 is the last remnant of the old school and is where the entrance was located. The park has one playground and a ball field. (Photograph by Elizabeth MacGuire.)

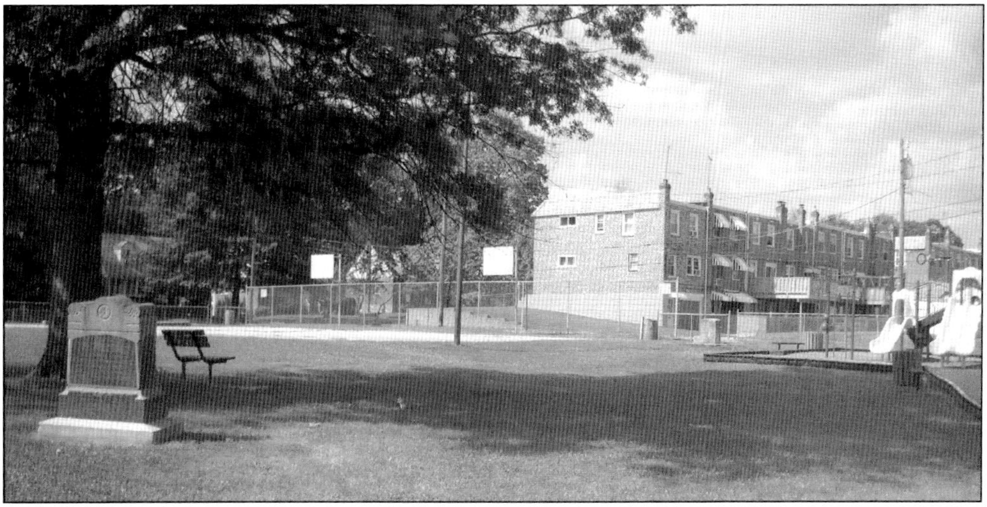

Westmont Drive Park, dedicated on July 4, 1954, provides neighborhood children with a safe place to play. It is the smallest of the five parks in Collingdale, having only one acre of land for the playground and another half-acre for the basketball court. Parents continue to fund improvements to the park, such as the new playground equipment visible at right in this July 2011 photograph. (Photograph by Elizabeth MacGuire.)

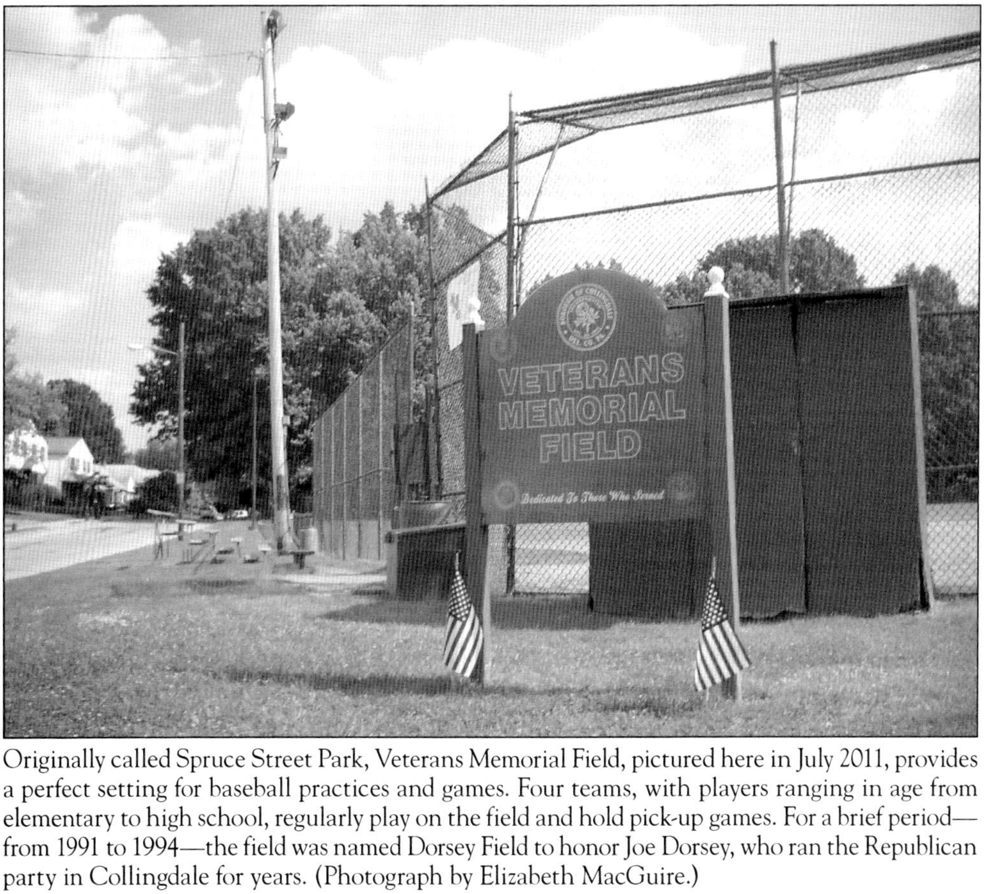

Originally called Spruce Street Park, Veterans Memorial Field, pictured here in July 2011, provides a perfect setting for baseball practices and games. Four teams, with players ranging in age from elementary to high school, regularly play on the field and hold pick-up games. For a brief period—from 1991 to 1994—the field was named Dorsey Field to honor Joe Dorsey, who ran the Republican party in Collingdale for years. (Photograph by Elizabeth MacGuire.)

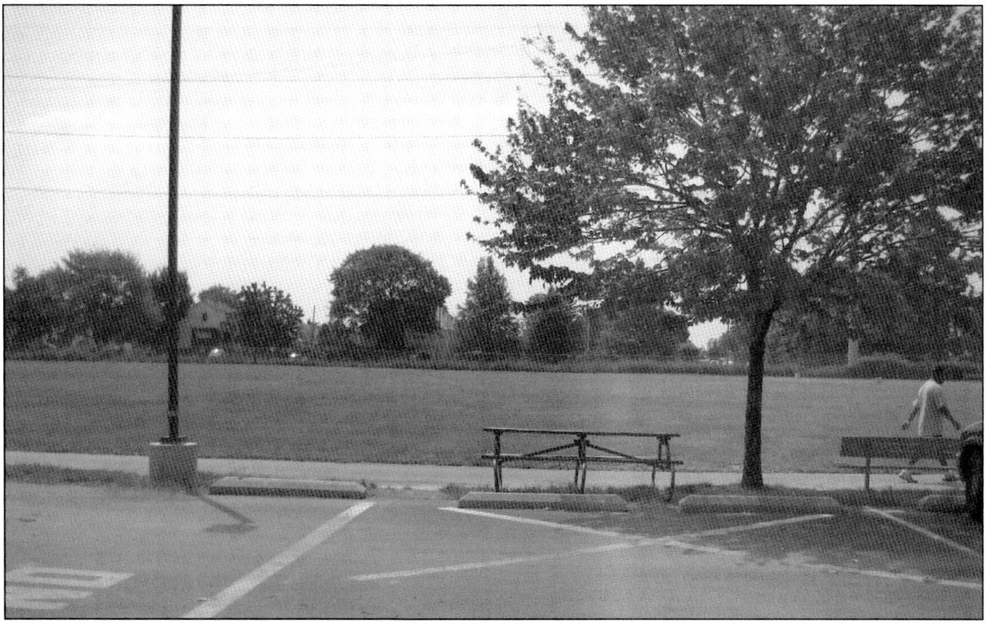

Dedicated in 2007, the Community Center Park consists of a baseball field, a football field, and a track around the perimeter. Originally the football field for Collingdale High School, the park, seen here in November 2011, has also been used for Fourth of July celebrations, field events, and sports such as lacrosse. (Photograph by Elizabeth MacGuire.)

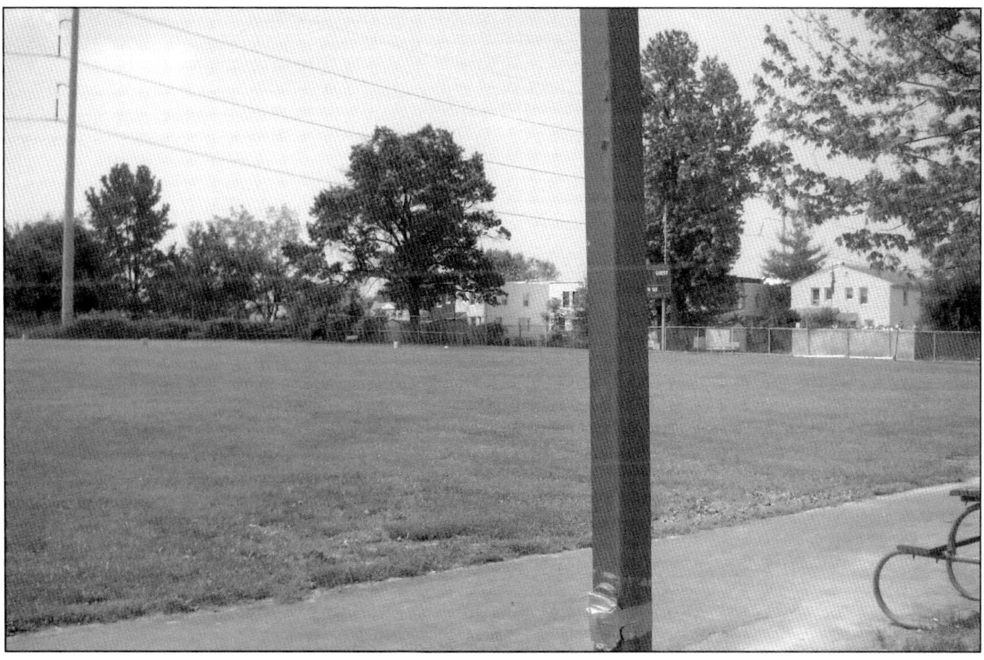

This November 2011 view of Community Center Park shows what spectators would have seen at the annual fireworks show. Behind the pole, the scoreboard stands ready for football games. To the left, at a certain time of day, one can see freight trains going down the old B&O tracks. The Collingdale Depot was next to the high school. After the B&O Railroad discontinued passenger service in 1958, the depot was demolished. (Photograph by Elizabeth MacGuire.)

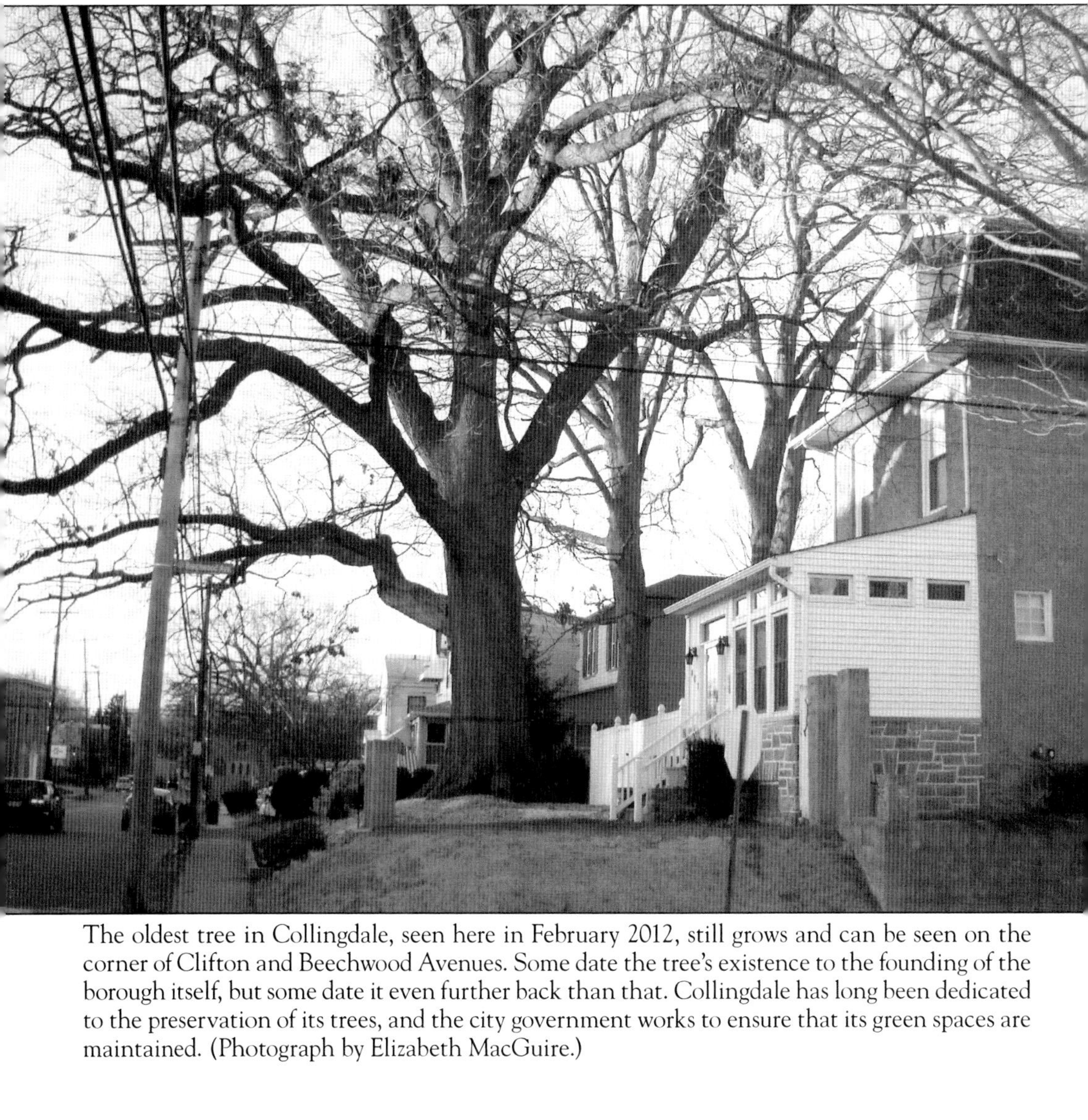

The oldest tree in Collingdale, seen here in February 2012, still grows and can be seen on the corner of Clifton and Beechwood Avenues. Some date the tree's existence to the founding of the borough itself, but some date it even further back than that. Collingdale has long been dedicated to the preservation of its trees, and the city government works to ensure that its green spaces are maintained. (Photograph by Elizabeth MacGuire.)

Two

Commuter Community
Trains, Trolleys, and Buses

As mentioned in the previous chapter and the introduction, transportation played a major role in the conception of the borough. Before the B&O Railroad tracks were laid, the only recourse for people traveling to Philadelphia or Wilmington was to traverse a muddy expanse that sometimes reached the top of wagon wheels or to cut through John Bunting's field to get to the track owned by the Philadelphia, Wilmington & Baltimore Railroad. The Philadelphia, Wilmington & Baltimore tracks were about a half-mile from Kings Highway (Chester Pike). In 1881, the B&O Railroad decided to buy Delaware Western Railroad's tracks, which cut closer to Darby borough. That action solidified the redirection of the railroad, which originally planned to form the line in another direction towards Philadelphia in the 1870s.

Once electric trolley services were introduced in 1894, there were more options for travel. Travel by trolley was convenient and cheap. Six lines and six different railway companies vied for travelers heading from Darby borough to points east and west, and two of these lines—the Philadelphia, Morton & Swarthmore Street Railway Company and the Media, Middleton, Aston & Chester Electric Railway Company—had routes that ran through Collingdale on Parker Avenue. A third trolley line, owned by the Philadelphia & Garrettford Street Railway Company, ran from a newly formed terminal at 69th Street to Collingdale. It was an ambitious endeavor for Philadelphia transit commissioner A. Merritt Taylor, but it paid off handsomely.

Buses replaced one of the trolley lines on Parker Avenue, which was renamed MacDade Boulevard on September 9, 1933, to honor Albert Dutton MacDade, a Pennsylvania state senator and common pleas court judge. The other trolley line that ran down Parker Avenue did not last long and was soon paved over. The third trolley line still runs today from Sharon Hill to the 69th Street Transportation Center.

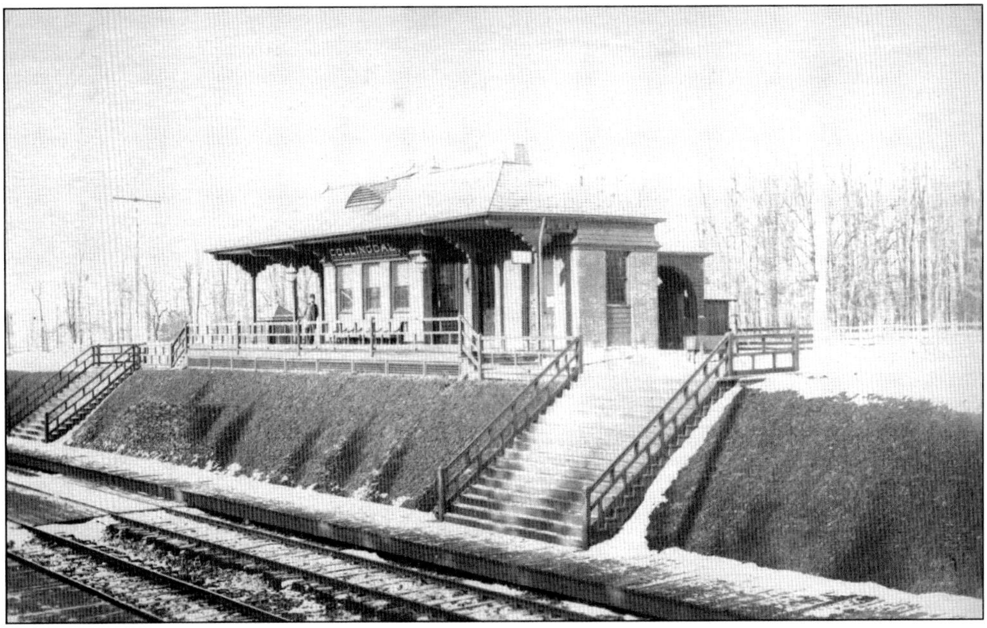

Pictured here in March 1892, the Collingdale B&O station provided passengers with an alternative to traipsing all the way to the Sharon Hill station on the Pennsylvania Railroad line. In its heyday, with six runs a day at its peak, B&O trains carried passengers as far as Washington, DC. (Courtesy of the Library Company of Philadelphia.)

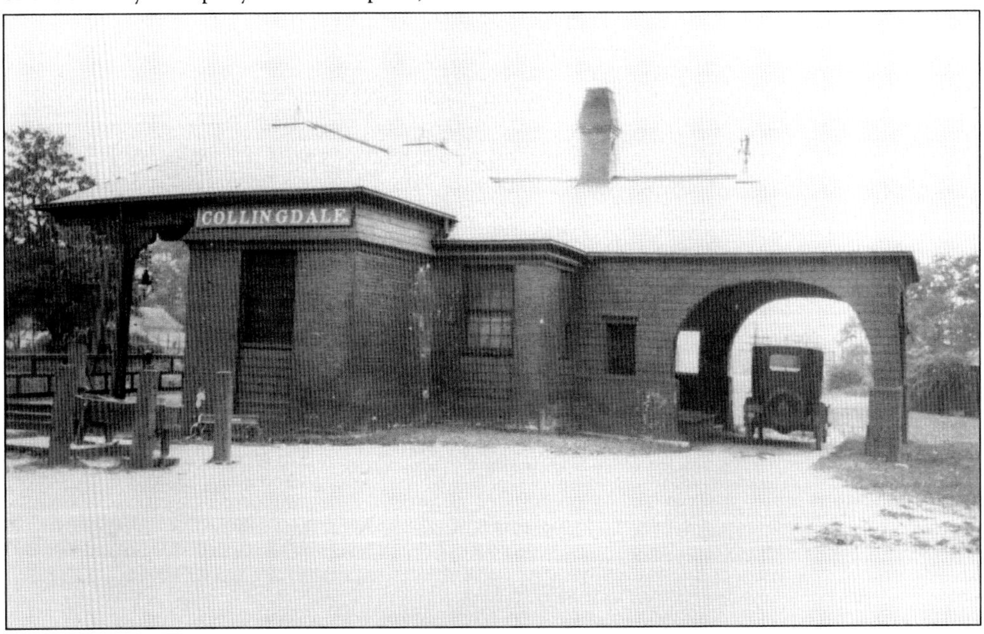

Passenger service on the B&O Railroad to the Collingdale station started in 1886 and was one of the main catalysts for the incorporation of the borough. When the railroad first started running trains on July 11 of that year, it had to work out a few kinks before it could accept passengers. By September 9, the railroad was ready to accept passengers. This picture, taken in 1926, shows some of the major changes, such as a paved parking lot, that occurred once automobiles were introduced. (Courtesy of Collingdale High School Alumni Association—Joe Dinmore collection.)

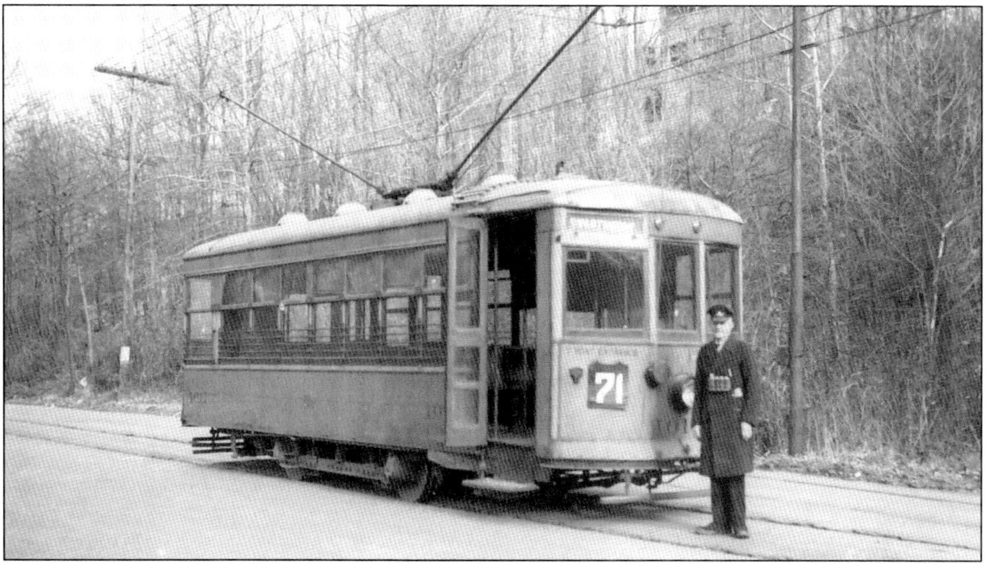

The Route 71 trolley line carried passengers from Darby to Media via Parker Avenue. An old J.G. Brill trolley car is pictured here on the Route 71 line at "Springfield Switch," sometimes known as the "Quarry Switch," which was in the west end of Morton on Yale Avenue before it crosses Swarthmore Avenue. Originally owned by the Philadelphia, Morton & Swarthmore Street Railway Company, this line became one of many acquired by the Philadelphia Transportation Company (PTC) in the early 1900s. (Courtesy of Stan Bowman.)

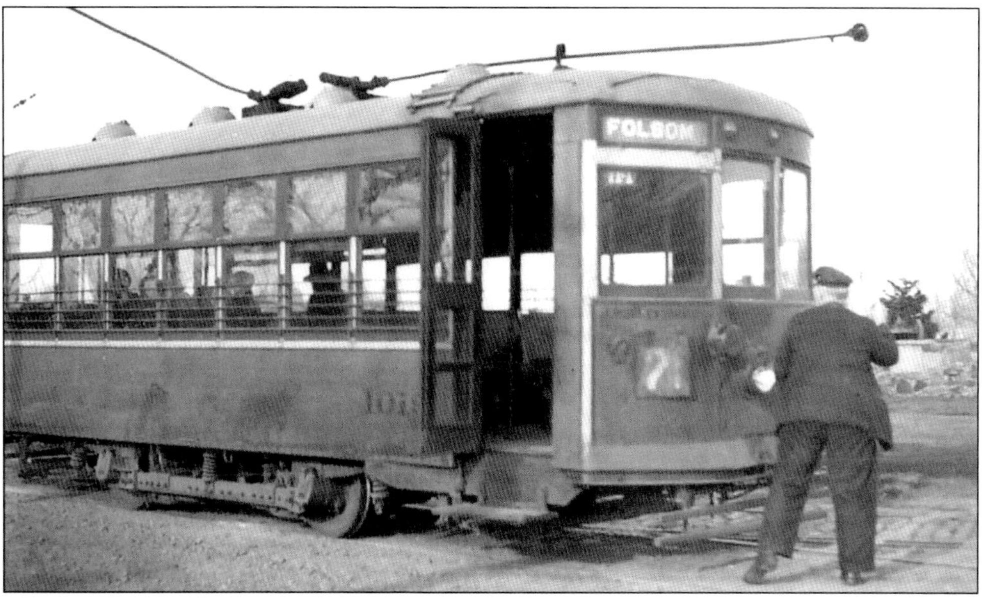

This March 1936 photograph shows another view of the J.G. Brill trolley on Route 71, pictured near the end of the line in Folsom. The motorman stands in front to guide the car to a stop near Sutton Avenue and MacDade Boulevard. Commuters often complained that the old J.G. Brill cars, which opened to the side and were drafty in the winter and sweltering in the summer, were noisy and broke down multiple times on the line. On December 7, 1932, a fatal trolley accident claimed the life of Henry Kitchens, a Collingdale police officer, as he directed traffic on Parker Avenue and Chester Pike. (Courtesy of Stan Bowman.)

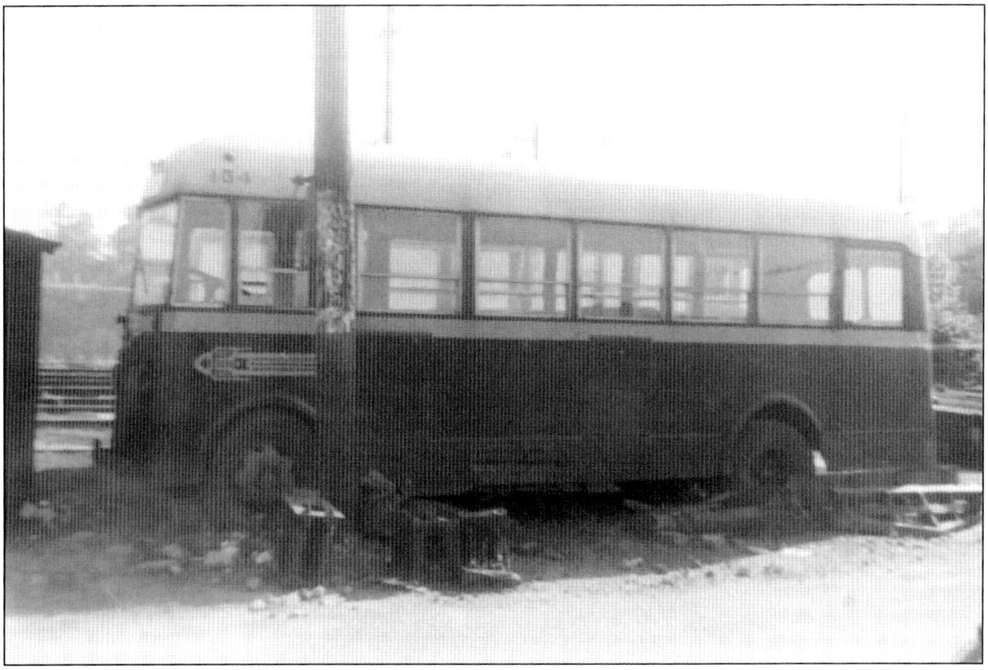

Buses such as this one replaced the trolley lines in the late 1930s. Three bus routes ran the trolley lines on what was then called the Red Arrow division of the PTC. Some bus routes were given letter descriptions, such as Route M, but the line going toward 69th Street remained a trolley line. (Photograph by Robert L. MacGuire)

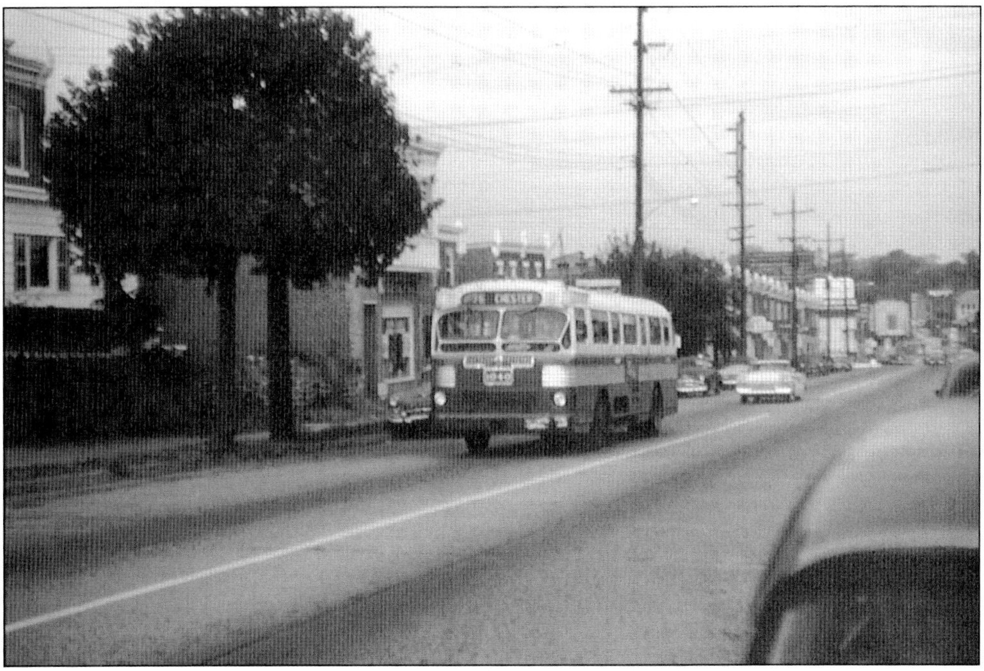

The Route 76, pictured here on its way to Chester in September 1950, took over from the Route 71 trolley line as part of the PTC in the late 1930s. After the Depression, many trolley companies went under or were merged with other companies. (Courtesy of Henry Adamcik.)

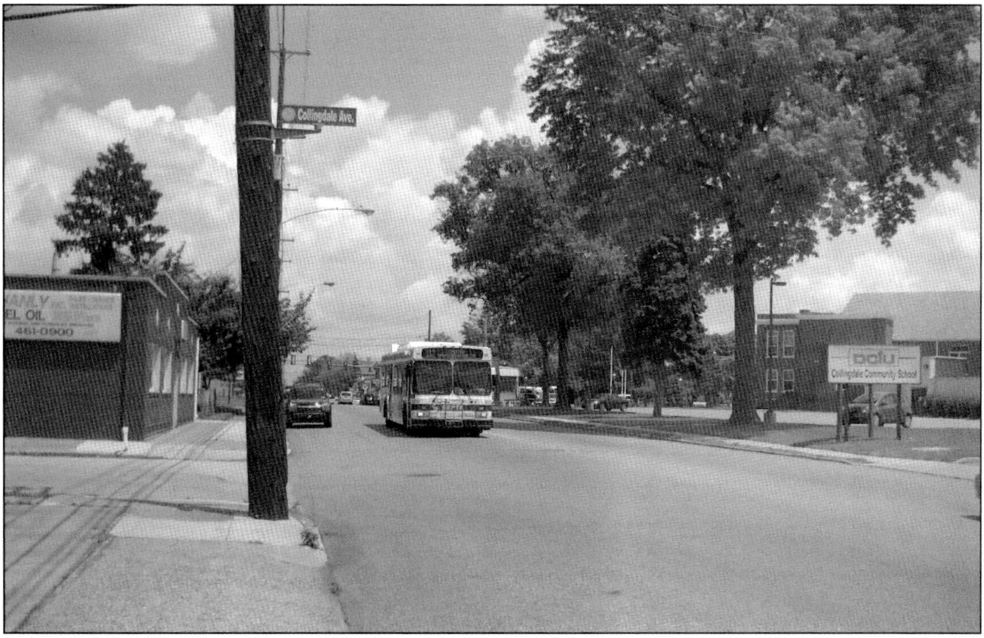

The Southeastern Pennsylvania Transportation Authority (SEPTA) officially took over the Red Arrow division of the PTC in 1970. Route M became Route 113 and traveled to Chester Transportation Center. In 2009, Route 113 was extended to Tri-State Mall. This photograph was taken in May 2012. (Photograph by Elizabeth MacGuire.)

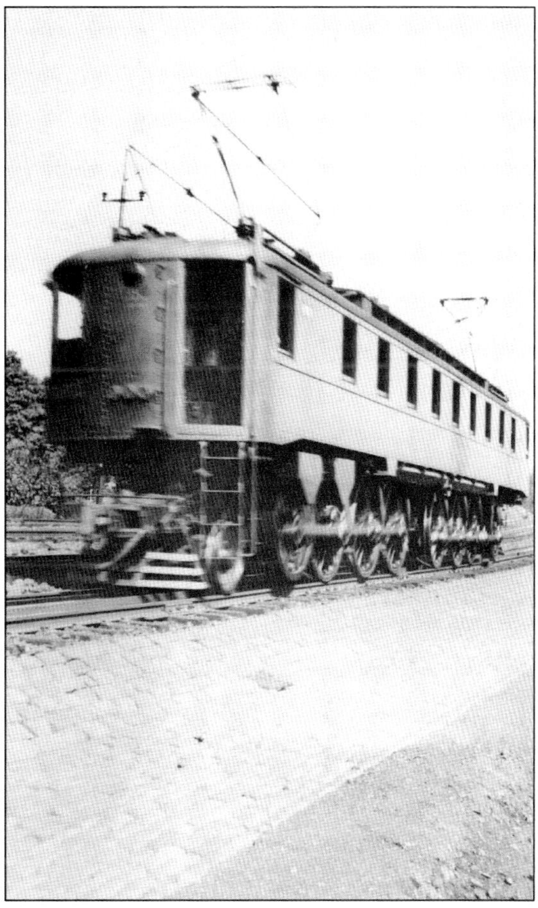

Service trolleys such as this one worked on all three lines that ran in Collingdale. In 1909, there were two other proposed trolley lines. One of the proposed lines went down Lincoln Avenue and the other went down Pusey Avenue. (Photograph by Robert L. MacGuire.)

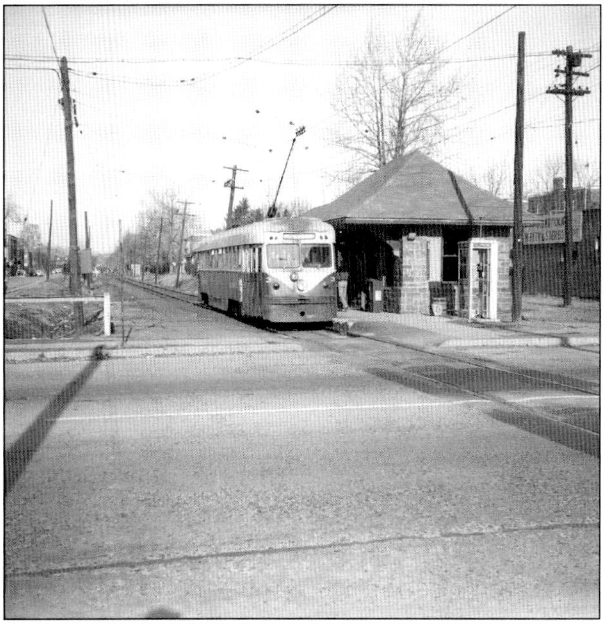

Trolley services on this line started in 1900, with the line going as far as Bywood Avenue. Philadelphia transit commissioner A. Merritt Taylor considered it his personal crusade to build a line that would serve the flourishing suburbs of present-day Upper Darby, Drexel Hill, and, eventually, Collingdale and Sharon Hill. Taylor's crusade succeeded, as the Collingdale station was dedicated on July 7, 1907. In this photograph taken on December 31, 1958, a Brilliner streetcar, built by J.G. Brill Co. in Philadelphia, waits at the Collingdale station before crossing MacDade Boulevard. (Photograph by Ed Havens.)

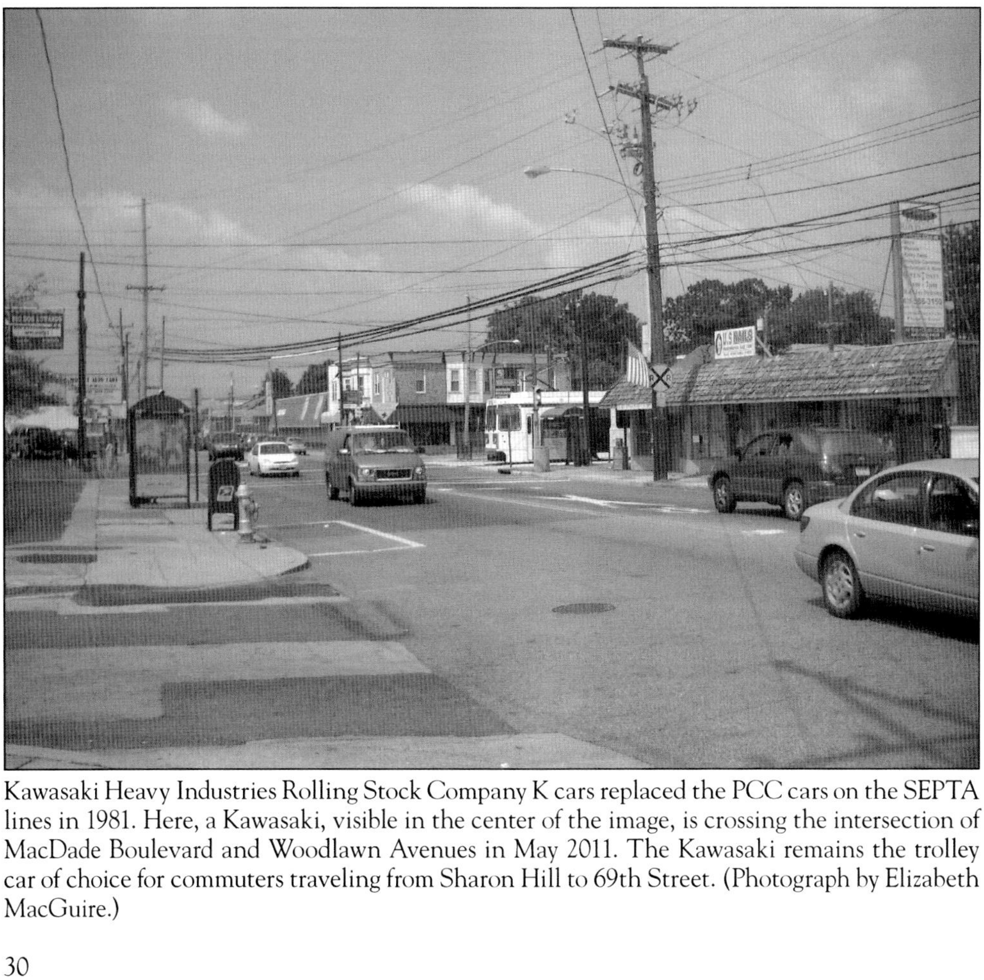

Kawasaki Heavy Industries Rolling Stock Company K cars replaced the PCC cars on the SEPTA lines in 1981. Here, a Kawasaki, visible in the center of the image, is crossing the intersection of MacDade Boulevard and Woodlawn Avenues in May 2011. The Kawasaki remains the trolley car of choice for commuters traveling from Sharon Hill to 69th Street. (Photograph by Elizabeth MacGuire.)

Three

Education Community
Living by the Golden Rule

Educating Collingdale's youth remained foremost in the minds of founding fathers Maximilian LaRoche and William McCausland. LaRoche had seven children and McCausland had five, all of whom needed solid educations. Many early inhabitants cited education as a prime motivator for settling in Collingdale.

From the beginning, Collingdale's commitment to education showed in the town government's concern and interest in the youngest members of the community. Margaret B. Harris, who moved to Collingdale with her brother Enon in the spring of 1886, wanted to do something to help the children, so she decided to start a school on the second floor of Pop Eliskey's candy store in March 1890, a full year and two months before Collingdale petitioned to become a borough.

Harris was not the only motivator, as others stepped forward and pressed for the space needed to teach schoolchildren in a better environment. By 1894, the area's first elementary school became a reality; called Bartram Avenue School because of where it was located, the school served students from kindergarten through eighth grade and only required a few adjustments when the population fluctuated and needs changed. An unidentified person donated the land for the school, which was renamed for Margaret B. Harris in 1937 and is still open today.

The children living in the other end of Collingdale had to attend school in two buildings that were rented out for that purpose until September 1914. Land was acquired that year by heirs of the Pusey family, and a school was built. To honor the Pusey family, and because the school was on Pusey Avenue, it was named Pusey Avenue Elementary School. Students from kindergarten through fourth grade attended the school until 1973. The school remained open for kindergarten students until it closed in 1979.

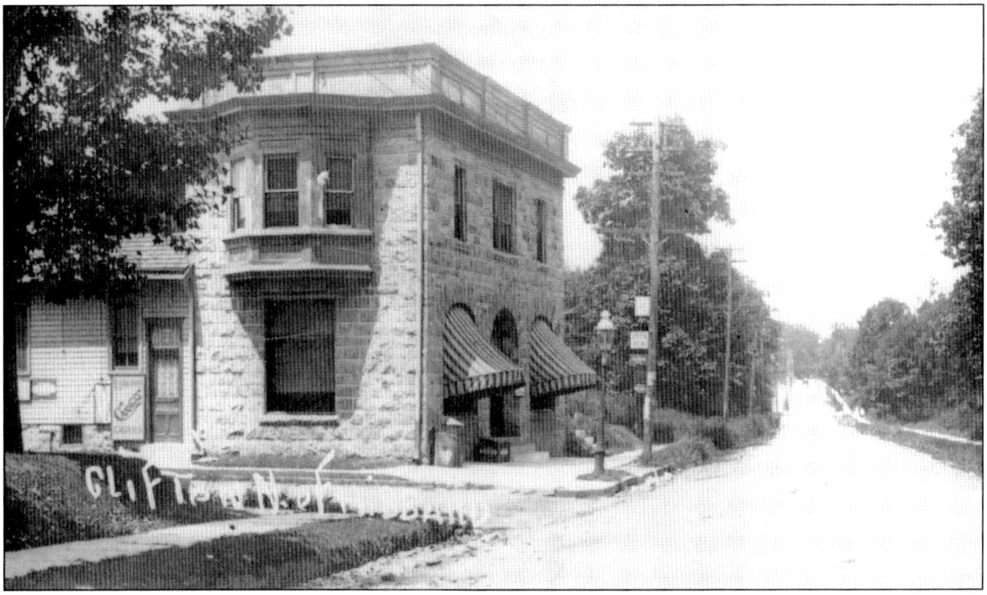

Pop Eliskey's store, shown here in 1910, was mainly a candy store, but also served as a schoolhouse before the Bartram Avenue School was built in 1894. (Courtesy of Keith Lockhart.)

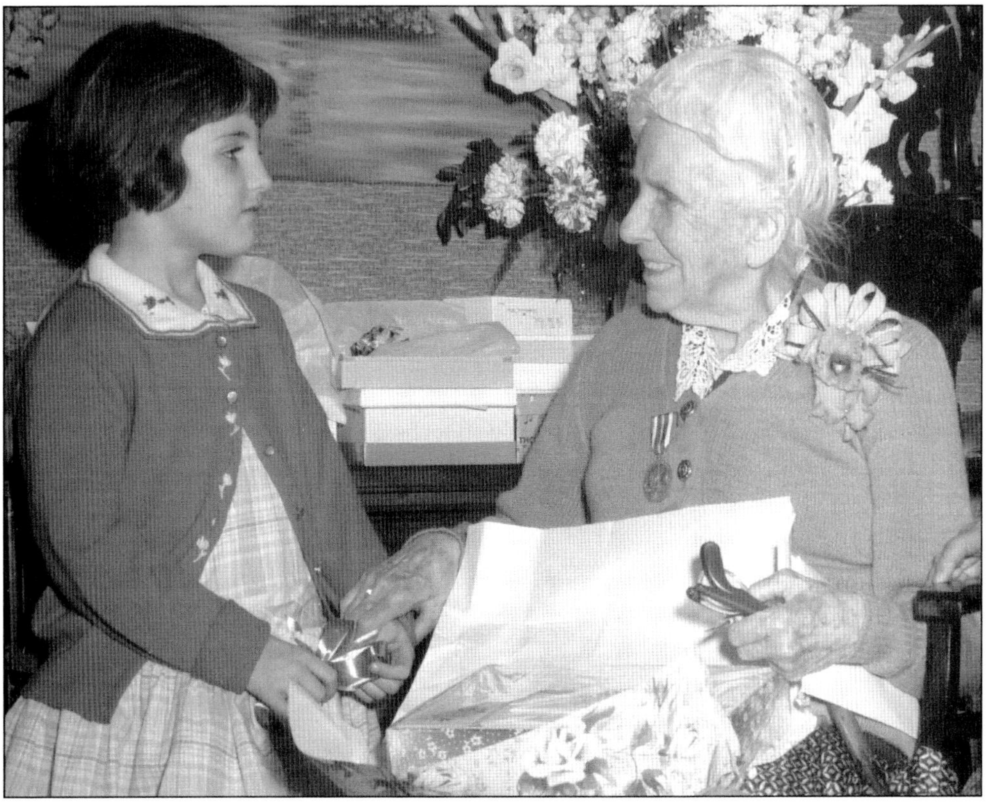

Margaret Brisbane Harris, pictured with her niece Helen during her 90th birthday celebration in 1959, was Collingdale's first schoolteacher. She served as both principal and teacher to thousands of children in the borough from 1890 to 1937, when she retired. (Courtesy of Helen Dick Deyo Moyer.)

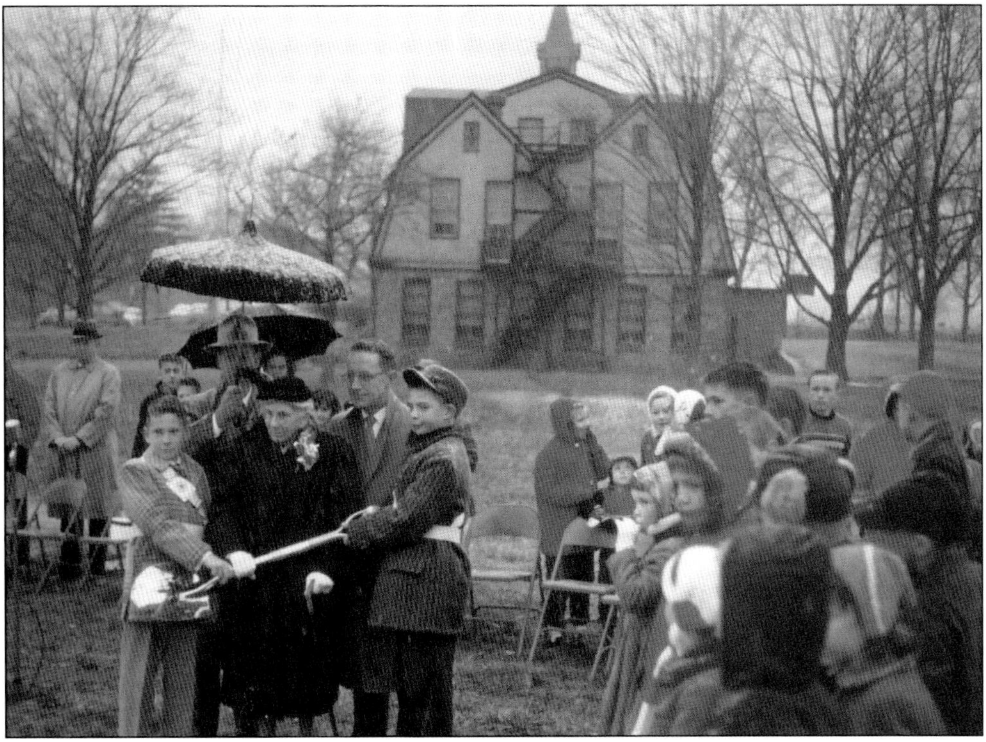

By the 1950s, when Collingdale's student population exploded, it became necessary to either move or demolish the old elementary school building. The decision to demolish the old building came in the summer of 1957. In this September 1957 picture, Margaret B. Harris shovels the first spade of dirt at the ground-breaking ceremony for the new Margaret B. Harris Elementary School. (Courtesy of Helen Dick Deyo Moyer.)

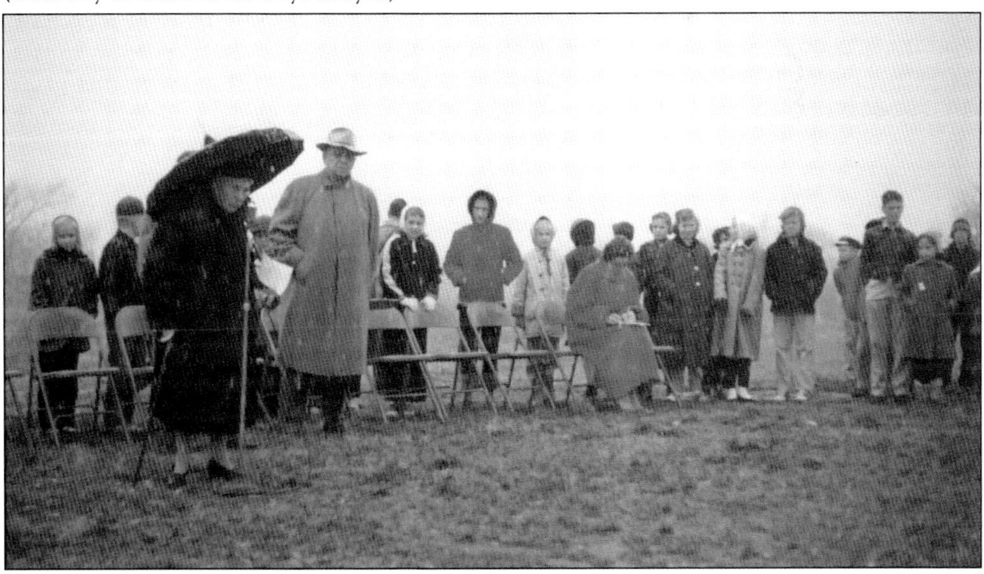

Margaret B. Harris prepares to read her speech during the September 1957 ground-breaking ceremony for the Margaret B. Harris Elementary School. Students listened as she dedicated the school and encouraged them to follow their dreams. (Courtesy of Helen Dick Deyo Moyer.)

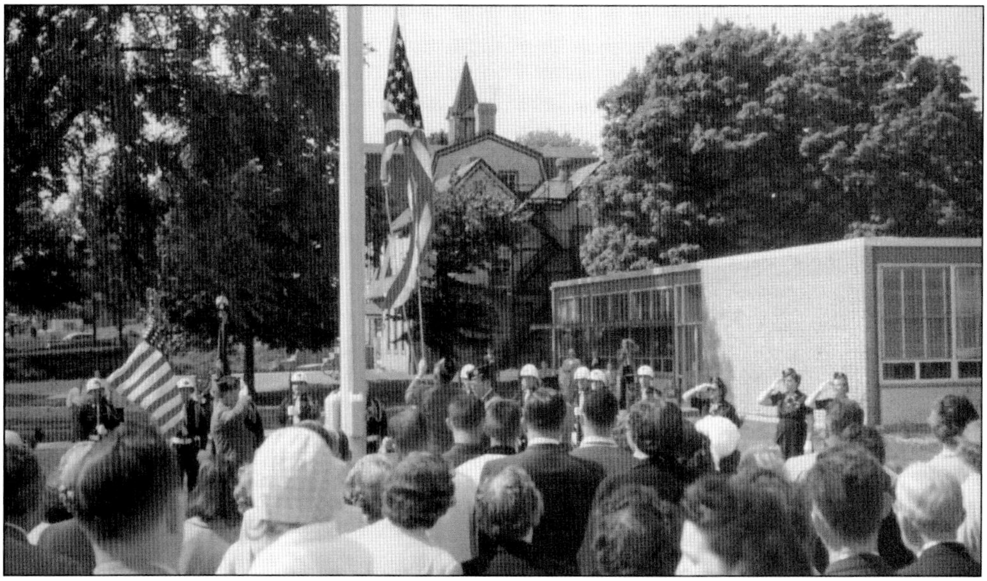

The dedication of the new Margaret B. Harris Elementary School was held on September 4, 1959. Compared to the ground-breaking ceremony held two years earlier, the dedication proceeded amidst perfect weather, with many of Collingdale's leading citizens in attendance. (Courtesy of Helen Dick Deyo Moyer and Collingdale High School Alumni Association.)

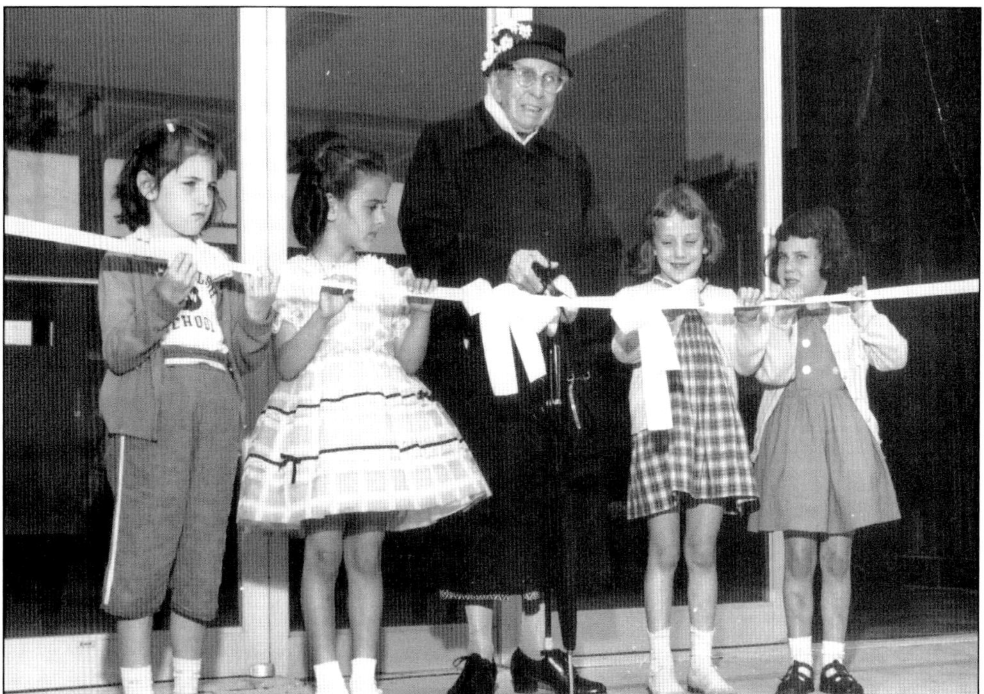

Margaret B. Harris, with the help of four kindergarten students, cuts the ceremonial ribbon to open the new Margaret B. Harris Elementary School. At that time, the school served kindergarten through sixth grades; until 1982, students transferred to Collingdale Junior/Senior High School for seventh through twelfth grades. (Courtesy of Helen Dick Deyo Moyer.)

Pusey Avenue Elementary School, established in September 1914, served students from the east side of town in kindergarten through fourth grades. Once a child reached fifth grade, he or she was sent to Margaret B. Harris Elementary to complete their elementary education. Here, a group of boys from the elementary school class of 1939 stand in front of the Pusey Avenue school. (Courtesy of Collingdale High School Alumni Association.)

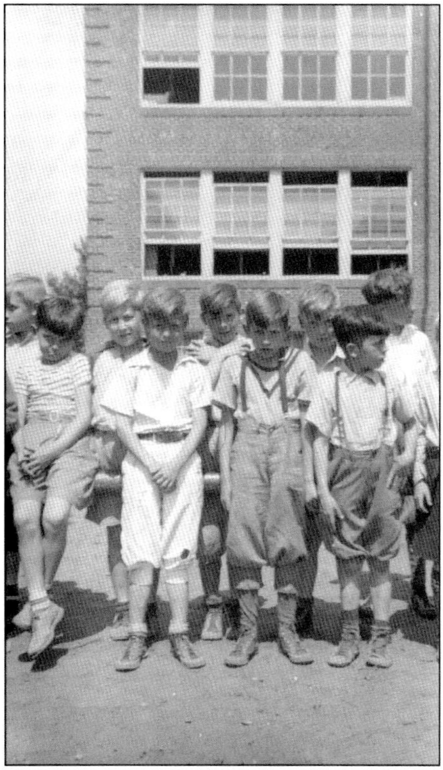

Considered by some as the last fourth grade class of Pusey Avenue Elementary School due to the discontinuation of third and fourth grade classes at Pusey, these students received special treatment as they were escorted to where they would begin classes in the new "pod" setting created for them. Many of these students recall treks to the high school gymnasium when it became too cold to work in their classrooms. This is a 1972–1973 class picture from Barksdale Studios. (Courtesy of the MacGuire family; photograph by Barksdale Studios.)

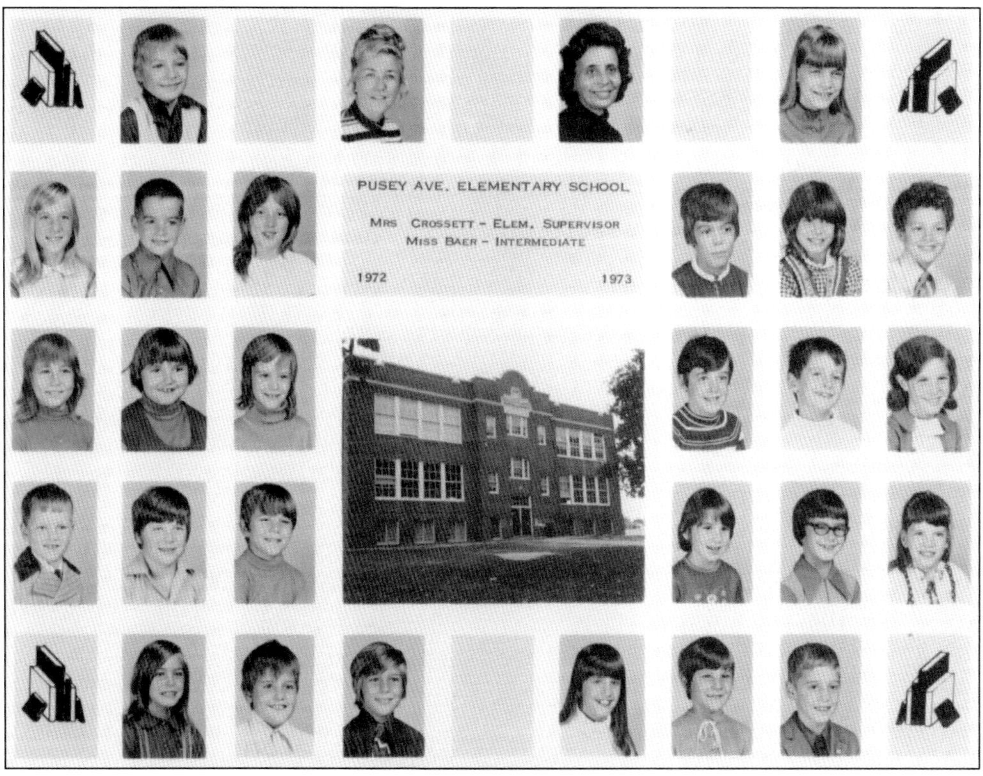

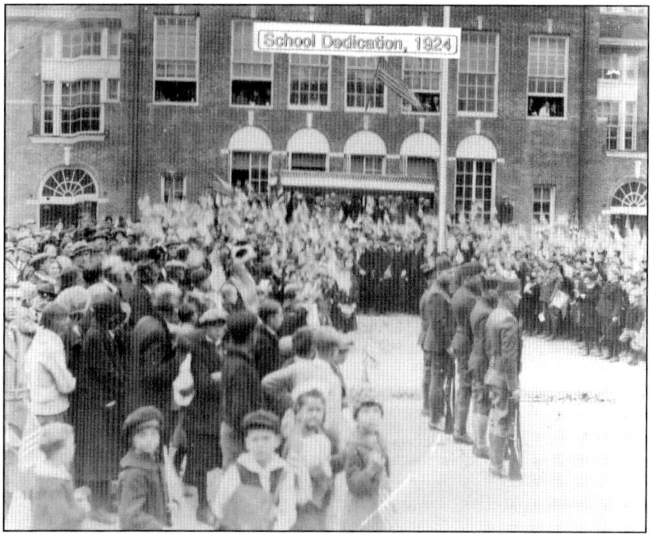

A grand parade celebrated the opening and dedication of the new Collingdale High School in 1924. The first students entered the school in September 1924 as part of a program that welcomed students who wanted to attend school after the eighth grade. Called "freshmen," the new students soon started extracurricular activities at their new school. (Courtesy of Collingdale High School Alumni Association—Carson Thompson collection; photograph by R.H. Howard.)

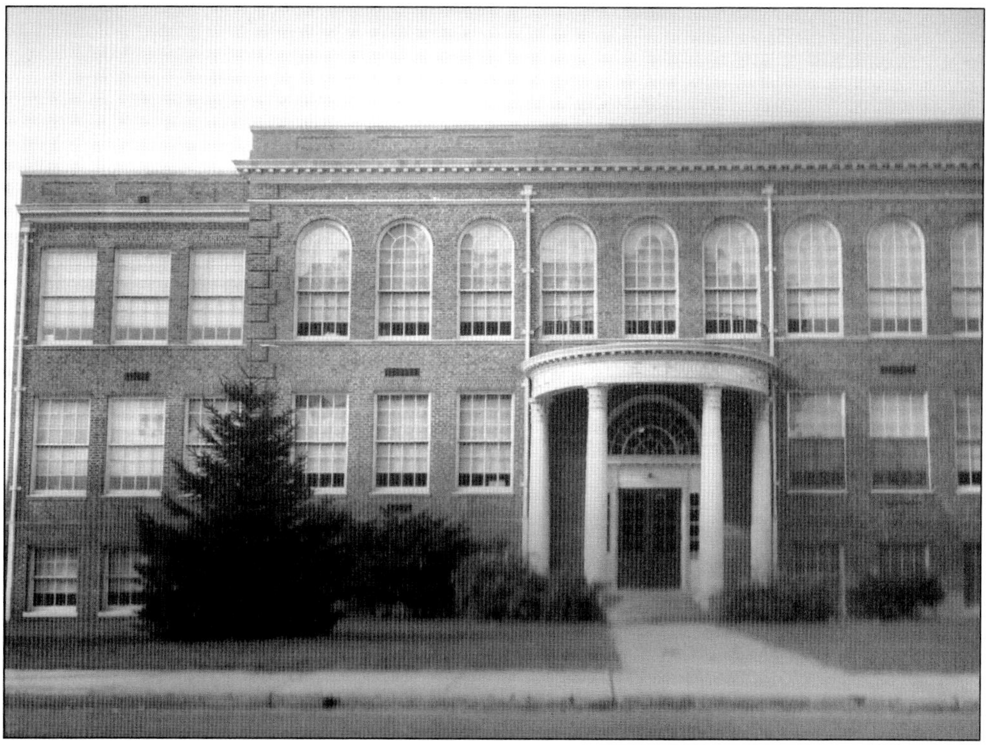

Collingdale High School had two buildings—one for the junior high, which was dedicated in 1924, and one for the senior high, which was dedicated in the early 1930s. At times, the trek between the two buildings became treacherous, especially when it rained. Students rejoiced when plans were made to join the two buildings with a covered walkway. The now famous columns seen here graced the senior high building, while the junior high building remained unadorned. (Courtesy of Collingdale High School Alumni Association—William Cox collection.)

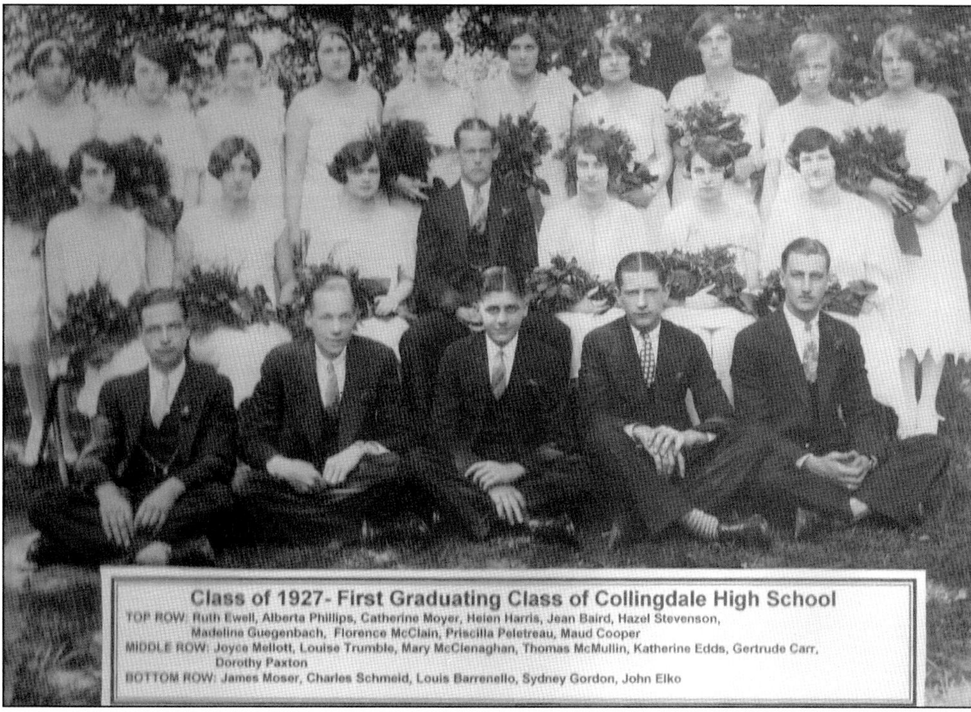

Collingdale High School's first senior class graduated on June 2, 1927. Many had high hopes for the future, but watched those dreams disappear with the stock market crash of 1929. Even so, this graduating class set precedents for many of the traditions and teams that followed. (Courtesy of Collingdale High School Alumni Association—Joe Dinmore collection.)

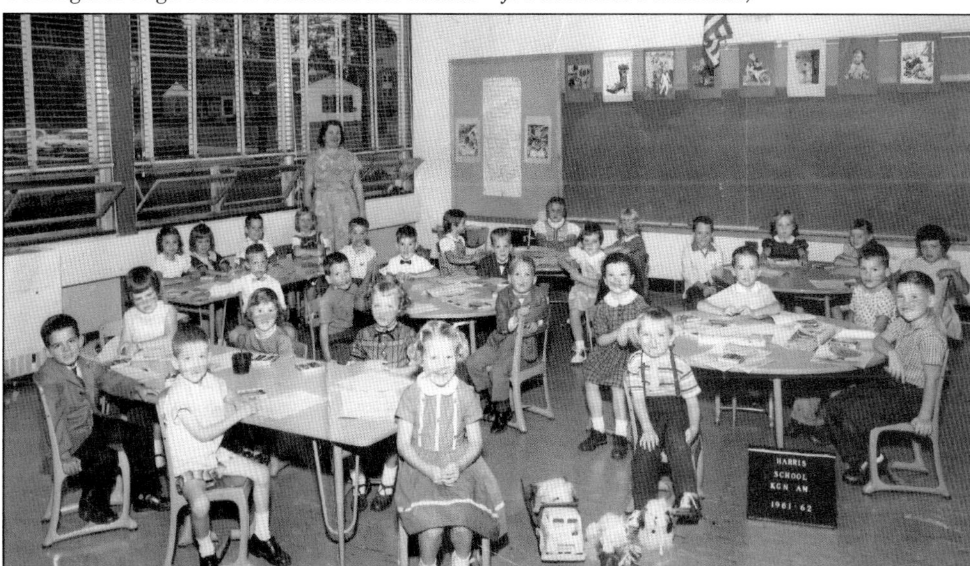

This May 1961 image shows Mrs. Bailey's kindergarten class at Margaret B. Harris Elementary in a typical classroom of the early 1960s. Students' memories of that day include making crafts and anticipating the activities that the class would participate in, along with older students, for May Day. (Courtesy of Tom Morse; photograph by Barksdale Studios.)

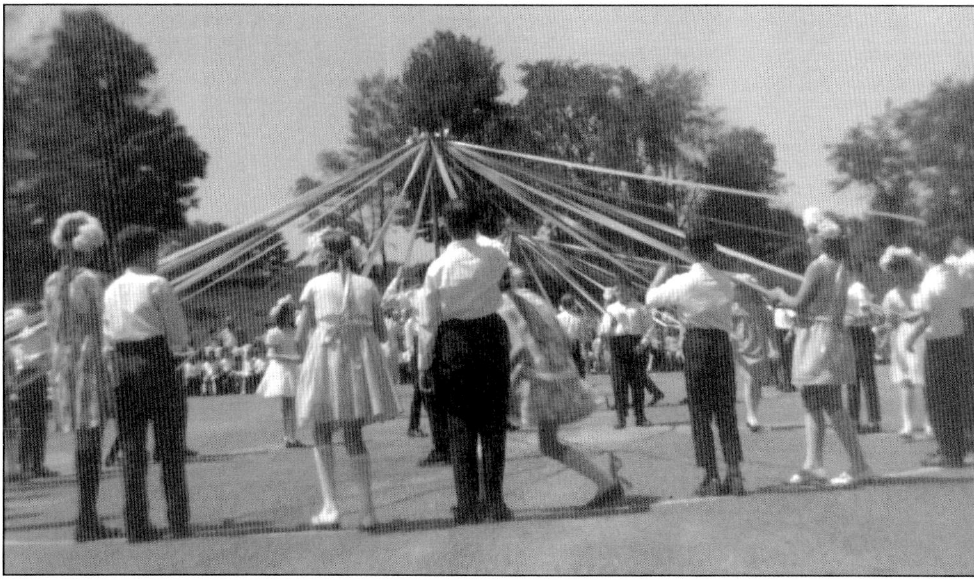

Children dance around the maypole as part of the 1969 May Day celebration. Activities were usually held outside and were anticipated for weeks as children prepared costumes and practiced songs. The maypole became a thing of the past in the mid-1970s as the celebration became more sports-oriented and less a celebration of spring. (Courtesy of Vicky Tuttle; photograph by Victor Tuttle.)

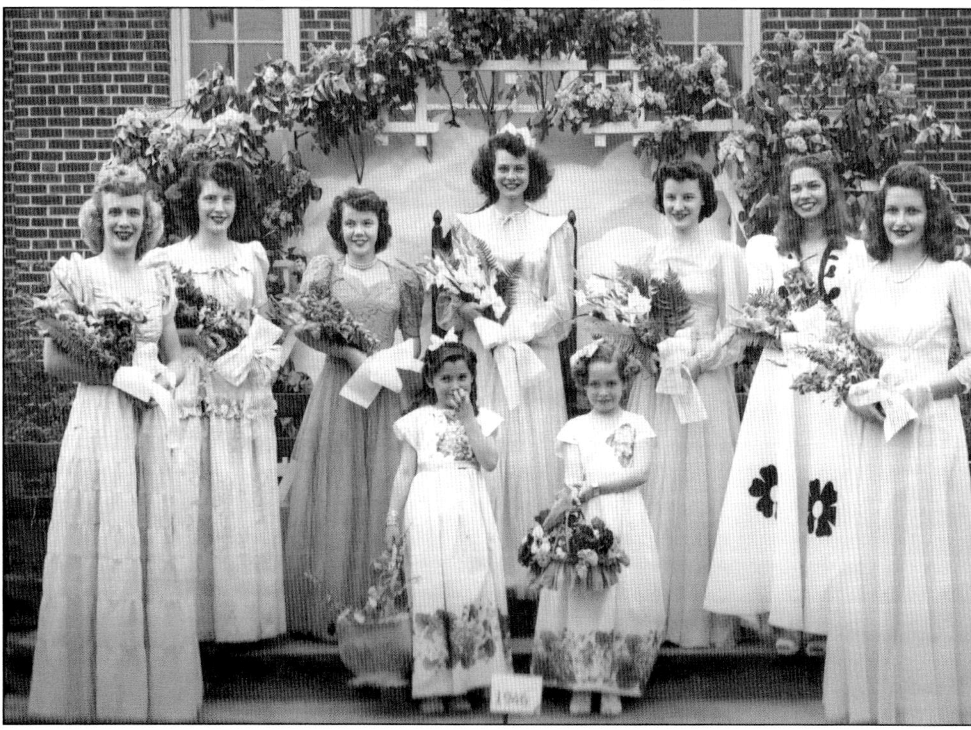

Mary Marquardt, crowned Collingdale's first May Queen in May 1946, poses with her court in front of the Collingdale Junior High School building. May Day celebrations often included the crowning of a May Queen and a parade. (Courtesy of Collingdale High School Alumni Association—William Cox collection.)

The Collingdale High School *ColHumS* student newspaper won awards from the Chester Pike Kiwanis Club for articles written about the effects of tobacco. In this photograph, William Gibson (left) presents Susan Wright, a CHS junior, with an award for her article "Should Teenagers Smoke?" from the January 1961 issue of *ColHumS*, which was presented as part of an essay contest sponsored by the National Tuberculosis and Columbia Scholastic Press Associations. (Courtesy of Collingdale High School Alumni Association—Susan Wright collection.)

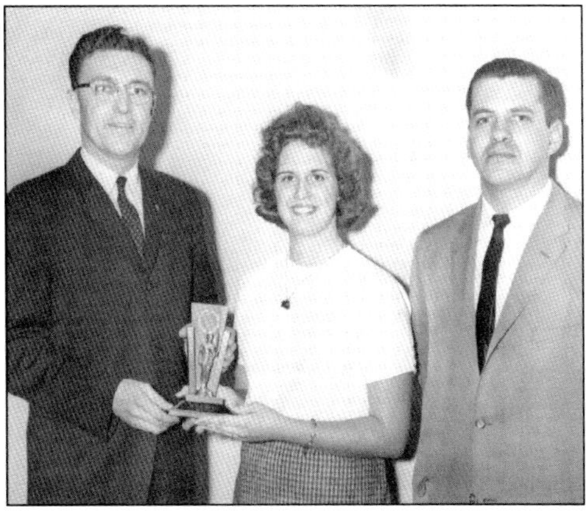

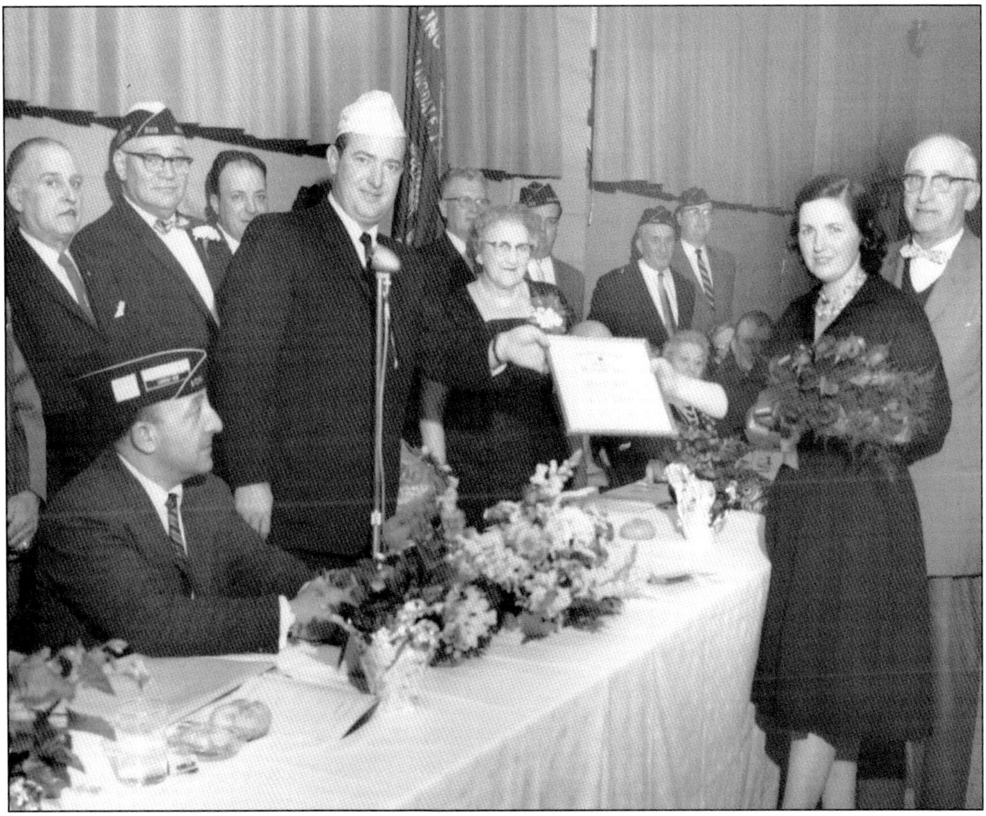

In this March 12, 1960, photograph taken at the 25th anniversary celebration of American Legion Post 669, Nancy Johnston, daughter of Burgess Charles Johnston, receives a Citation for Meritorious Service for her work in improving library standards. Presenting her with the citation are Dept. Commander William Malone and the president of the State Auxiliary, Mrs. Paul Daque. Nancy Johnston served as the chairwoman of the Library Improvement Committee sponsored by the Junior Women's Club of Collingdale. Standing behind her is her father, Charles Johnston. (Courtesy of Nancy Johnston Collier; photograph by *Upper Darby News*.)

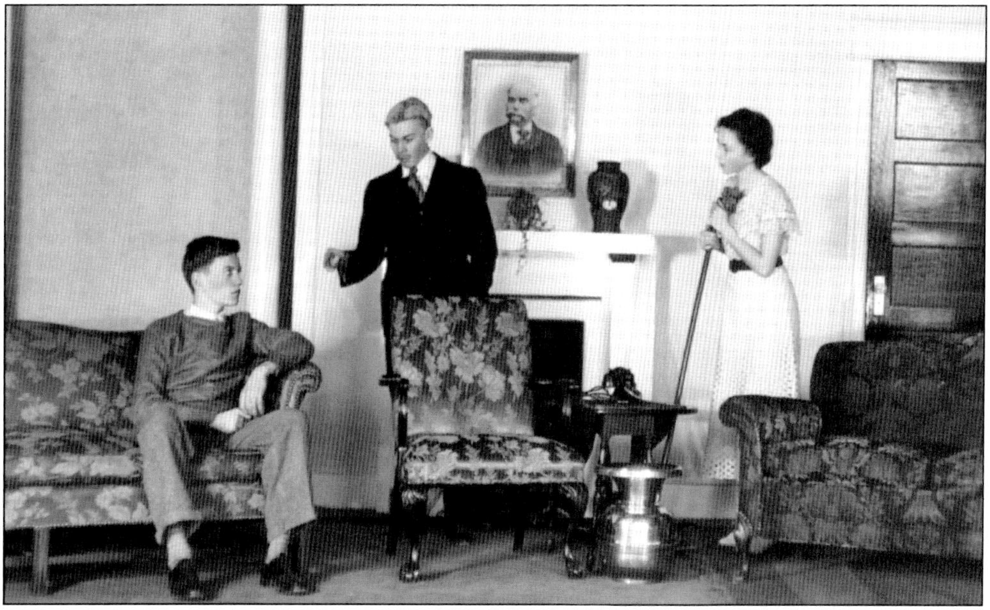

High school theater played a huge role at the school, making life interesting and providing an outlet for many youngsters. In the junior class presentation of *Big Hearted Herbert*, performed on March 20 and 21, 1936, John Beattie (center) played Herbert Kalness, while Mary Wechter played Alice Kalness (Herbert's daughter) and Fred "Bob" Lyon played Andrew Goodrich, Alice's fiancé. (Courtesy of Collingdale High School Alumni Association—Ann Speer collection.)

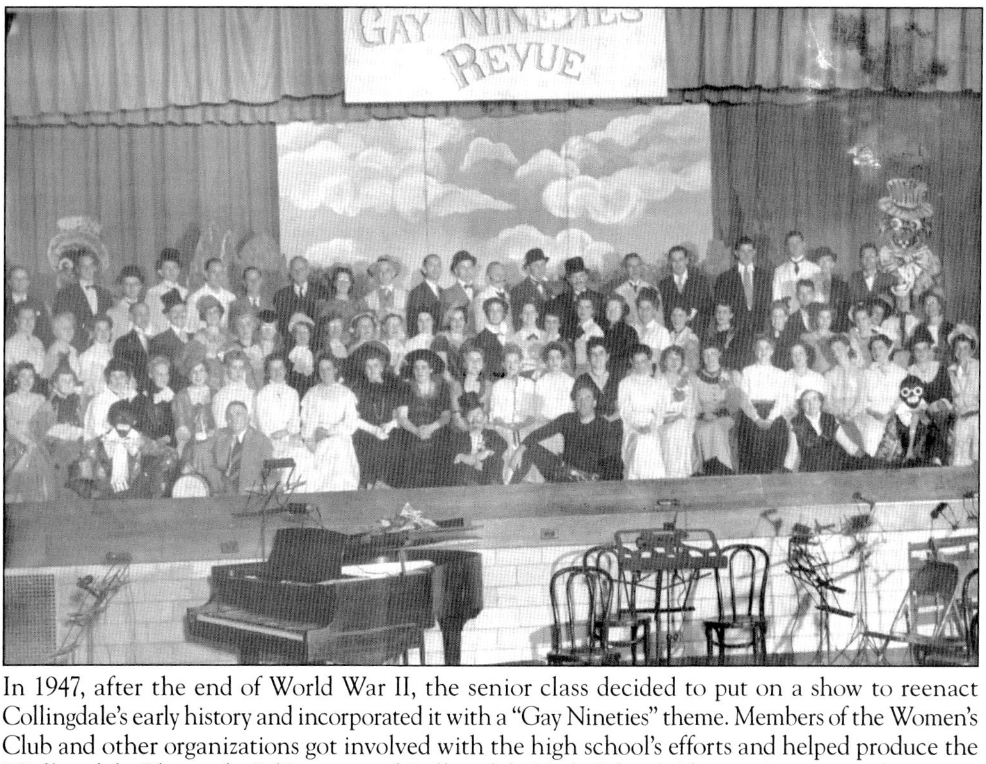

In 1947, after the end of World War II, the senior class decided to put on a show to reenact Collingdale's early history and incorporated it with a "Gay Nineties" theme. Members of the Women's Club and other organizations got involved with the high school's efforts and helped produce the "Collingdale Chronicles." (Courtesy of Collingdale High School Alumni Association.)

Hello Dolly, staged for three nights in May 1979 at the Collingdale High School auditorium, was the fourth Southeast Delco School District musical. Set design, costumes, and lighting were all done by students under the supervision of three teachers. (Photograph by Betty R. MacGuire.)

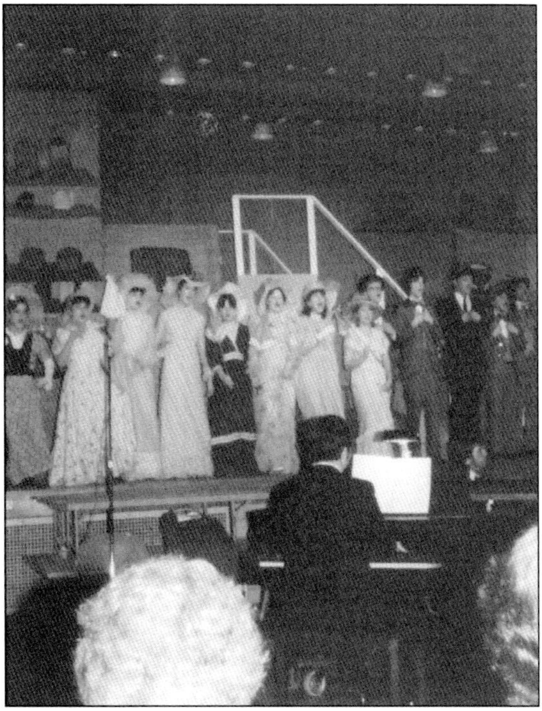

In this 1971 image, Ms. Joan Messinger ushers children out of the school building and directs them to place their chairs on the playground. Masks adorn the faces of the children, who were eager to portray their favorite characters. (Courtesy of Vicky Tuttle; photograph by Elizabeth Tuttle.)

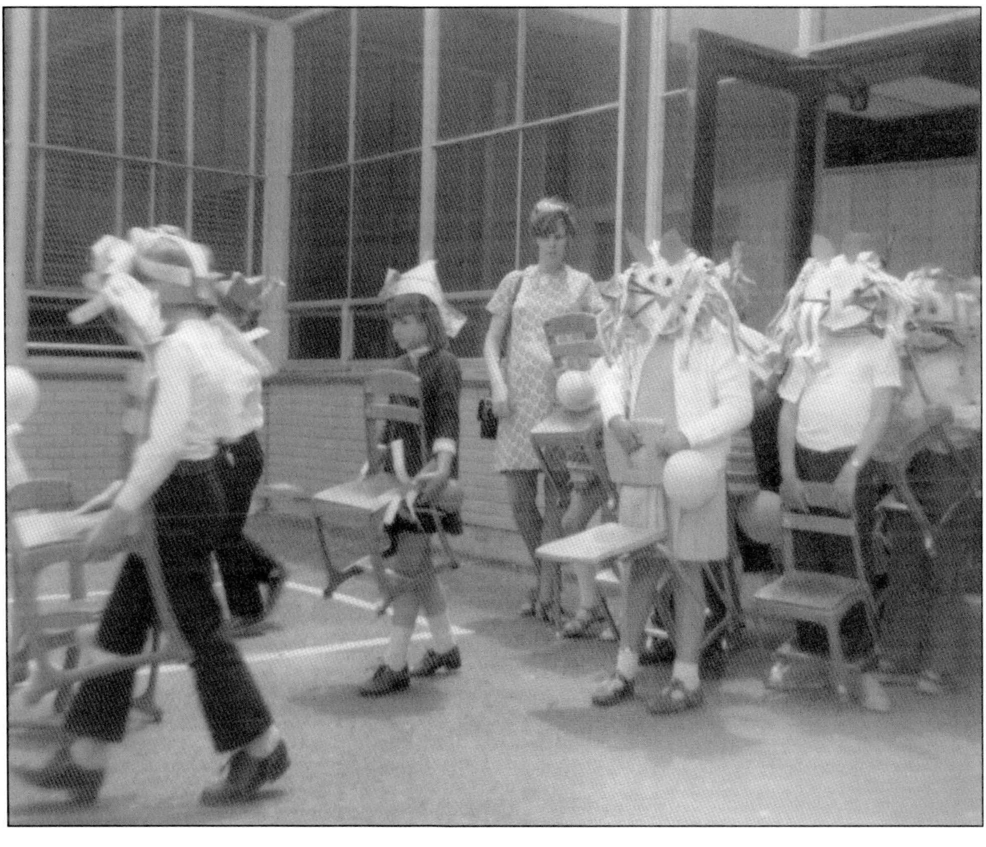

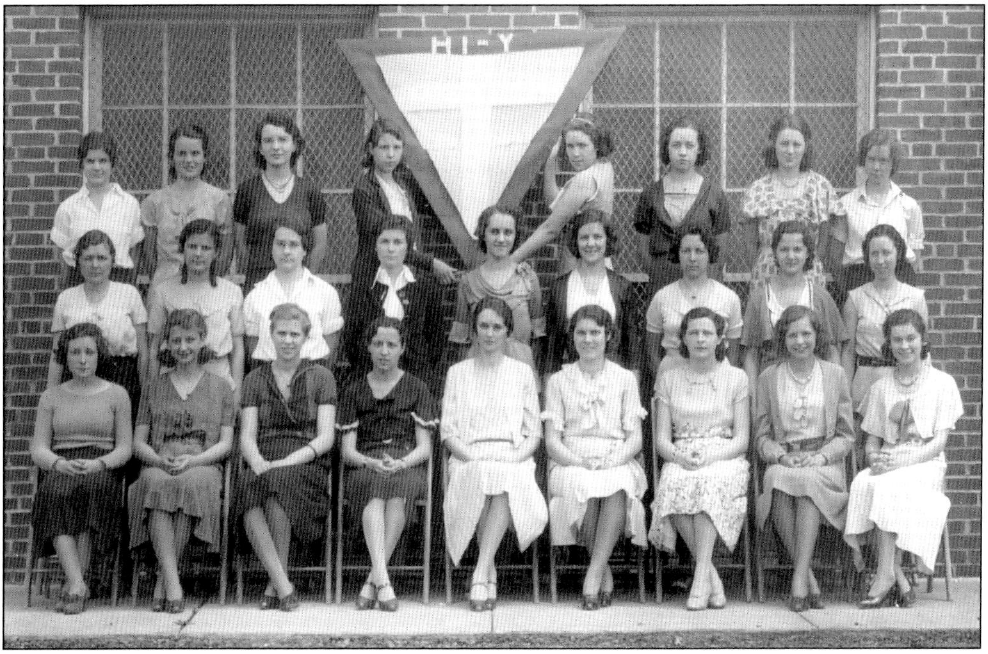

Numerous clubs kept students busy after school. Some of these clubs reflected the times in which the students lived. Debate clubs were popular, as well as Hi-Y clubs started in conjunction with the YMCA. Collingdale's Hi-Y girls' club started in 1925, and the boys' club started in 1931. The 1936 girls' Hi-Y club is pictured here. (Courtesy of Collingdale High School Alumni Association.)

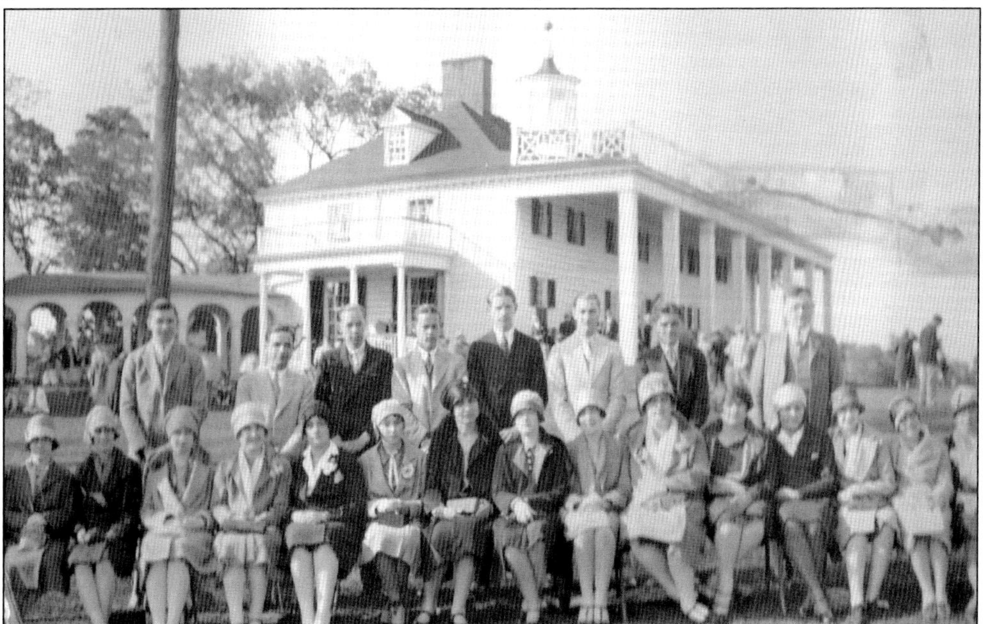

One of the most popular outings for students was the annual trip to Washington, DC. Since the B&O Railroad ran just behind the high school, students could hop on the train and be in Washington in three hours or less. In this 1927 photograph, students from the senior class pose for a picture at Mount Vernon. (Courtesy of Collingdale High School Alumni Association.)

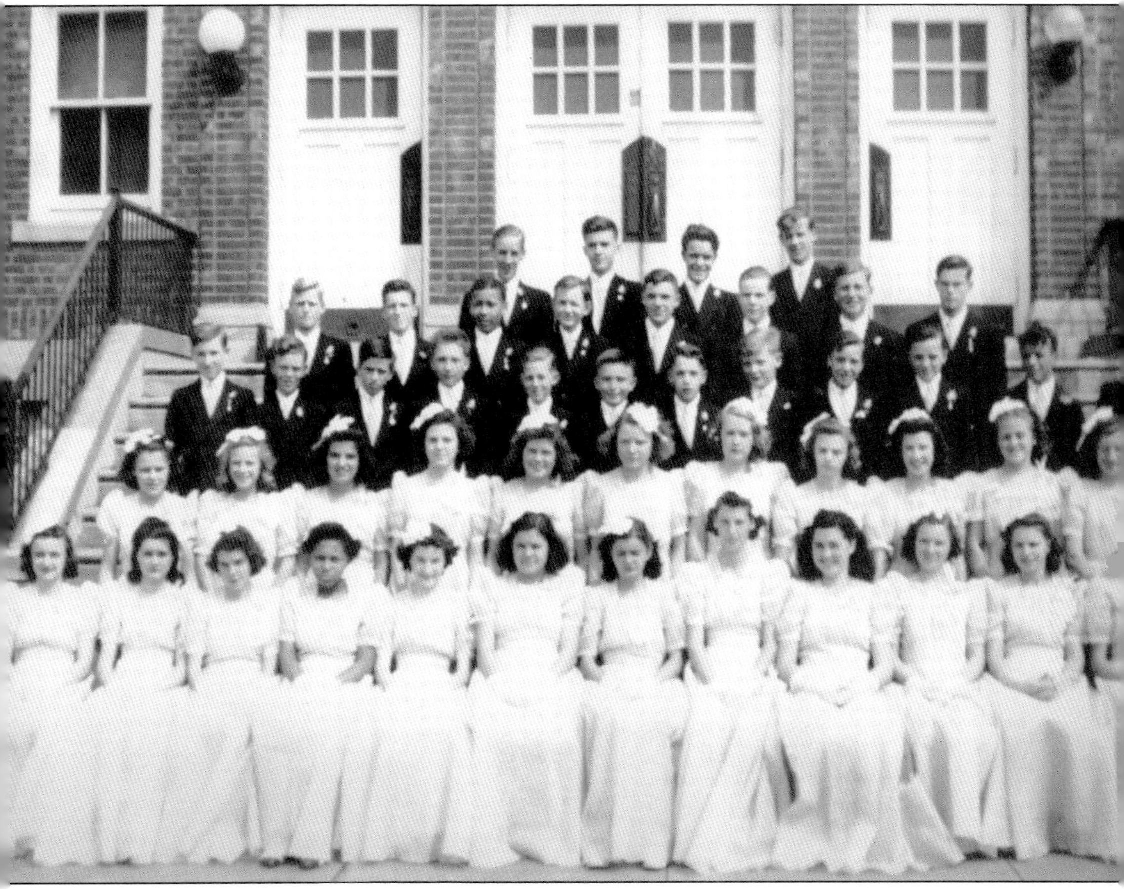

Saint Joseph School opened its doors to students on January 22, 1917, with a starting class of 65 students. By 1928, enrollment had doubled and a new addition to the building became necessary. During the Depression, students helped support each other and the community. The graduating eighth grade class of 1941 is pictured here. (Courtesy of Eileen Johnston Collins.)

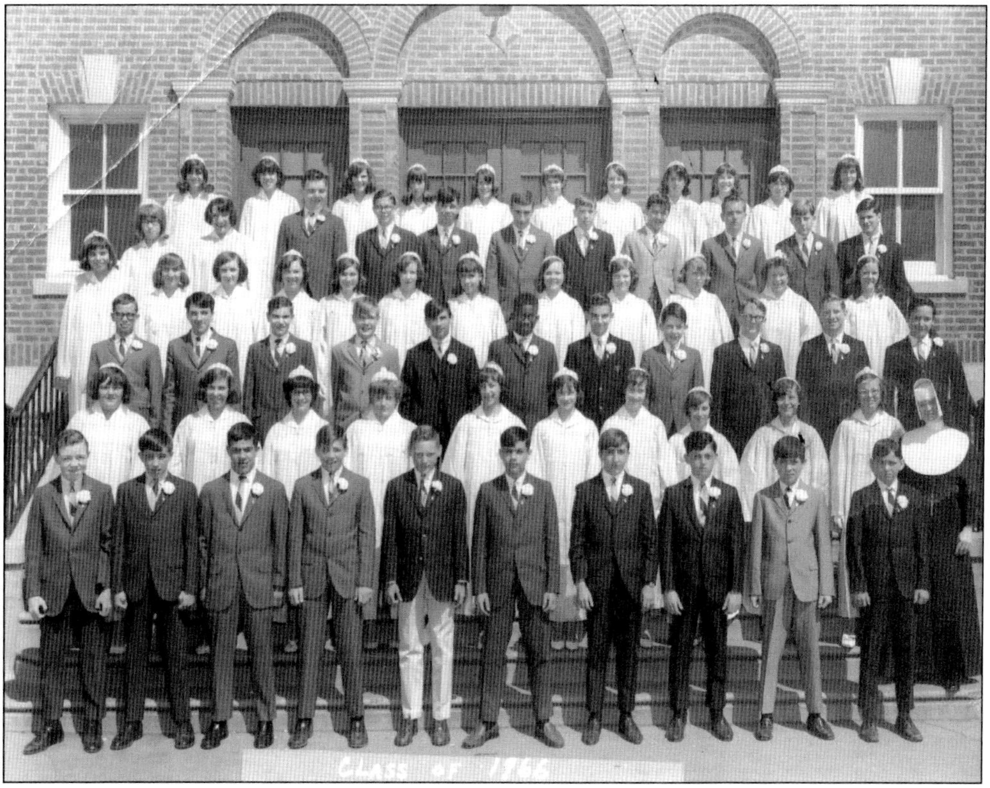

Saint Joseph School played a significant role in the community by providing an alternative to public education for students in kindergarten through eighth grade. Known for its strict adherence to moral values and quality education, St. Joe's (as it was affectionately called) produced well-rounded and stable students ready to continue their education at either Monsignor Bonner High School (for boys), or Archbishop Prendergast High School (for girls). Saint Joseph School closed its doors in September 2010 after 93 years serving the children of the community. The graduating eighth grade class of 1966 is pictured here. (Courtesy of James Mazzotta.)

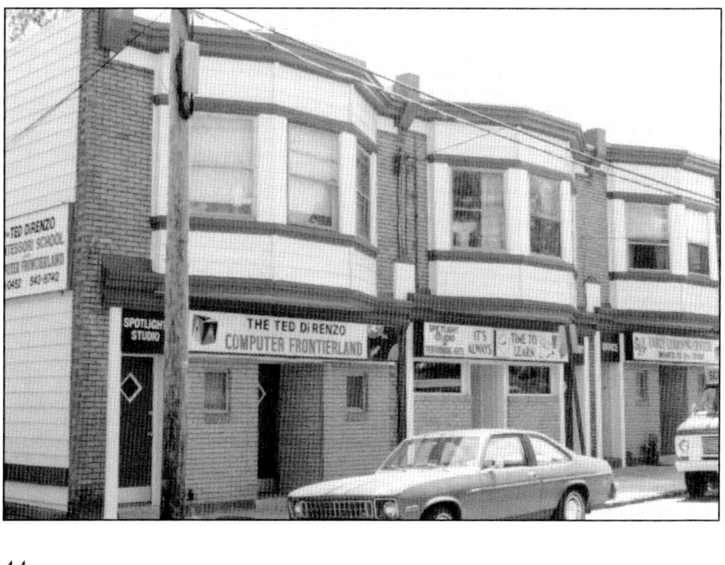

Nursery schools for the youngest members of the community became common in the 1970s, when more women started entering the workplace. Ted DiRenzo Montessori School first opened the doors at this Clifton Avenue location in September 1969 with only four pupils. (Courtesy of Connie DiRenzo.)

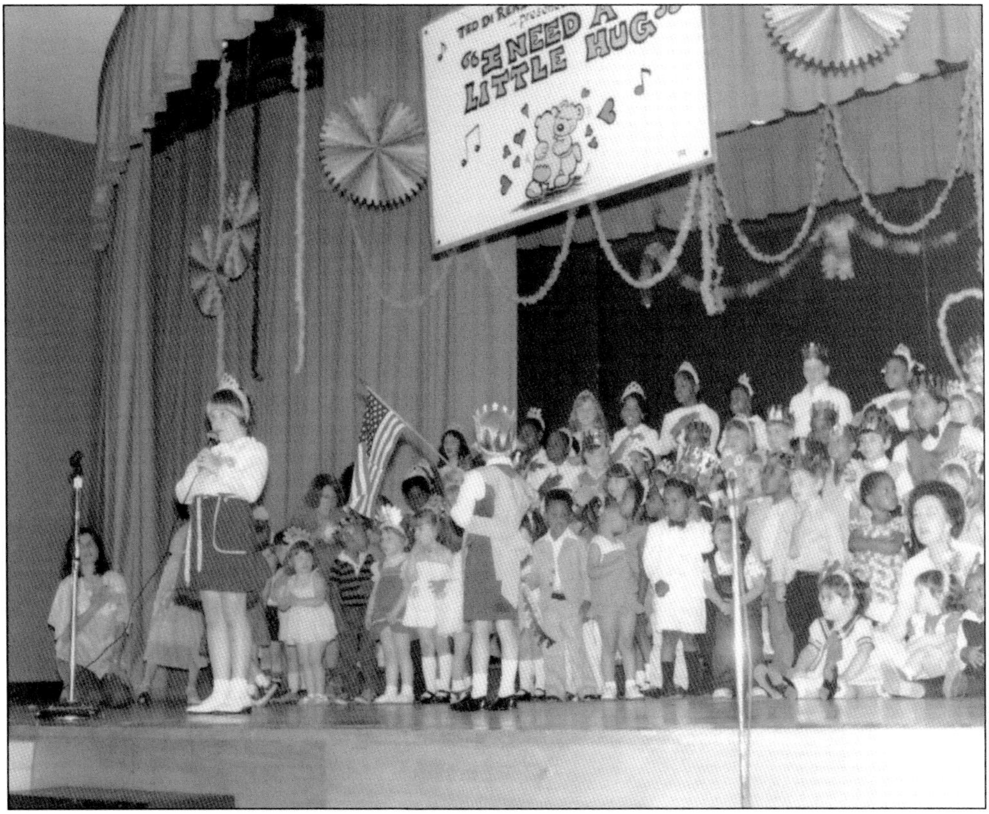

Part of the curriculum at Ted DiRenzo Montessori School provides children with ample opportunities to showcase their talents. Events like the Thanksgiving and Christmas pageants focus on activities in performing arts, history, and self esteem. The highlight of each school year is the graduation celebration, held to coincide with older children's graduations from other grades. Most of the celebrations, like this one from 1980, have a theme. (Courtesy of Connie DiRenzo.)

By 1972, the Ted DiRenzo Montessori School had grown from four pupils to eighty, which necessitated a move to larger quarters. Fortunately, the school was able to acquire a building on Bartram Avenue and renovate it to suit their needs. After many renovations, the school, pictured in May 2011, became an accredited private academic institution and grew to accommodate 120 students, serving children ranging in age from infants to sixth graders. (Photograph by Elizabeth MacGuire.)

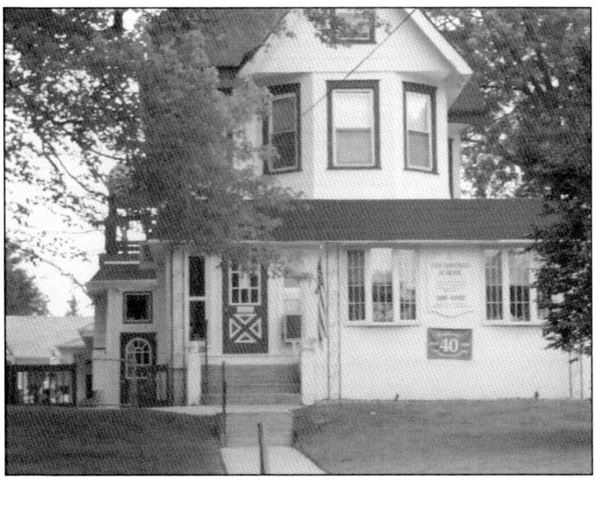

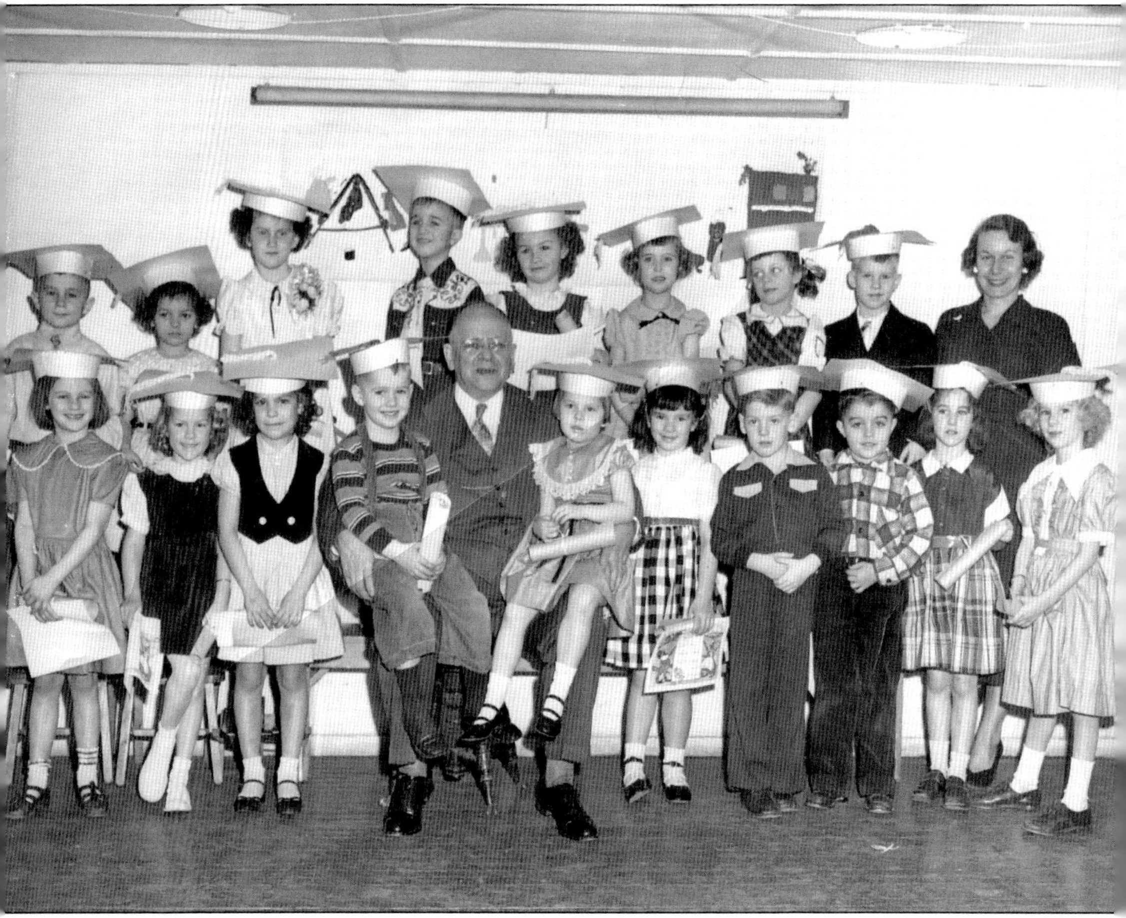

Faber Stengel, superintendent of Collingdale School District, took an active interest in his students. He attended sporting events, cheering for the players and admonishing those who were out of line. Pictured here with the 1953 kindergarten class at Harris Elementary School, Stengel presented each student in the graduating class with a diploma. (Courtesy of Collingdale High School Alumni Association.)

Four

Civic Community
Government, Businesses, and Rescue Services

When Collingdale borough officially incorporated on December 23, 1891, the first order of business was to establish the local governing council, whose responsibilities would include setting up ordinances to provide necessary services and ensuring that the fledging community would continue to grow. The first council consisted of six men whose interest in the community's continued existence ensured that necessary governmental procedures would be followed. The council took roughly three weeks to form. The initial meeting, held on January 10, 1892, established seven departments and appointed Maximilian LaRoche as the first burgess.

Two of LaRoche's first acts as burgess were establishing land boundaries in the borough and commissioning Enon Harris to map out the borough streets. Rather soon after Harris completed the map, other improvements took place, such as lighting—done by the Pennsylvania Globe Gas & Light Company at a cost of $25 per month.

The first businesses established in Collingdale included a woodturning factory, a flourishing floral business, and a post office; the floral business and the woodturning factory were LaRoche's businesses. His large greenhouses spanned six acres and had huge glass roofs, providing a showcase for roses and chrysanthemums. The Collingdale borough's seal honors LaRoche's passion for roses, which were his specialty.

Civic organizations formed to meet community needs. Some, like the fire departments, had been established from the beginning, while others arose as the need became apparent. An example of this was the Women's Club that filled the community's need for a public library and dissolved in the early 1970s.

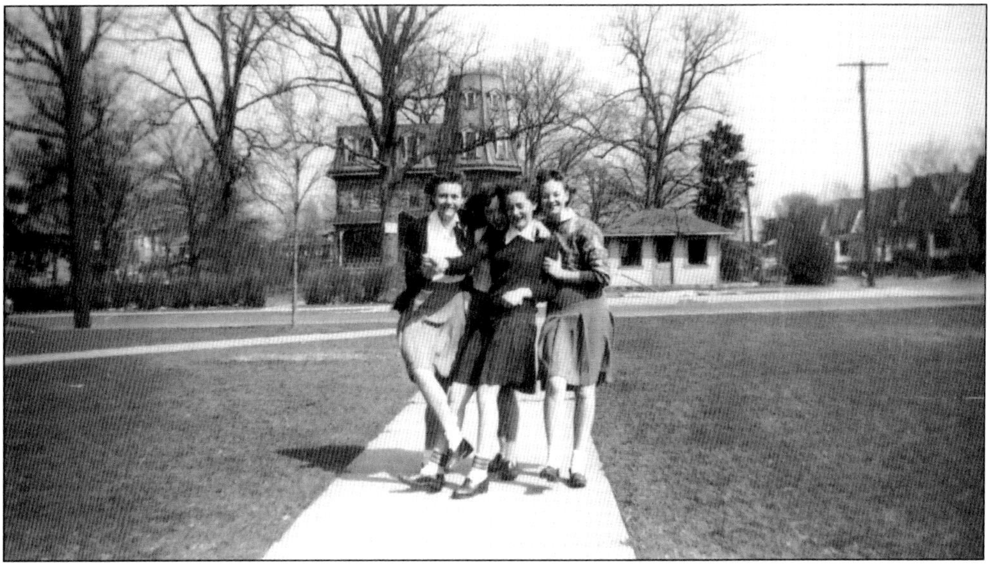

Maximilian LaRoche, the first burgess of Collingdale, lived in the house in the background from the time he accepted the position of burgess in 1891 until he left in 1904 due to a dispute with the borough council. This mid-1940s photograph shows, from left to right, Joan Dawson, Barbara Hunter, and two unidentified girls on the lawn of the high school, which faced the mansion. (Courtesy of Collingdale High School Alumni Association—Ann Speer collection.)

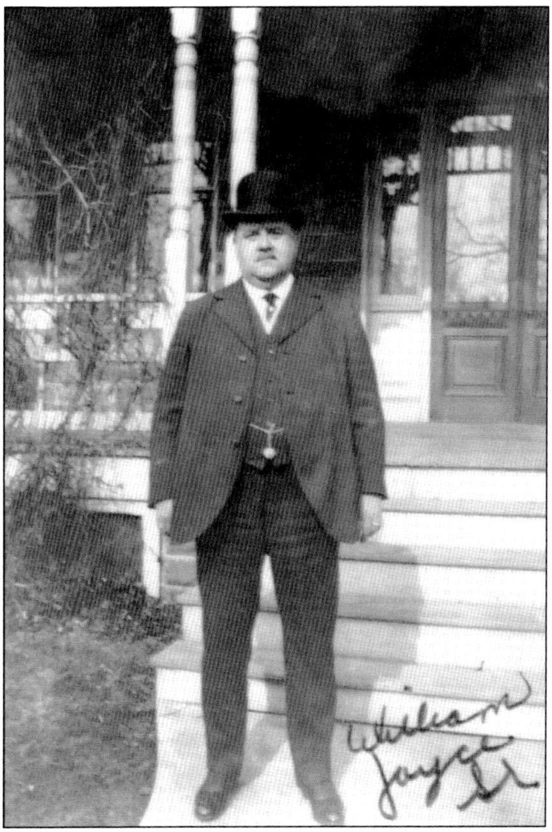

William Joyce, the third burgess of Collingdale, had a lively interest in the improvement of the borough. When he took over from Joseph Beswick in January 1909, Joyce worked with the existing council to provide new services related to transportation and infrastructure. Even after his term ended in January 1913, Joyce kept a hand in community affairs. (Courtesy of Keith Lockhart.)

Charles Johnston, pictured in his living room in 1958, became the last burgess of Collingdale when a Pennsylvania state ruling in 1961 changed the title to mayor. Technically, Johnston also became the first mayor of Collingdale, since the change occurred before he left office in January 1962. (Courtesy of Nancy Johnston Collier.)

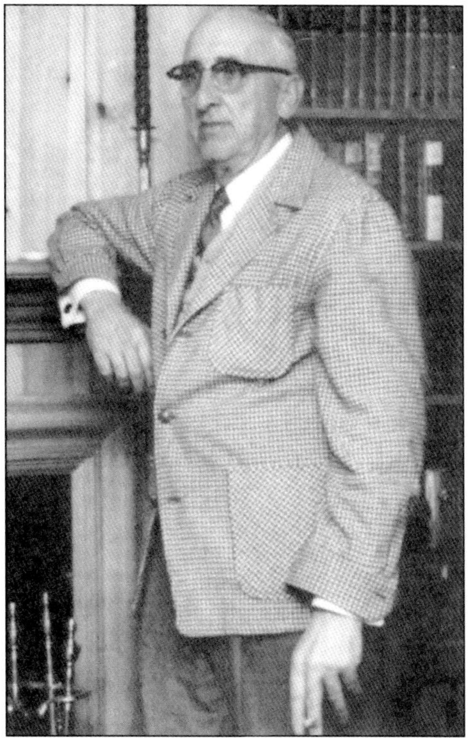

Frank Kelly, pictured here in 1991, is the longest-running mayor in Delaware County, after 42 consecutive years as mayor of Collingdale. Kelly entered the office on January 5, 1970. One of his greatest accomplishments as mayor was helping save the Collingdale High School building from demolition. An equally important accomplishment was the acquisition of land for Collingdale Park in 1972. (Photograph by Ann Neborak.)

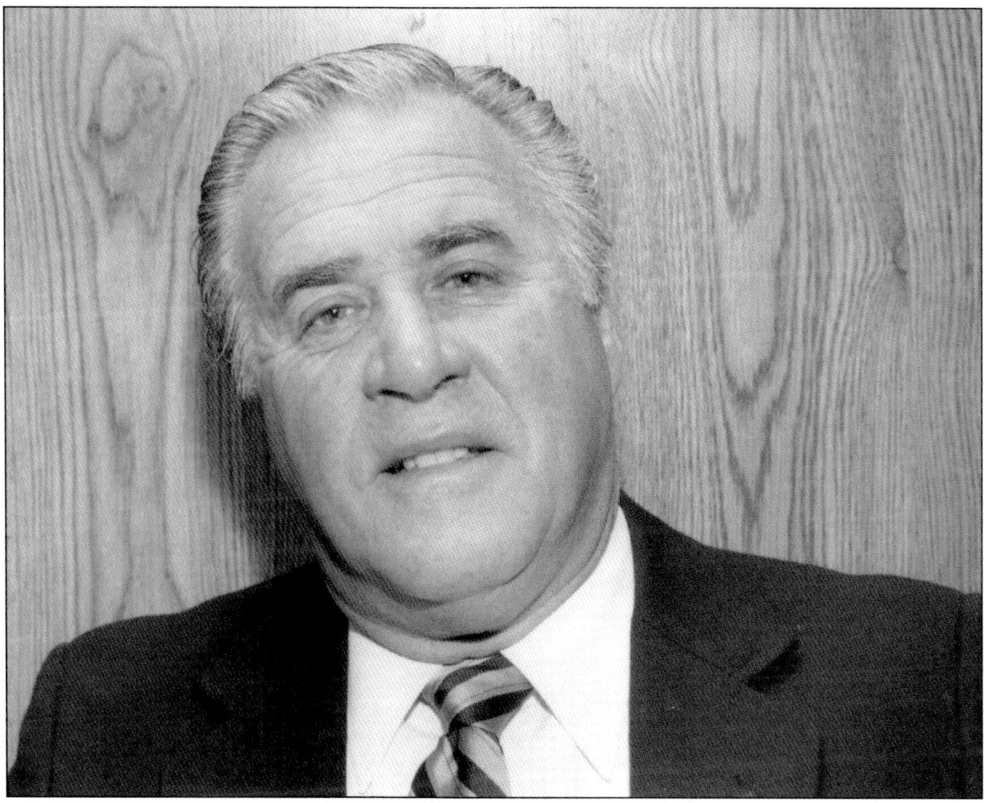

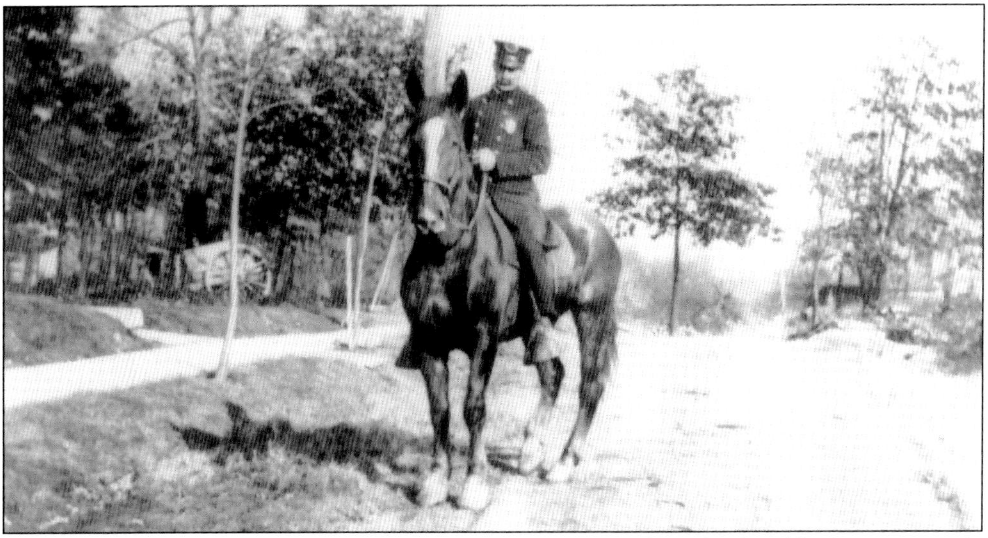

Isaac Diehl was considered by most to be Collingdale's first police chief, and had an active role in the community. Some have described him as a jack of all trades. He served as a sanitation supervisor and helped oversee the installation of Collingdale's first sewer system. He also served as a member of the first volunteer fire department and was active in Collingdale's police department from January 8, 1912, until March 1916. He became captain of Collingdale Fire Company No. 1 during the influenza pandemic of 1918. (Courtesy of Jim Powers.)

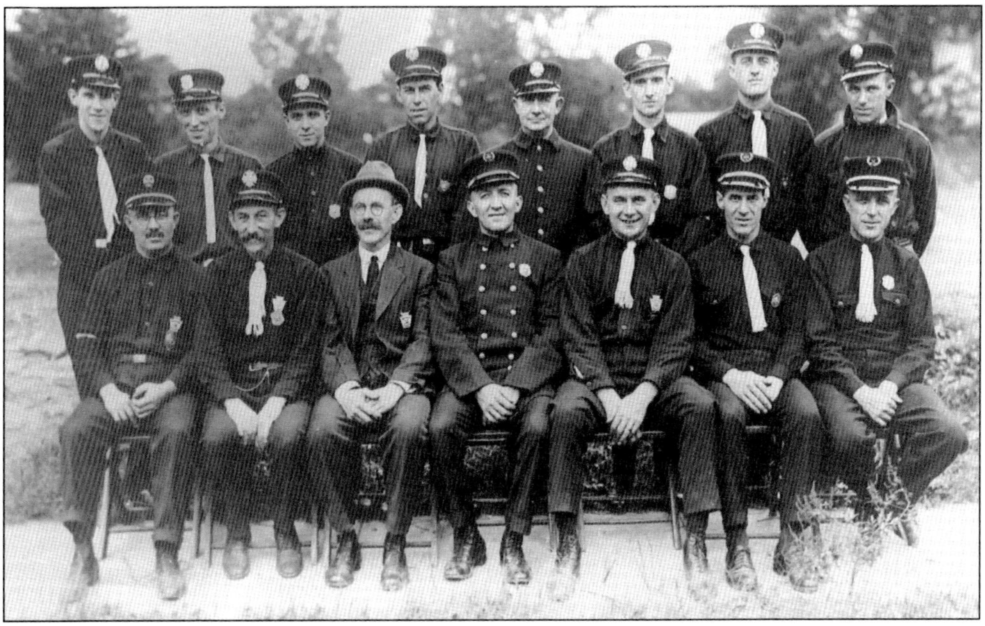

By 1911, criminal activity had increased to the point that the lone police officer assigned to the borough could not handle it all by himself. Borough officials decided to put together a committee, which created a volunteer police force. This 1915 photograph shows the volunteer police force posing in a field near the borough hall on Clifton Avenue. Andrew Voss, Chauney E. Bryant, Isaac Diehl, Thomas Dorsey, and William H. Hick Jr. were mentioned as part of this volunteer police force in a *Chester Times* article from September 9, 1915. (Courtesy of Stynor Carter and Fred Howell Sr.)

William Fitzpatrick served as Collingdale's first official chief of police. He was sworn in on January 2, 1928, and served until his retirement in 1948. During his tenure, Fitzpatrick initiated an efficient system of tracking criminals and instituted various changes that improved the reliability of service to the citizens of the community. (Courtesy of Sally Henry.)

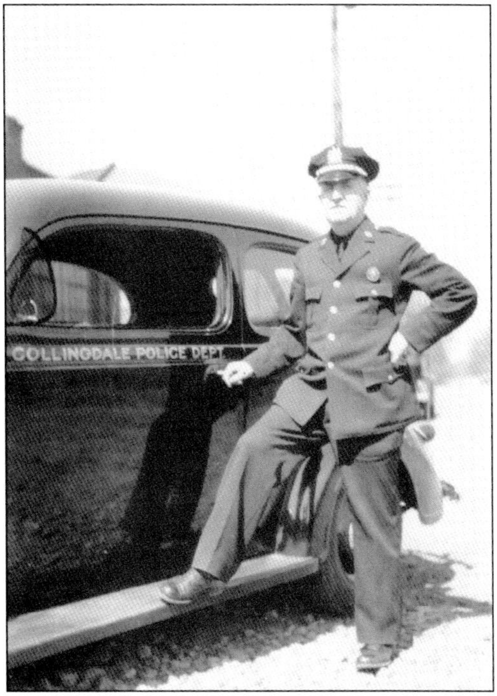

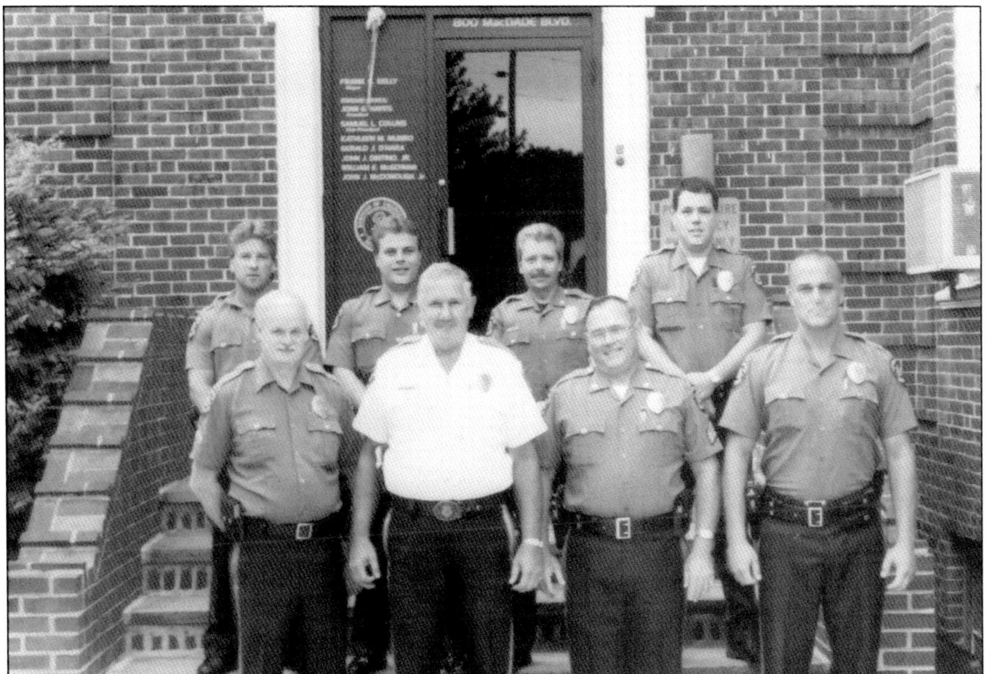

The police department continues to work in the community and sponsors various programs, such as DARE (Drug Abuse Resistance Education), which teaches children about the dangers of drugs and alcohol. In this 1991 photograph, the officers are, from left to right, (first row) Cpl. John Singley, Chief Robert Morris, John Hewlings, and Frank McKone; (second row) Jim Clifton, Dan Fynes, Charles Laut, and Robert Adams. (Courtesy of Jim Powers.)

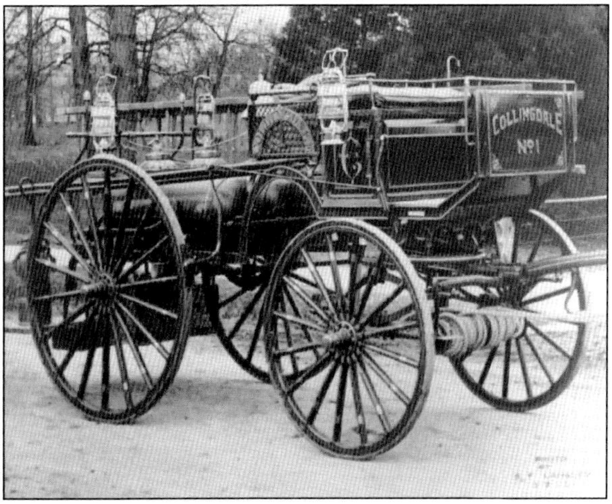

Collingdale Fire Company No. 1, the sixth member of the Delaware County Firemen's Association, has a rich history of serving the borough and surrounding communities. Established on October 6, 1906, the all-volunteer fire company responds to emergencies, provides fire safety classes, and sponsors events. This is Collingdale Fire Company No. 1's first fire engine, a chemical tank that could be moved via either horsepower or manpower. (Courtesy of Stynor Carter; photograph by S.P. Langley.)

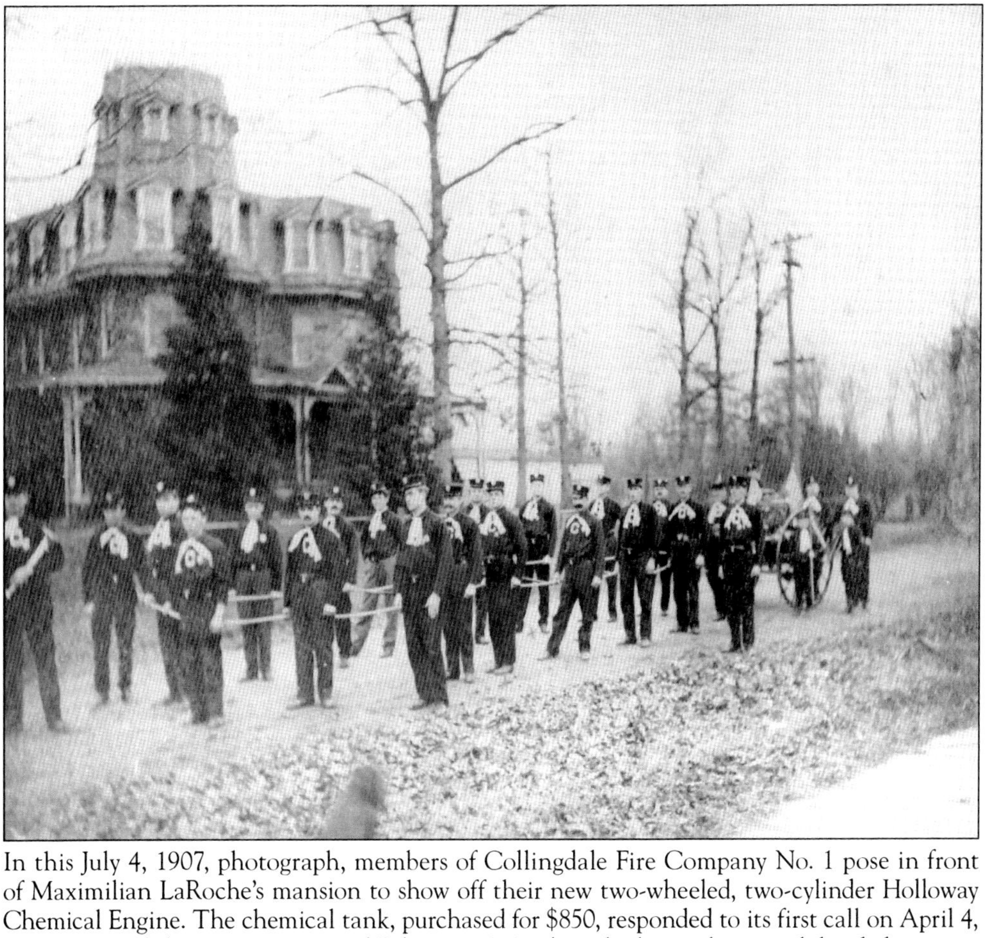

In this July 4, 1907, photograph, members of Collingdale Fire Company No. 1 pose in front of Maximilian LaRoche's mansion to show off their new two-wheeled, two-cylinder Holloway Chemical Engine. The chemical tank, purchased for $850, responded to its first call on April 4, 1907. It served the community until February 1919, when the borough council decided to retire the apparatus and purchase a new truck. (Courtesy of Stynor Carter.)

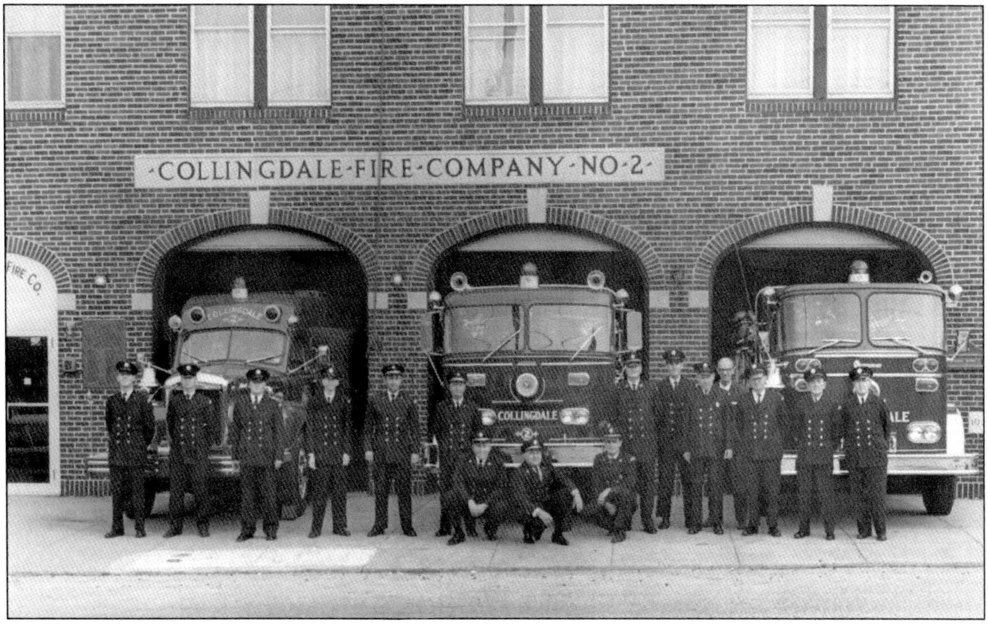

Collingdale Fire Company No. 2 members pose in front of the firehouse in this 1967 photograph. Established in October 1916 to fulfill the needs of residents of the lower half of Collingdale, this all-volunteer company supported and served alongside their fellow firemen in the community. (Courtesy of Collingdale Fire Company No. 2.)

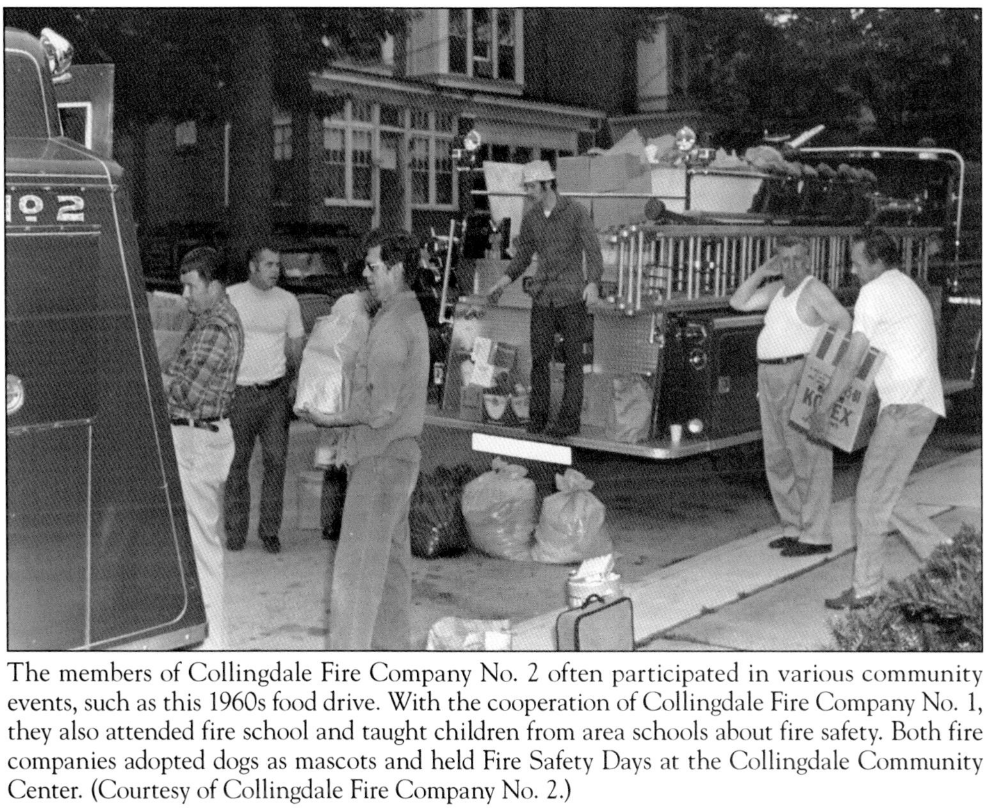

The members of Collingdale Fire Company No. 2 often participated in various community events, such as this 1960s food drive. With the cooperation of Collingdale Fire Company No. 1, they also attended fire school and taught children from area schools about fire safety. Both fire companies adopted dogs as mascots and held Fire Safety Days at the Collingdale Community Center. (Courtesy of Collingdale Fire Company No. 2.)

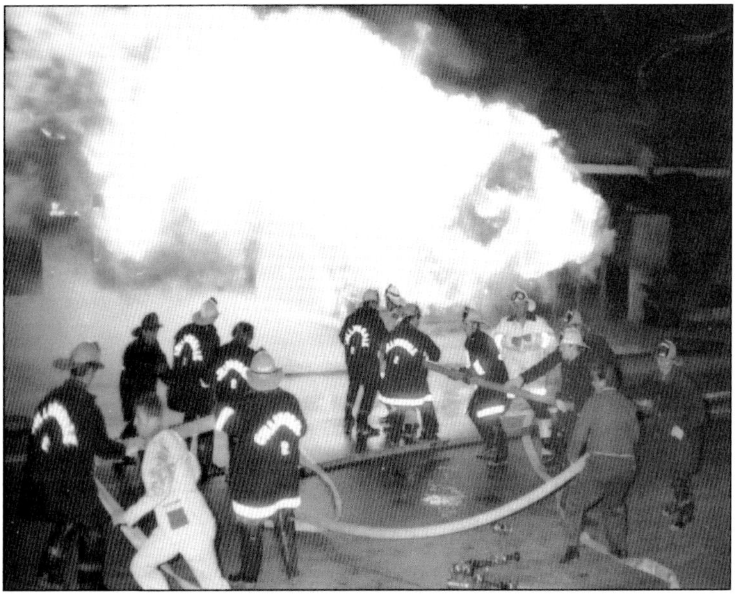

An early morning blaze destroyed the Janess Plumbing and Building Supply building on April 22, 1971. Both Collingdale fire companies responded to the fire. Amazingly, only one fatality occurred—Walter "Bud" Bley suffered a heart attack while running hose line on Rhodes Avenue. (Courtesy of Collingdale Fire Company No. 2; photograph by Keith Urban.)

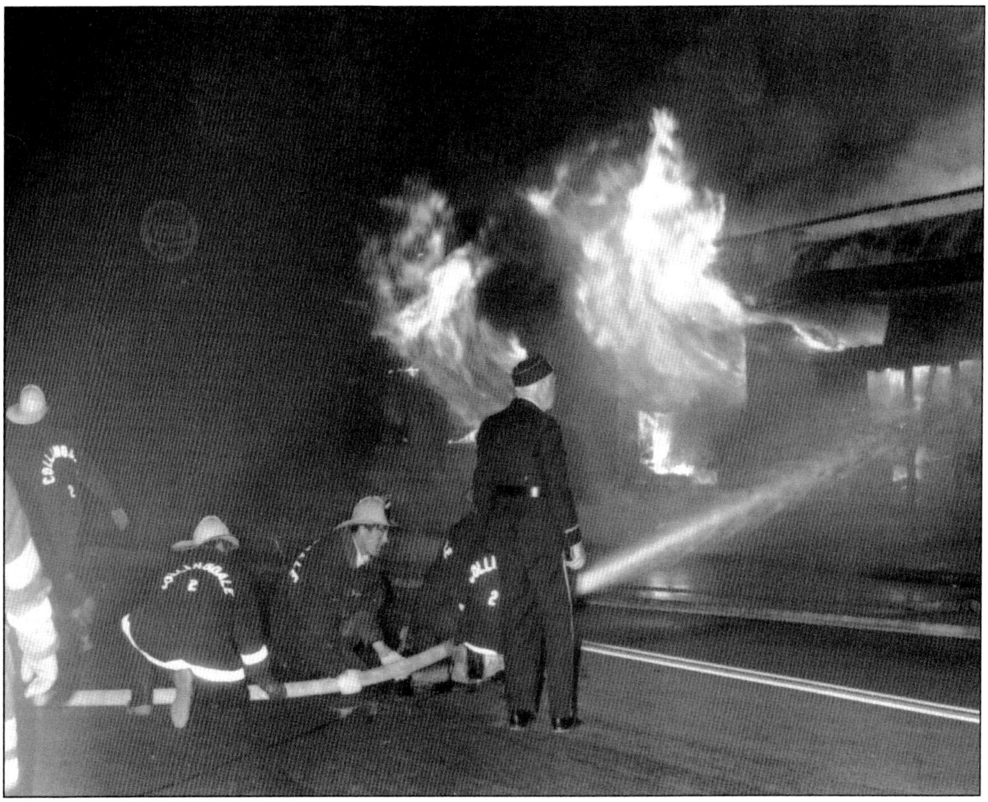

Another photograph of the Janess fire shows one of the older fire captains directing the younger men in their valiant fight to save the building. The Ply-Gems building was also destroyed in the blaze. No businesses replaced those two at that location; it remains a parking lot for the Church of the Nazarene and other businesses on the corner of Staley and Rhodes Avenues. (Courtesy of Collingdale Fire Company No. 2; photograph by Keith Urban.)

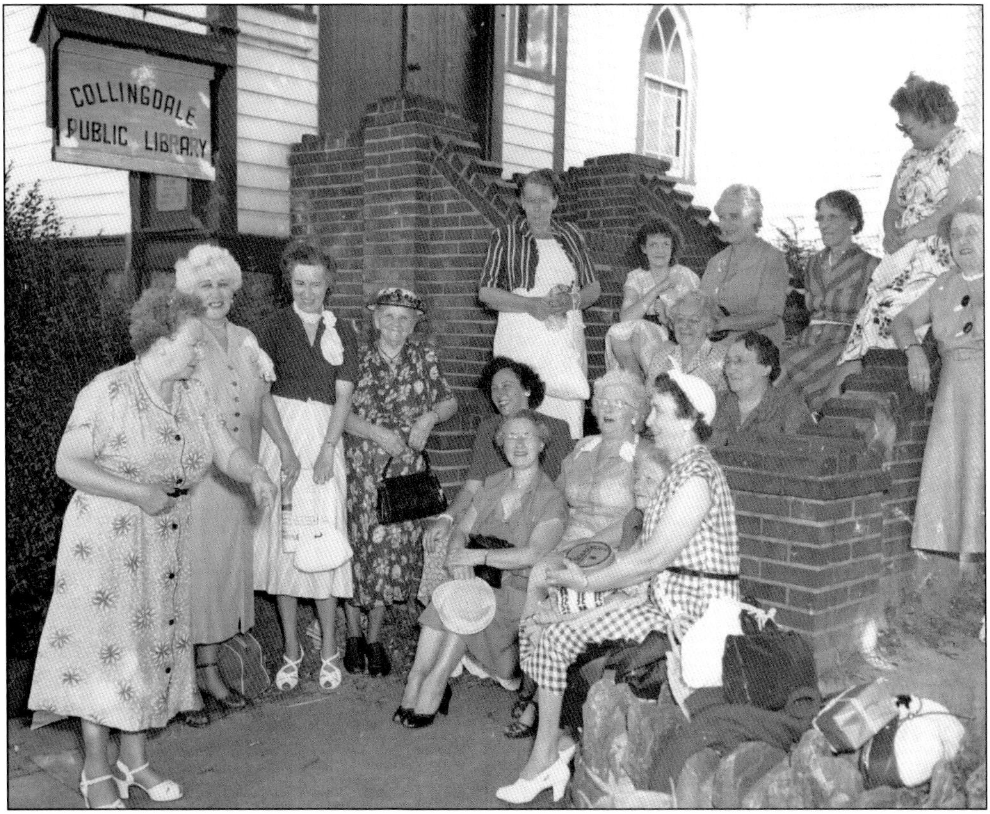

The Women's Club, formed on September 17, 1936, established a public library as one of their first orders of business. The women also worked hard for many community efforts, including blood drives. This 1952 photograph shows the members of the Women's Club in front of the library as they wait to board a bus to Ship Bottom, New Jersey. (Courtesy of the Collingdale Library Association.)

The Collingdale Public Library has served students and the community since May 1937. The building seen here in May 2011 was not the first; the first public library was on Clifton Avenue, and the second was the old Trinity Episcopal rectory, which was rented for $25 per month. This building was constructed in 1976 and dedicated on October 12, 1978. (Photograph by Elizabeth MacGuire.)

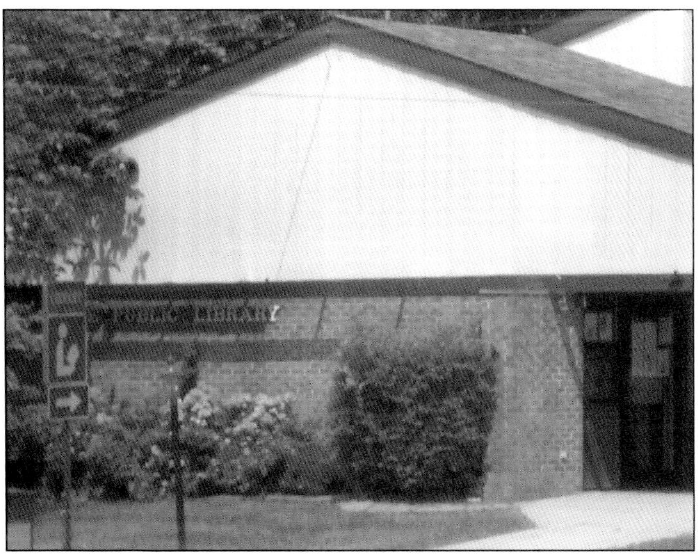

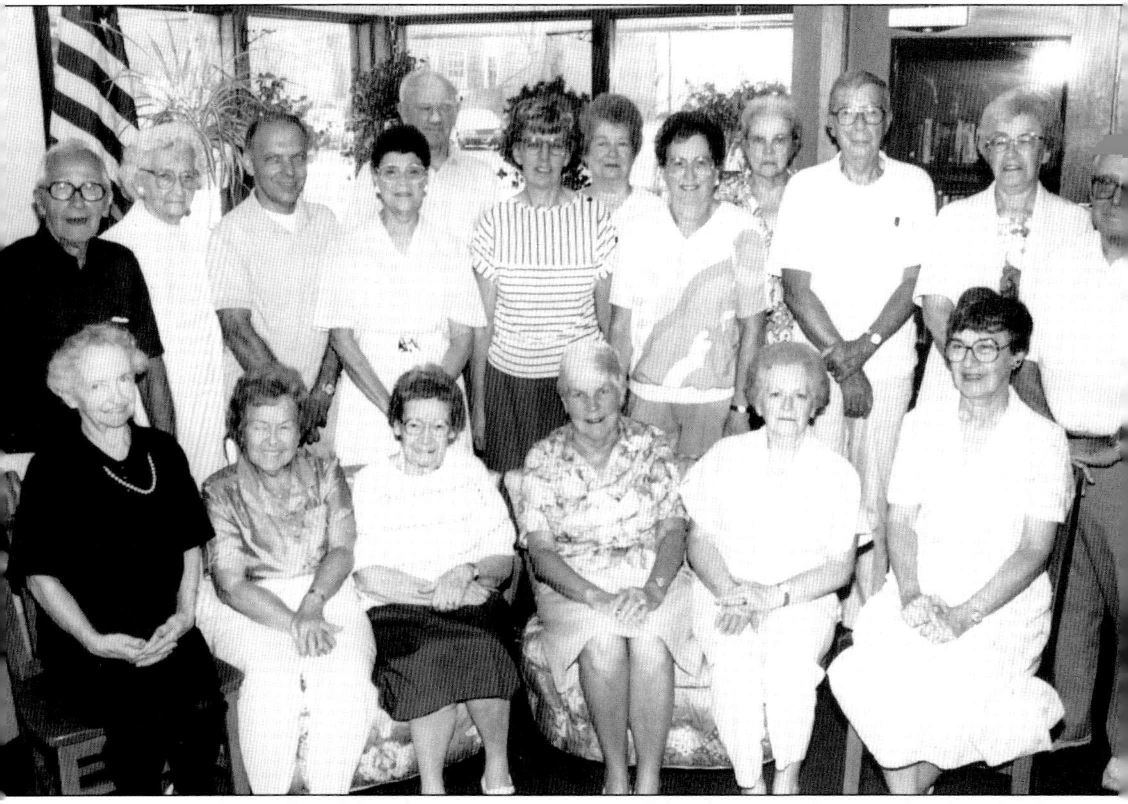

Members of the Collingdale Library Association posed for this 1991 photograph taken for the 100th anniversary of Collingdale borough. Pictured from left to right are (first row) Agnes Sweney, Betty Welch, Molly Ottey, Dot Whitaker, Martha Appleman, and Carol Savage; (second row) Joe Salus, Dot Taylor, Bob Crossetti, Mildred Cooney, Bob Grenfell, Fran Allen, Nancy Grenfell, Jean Crozier, Dot Davis, Harold Savage, Gert Hylan, and Gene Appleman. (Courtesy of Keith Lockhart; photograph by Anne Neborak.)

Five

Patriotic Community

Parades, Ceremonies, and Other Special Events

Collingdale celebrated its veterans and war casualties on Memorial Day and, until recently, Veteran's Day with ceremonies and parades. Two organizations formed to serve veterans and their families; one of them, the American Legion Post 669, was established on October 10, 1934, and served the community through various programs. After World War II, returning veterans felt the need for services that the American Legion could not provide and wanted a way to honor fallen comrades who died in foreign lands. Thus, the Joseph Marshall–Donald R. McKay VFW Post 5428 mustered on May 23, 1952, and provided an avenue for veterans and their families to provide for veterans who served overseas.

The World War I monument in Collingdale Park served as a reminder to Collingdale residents of the sacrifice made by brave men who died in the "war to end all wars." Every Memorial Day, a parade would stop at the monument for a half-hour ceremony that honored veterans and those lost in the war. The parade was discontinued in the late 1980s, but the ceremony continued. By 1996, concerned citizens felt there was a need for all veterans and fallen soldiers to be honored and remembered.

On Veteran's Day (November 8) in 1997, a new monument was dedicated for Collingdale veterans and fallen soldiers. The All Wars Memorial lists the names of all Collingdale residents known to have participated in action up to that date.

Collingdale celebrated its 30th, 50th, 75th, and 100th anniversaries with parades and other special events, such as costume contests. Some older residents fondly recall the huge diamond jubilee parade. Fourth of July was a time for fireworks, parades and games, and the main parade, in its heyday, boasted two bands and various floats.

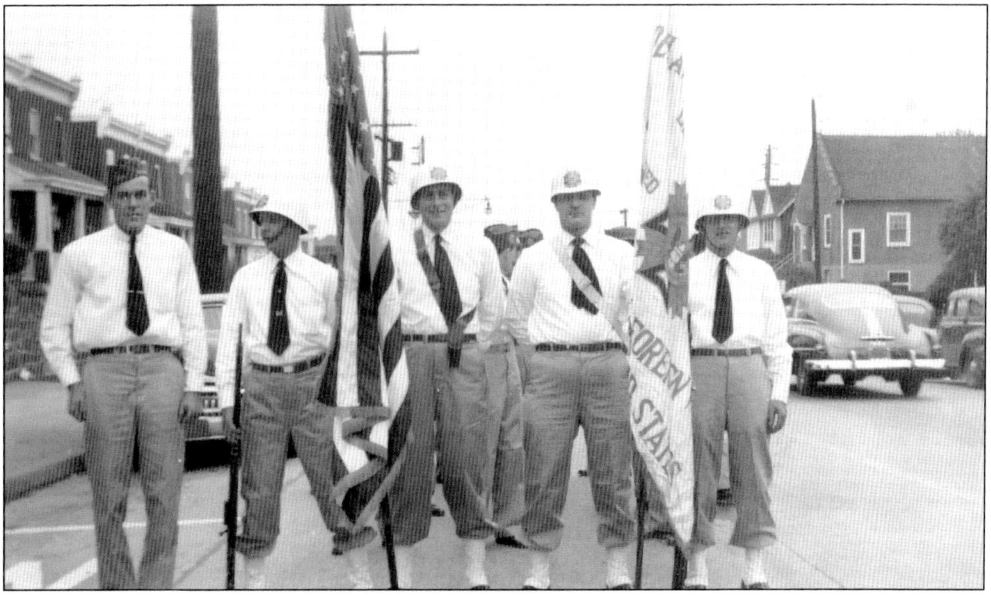

One of the first acts of the newly formed VFW was to march in the Memorial Day parade held on May 30, 1952. Pictured here are, from left to right, VFW founder Harry O'Hagan, whose tavern hosted VFW meetings until a building could be constructed; John Jones; Pat DiCristo; George Boot, and unidentified. Behind them, a group of men form a line as they prepare to march down MacDade Boulevard. (Courtesy of Chuck Meehan, Marshall-McKay VFW Post 5248.)

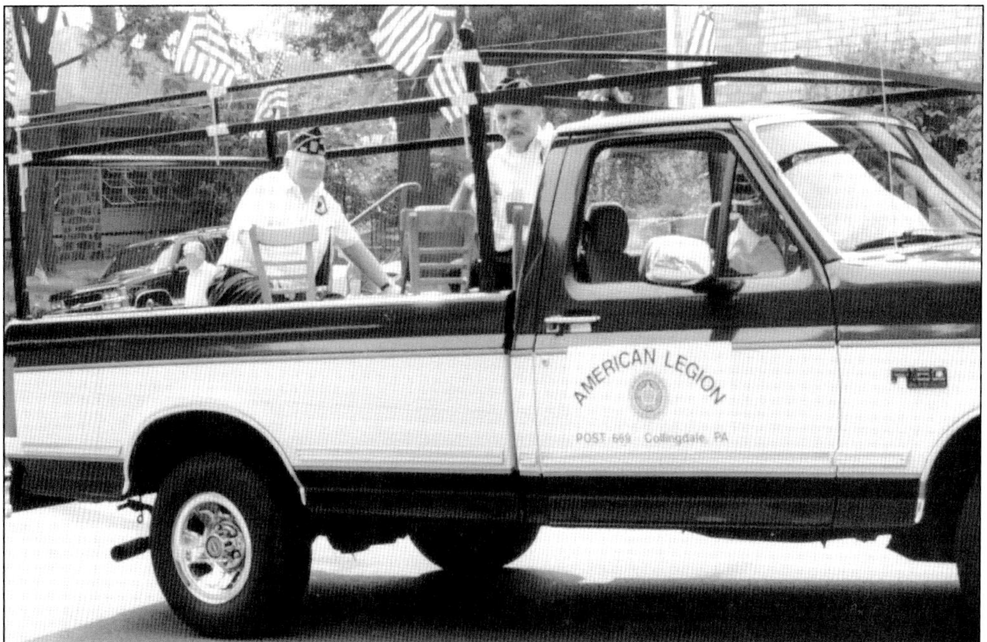

American Legion Post 669 remained fairly active until the late 1960s, and continued to award deserving youngsters for actions that exhibited Americanism until the mid-1970s. Here, Harry Butler (left) and an unidentified man ride in the back of a truck as part of a Memorial Day parade in the late 1980s. (Courtesy of Chuck Meehan, Marshall-McKay VFW Post 5248.)

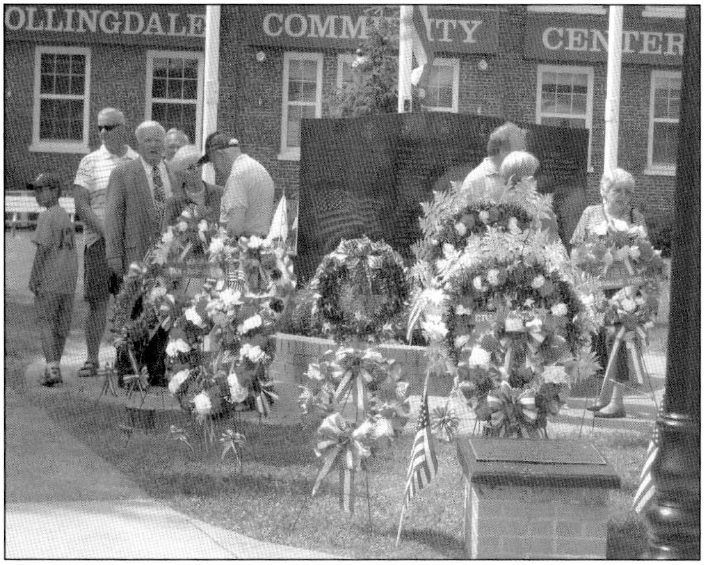

Veterans and other civic organizations gather to honor the dead at the All Wars Memorial in this scene from Memorial Day in 2011. Each organization places a wreath in front of the memorial when their organization is called to do so. Both of the fire departments and the police department are always well represented, along with the veterans' organizations. (Photograph by Elizabeth MacGuire.)

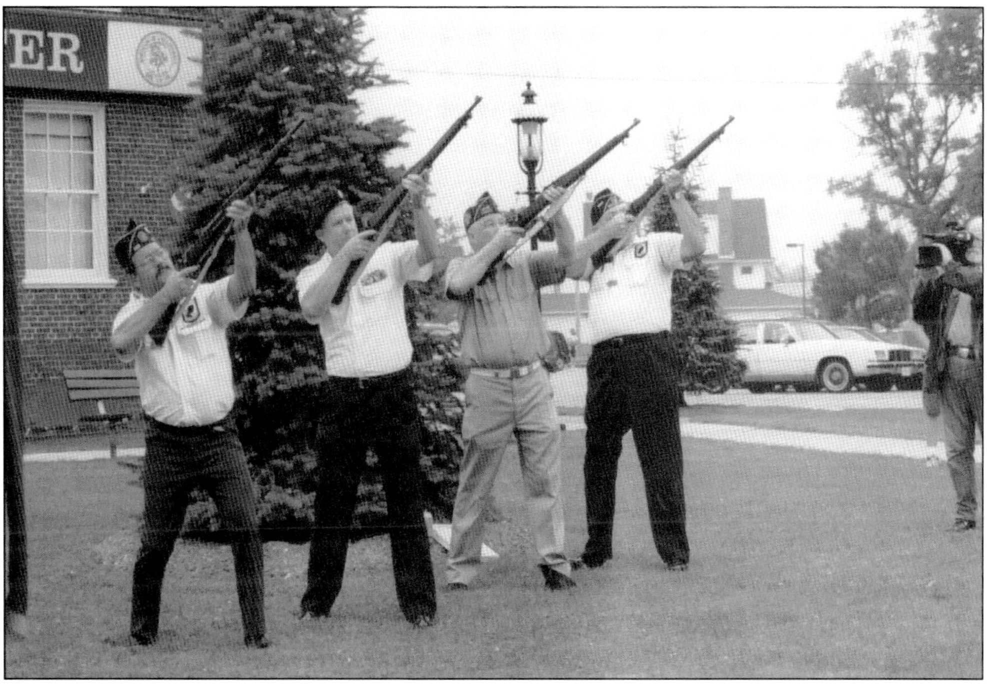

On Memorial Day in 1998, members of VFW Post 5428 and American Legion Post 669 fire a 21-gun salute to honor those lost in battle. When the American Legion Post 669 disbanded in the late 1990s, the VFW post allowed the remaining members to become part of their group. Most, however, decided to join up with other American Legion posts in the surrounding communities due to strict guidelines that specify that members of the VFW had to have served in combat overseas. (Courtesy of Chuck Meehan, Marshall-McKay VFW Post 5248.)

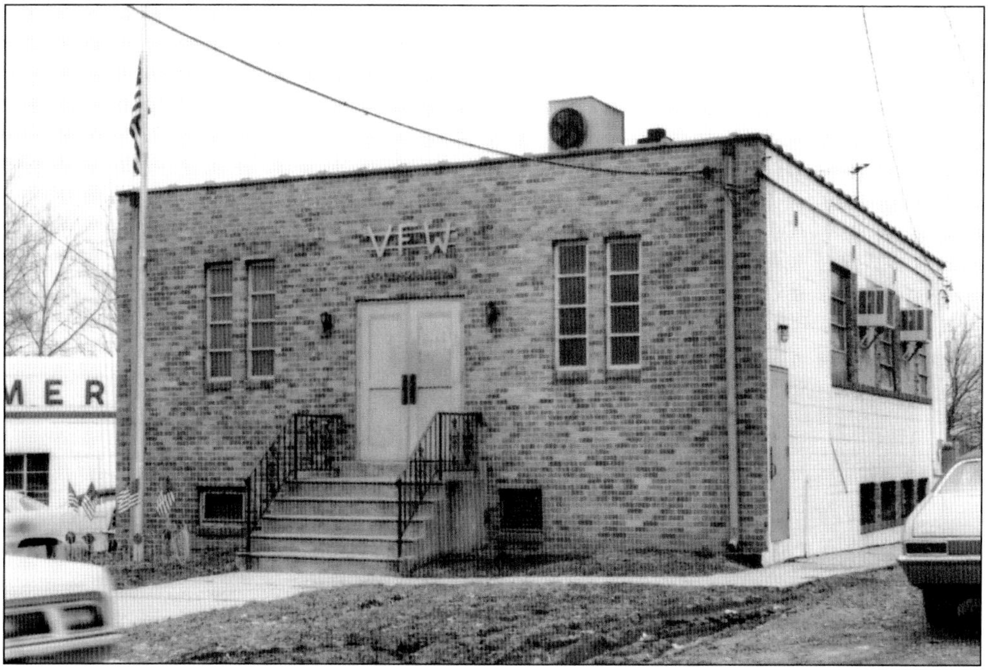

The VFW sponsored two Boy Scout troops in the 1980s and held various functions in this building in the 1960s and 1970s. Built in December 1959, the building boasted a large banquet room, a kitchen, a pool table, and a meeting area where members could relax. During the early years, many dances were held, and a women's auxiliary was formed to complement the men's efforts on behalf of returning servicemen. (Courtesy of Chuck Meehan, Marshall-McKay VFW Post 5248.)

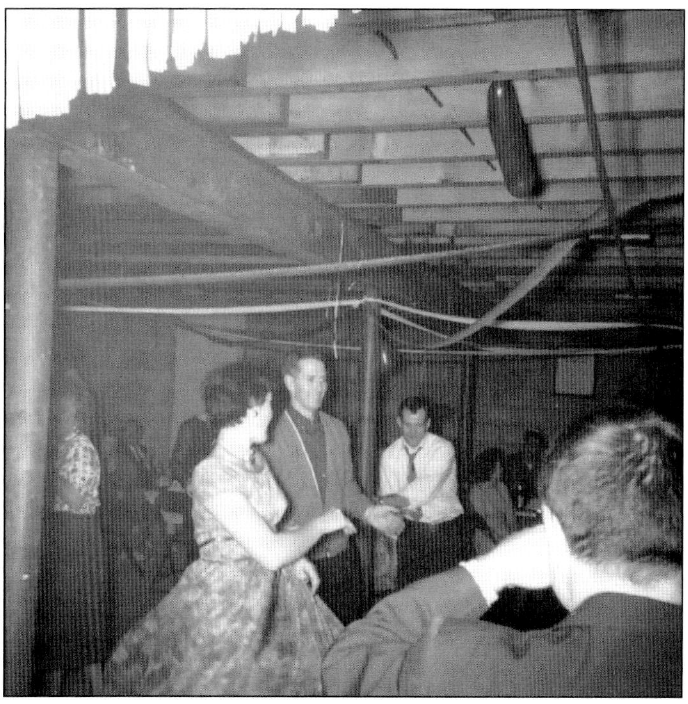

One of the founders of the VFW women's auxiliary was Betty Huddy, shown here dancing at a celebration held in January 1960 to christen the new building. Huddy remained active until the women's auxiliary was disbanded in 1986. Her efforts among the young women of the community were well known, and many programs were started under her capable hands. (Courtesy of Chuck Meehan, Marshall-McKay VFW Post 5248.)

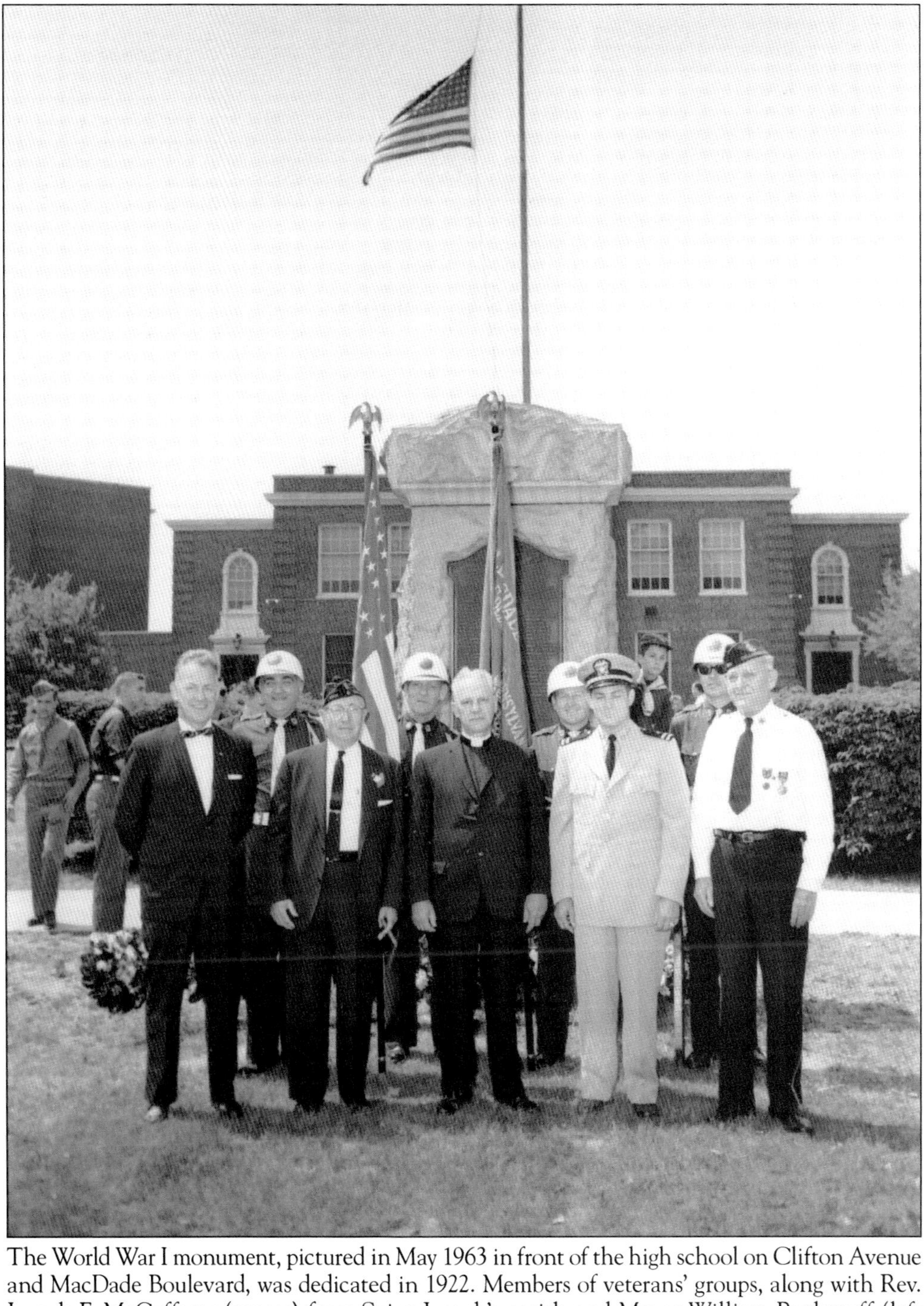

The World War I monument, pictured in May 1963 in front of the high school on Clifton Avenue and MacDade Boulevard, was dedicated in 1922. Members of veterans' groups, along with Rev. Joseph F. McCafferty (center) from Saint Joseph's parish and Mayor William Ruthrauff (left center) proudly posed in front of the monument. (Courtesy of Donald Bird—Joe Bird collection; photograph by John Harris Studios.)

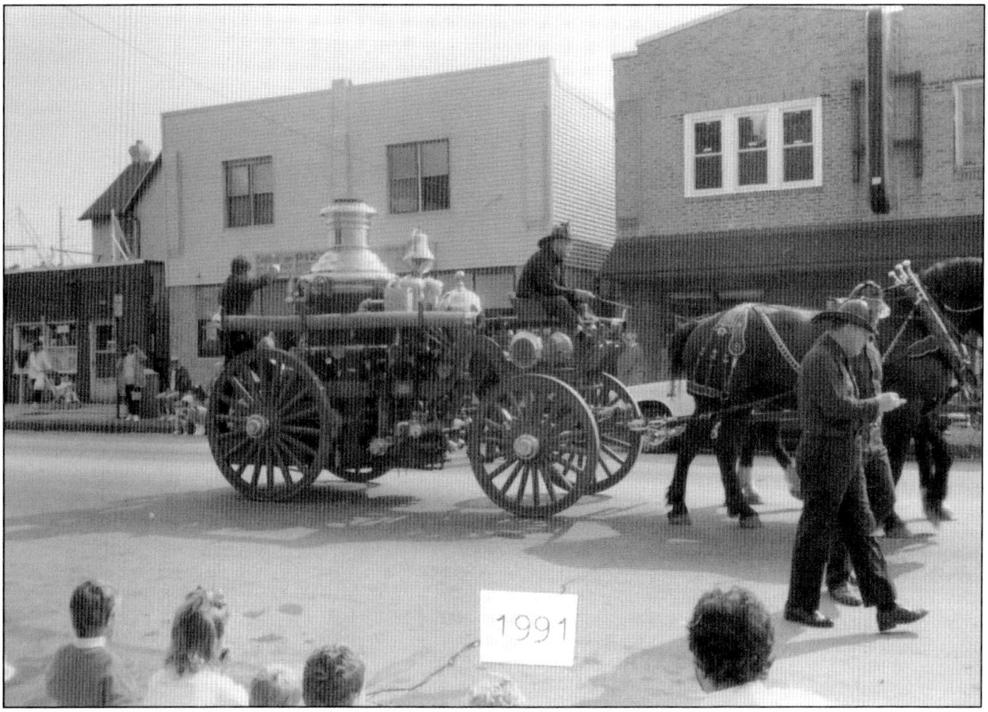

Borough anniversaries were a time to celebrate. For the 100th anniversary of Collingdale borough, celebrated in 1991, the parade had a patriotic theme. Antique fire equipment, such as the chemical tank seen here, and cars promenaded down MacDade Boulevard. (Courtesy of Collingdale High School Alumni Association.)

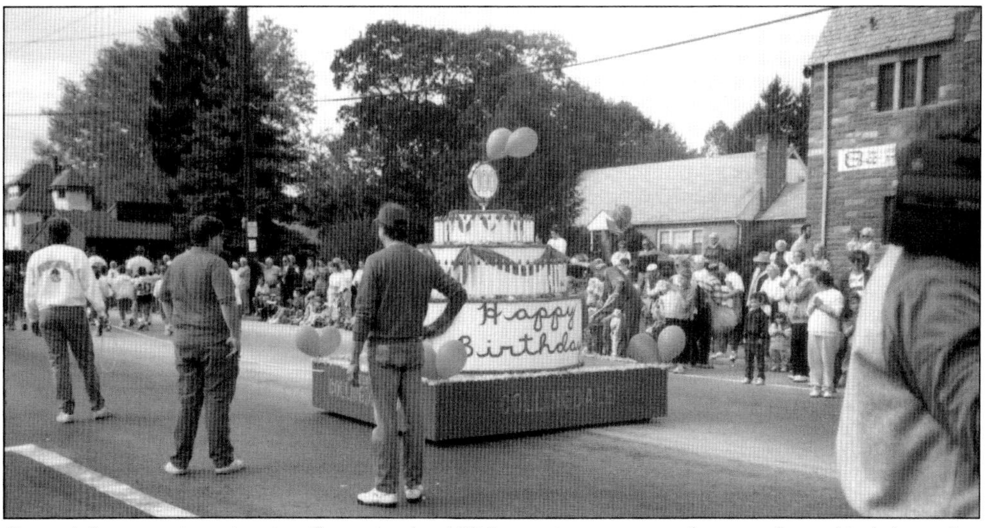

One of the most imaginative floats in the 100th anniversary parade was a huge birthday cake. Members of the borough's sports teams worked on this float. In front of the float (at left in the photograph) is the championship Collingdale Bulldogs football team from the Collingdale Athletics Club. (Courtesy of Collingdale High School Alumni Association.)

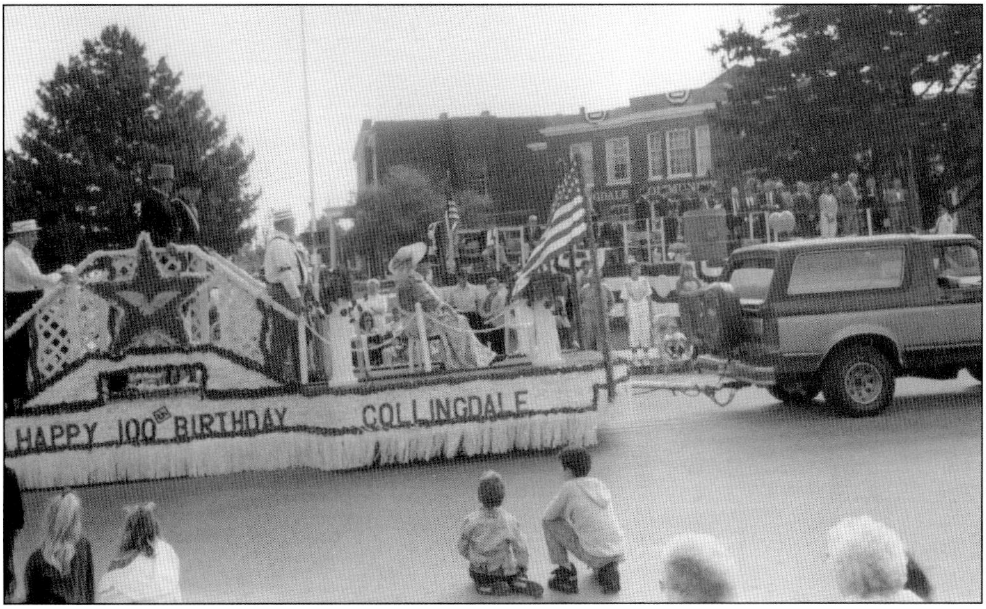

The float pictured here featured members of the borough council and other citizens dressed in period costume from the time of the founding of Collingdale. The mayor and members of the police and fire departments judged parade entries from the stand in front of the Community Center. (Courtesy of Collingdale High School Alumni Association.)

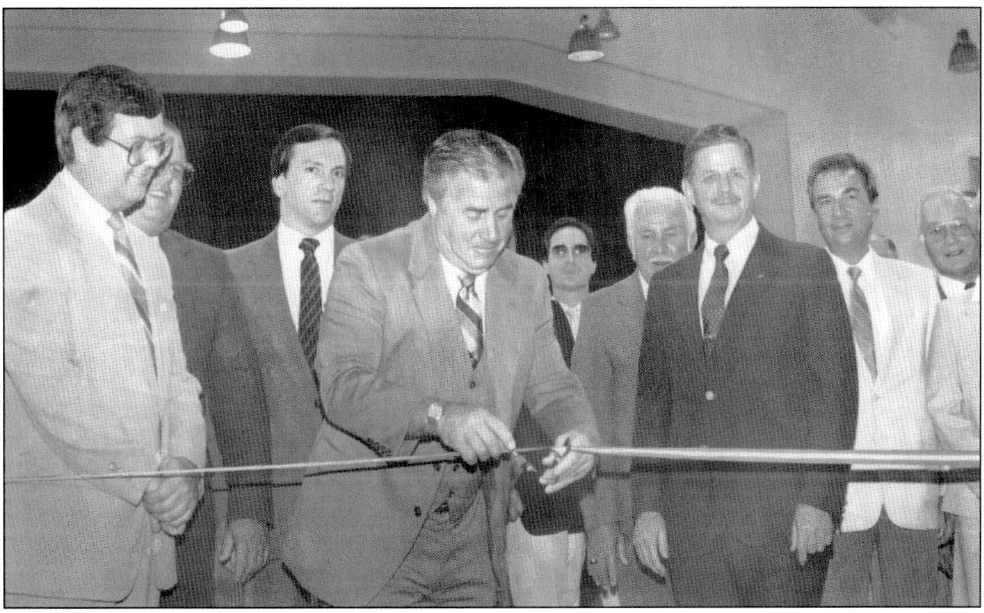

Mayor Frank Kelly cuts the ribbon for the new Collingdale Community Center in this image taken on September 6, 1986. The ceremony had a special meaning to Collingdale High School alumni concerned that their old school would be demolished. On hand to witness the ceremony were, from left to right, Congressman Curt Weldon, State Senator F. Joseph Loeper, State Representative Ron Raymond, Mayor Frank Kelly, Borough Councilman James Powers, Borough Councilman Sam Collins, president of the borough council Jack Hayes, Borough Councilman John Dintino, and Sheriff John Taylor. (Courtesy of Keith Lockhart and Jim Powers.)

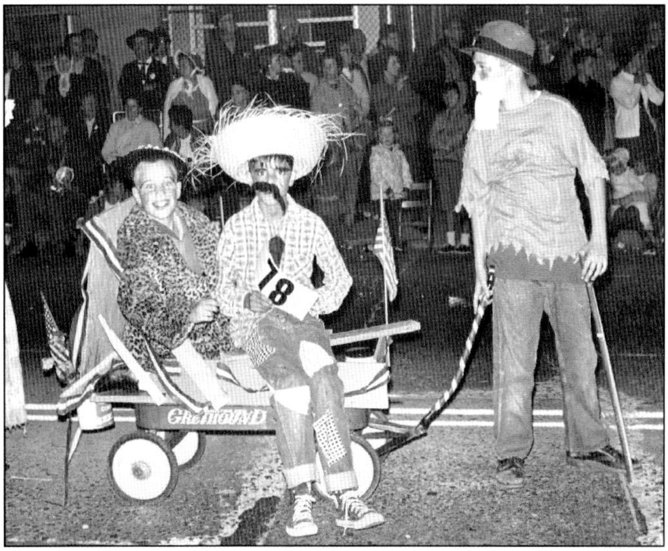

Three young boys parade down the street in the 75th anniversary parade held on October 15, 1966. Many residents dressed in period costume in accordance with "laws" that were enacted to ensure everyone participated in the festivities. Men were required by one of the laws to wear beards. Two of the young boys honor the law by sporting mustaches and beards. (Courtesy of Stynor Carter and Fred Howell Sr.)

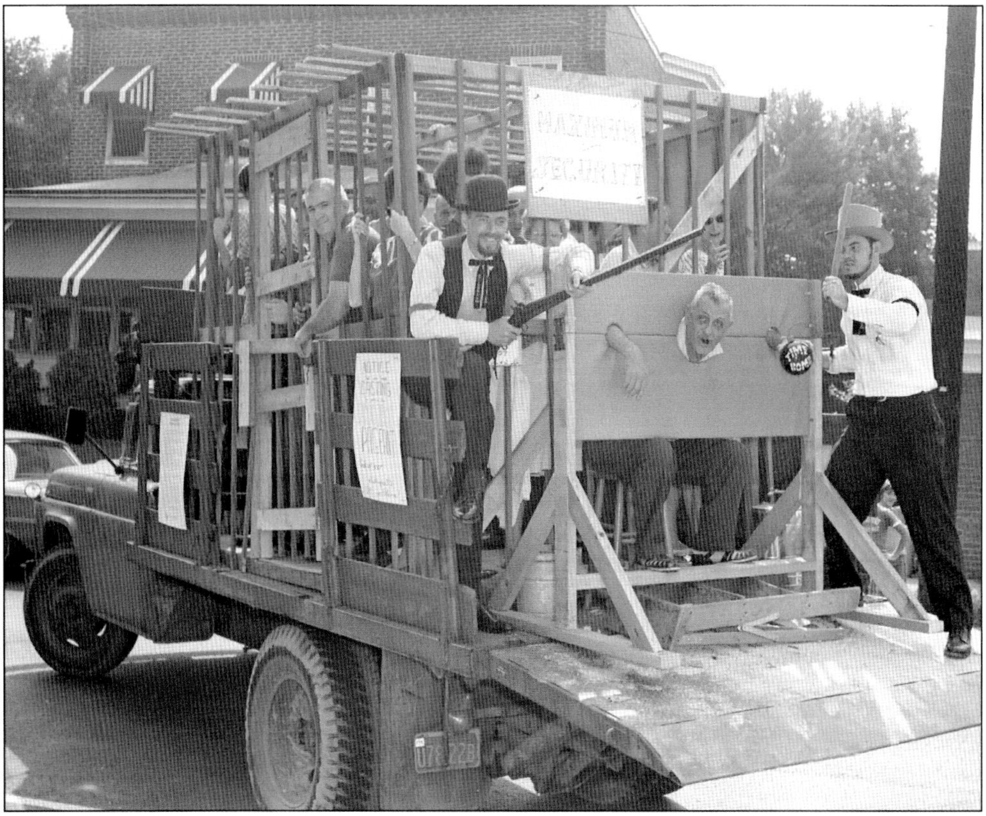

One of the many events of the 1966 Diamond Jubilee Celebration was the "arrest" of any man caught without a beard. Men good-naturedly volunteered to dress up in period costume and ride in a mock-up of a stockade, complete with stocks and a cage to hold the beardless men. Many residents recall the camaraderie that occurred as a result. (Courtesy of Stynor Carter and Fred Howell Sr.)

In this picture, the Brookhaven Junior High School Crusaders Drum and Bugle Corps joins the 75th anniversary parade, along with many other high school bands performing in competition. Winners of the marching band competition, held as part of the celebration, included the Crusaders Drum and Bugle Corps, which came in first. (Courtesy of Stynor Carter and Fred Howell Sr.)

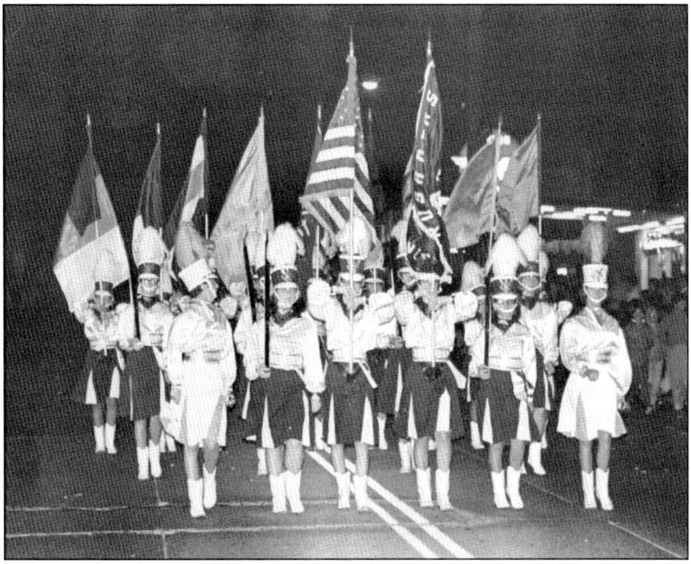

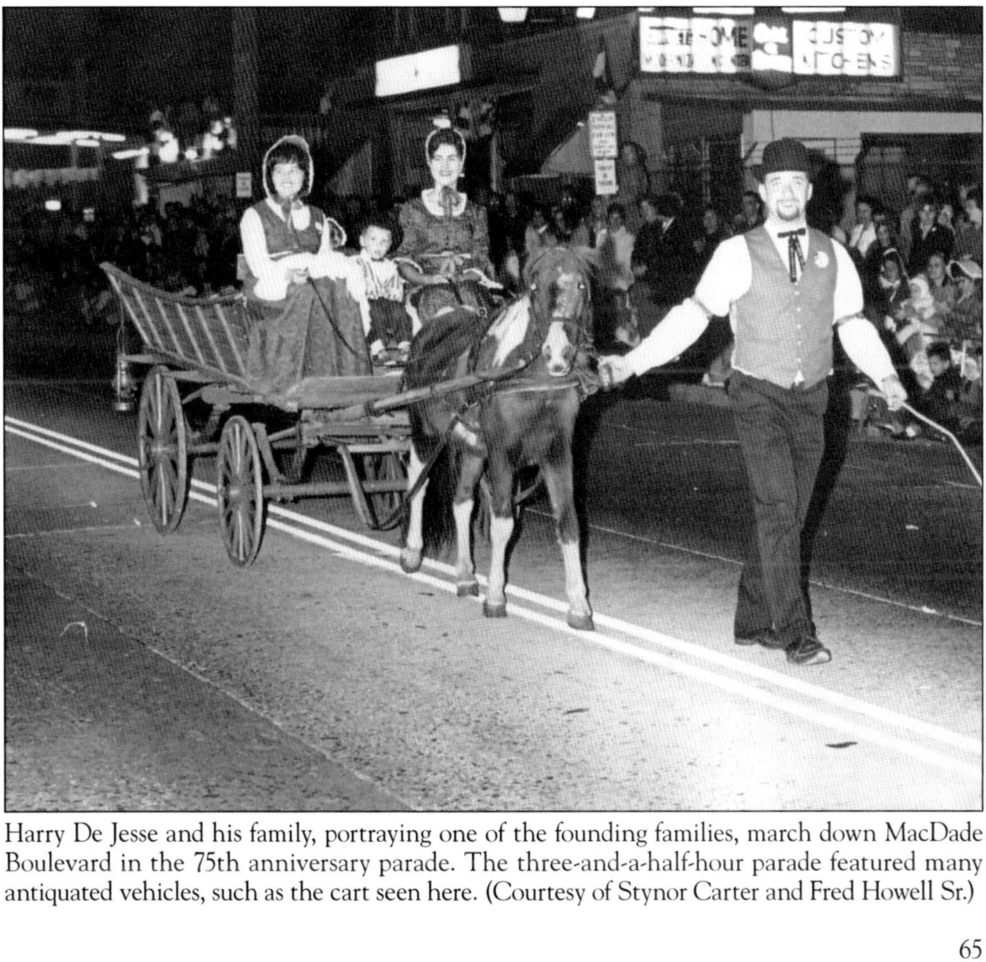

Harry De Jesse and his family, portraying one of the founding families, march down MacDade Boulevard in the 75th anniversary parade. The three-and-a-half-hour parade featured many antiquated vehicles, such as the cart seen here. (Courtesy of Stynor Carter and Fred Howell Sr.)

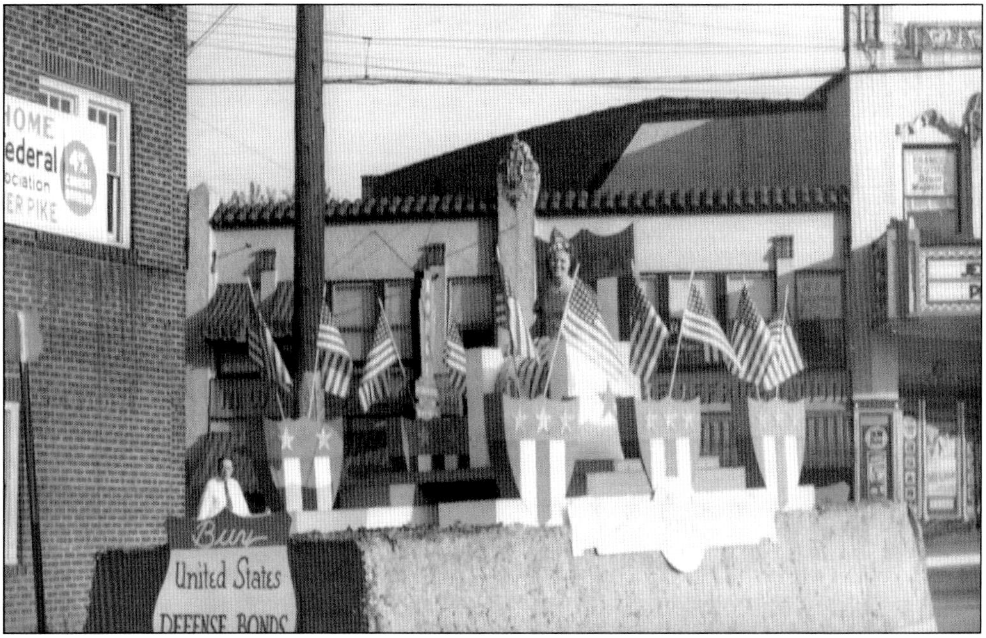

The 50th anniversary parade in 1941 featured a war bond float with Miss Pennsylvania riding atop it. Most of the small towns around the state also featured this float as a way to encourage citizens to buy war bonds. In this photograph, the float is on the corner of MacDade Boulevard and Chester Pike. The Wendy movie theater marquee is partially visible across the street at right. (Courtesy of Collingdale High School Alumni Association.)

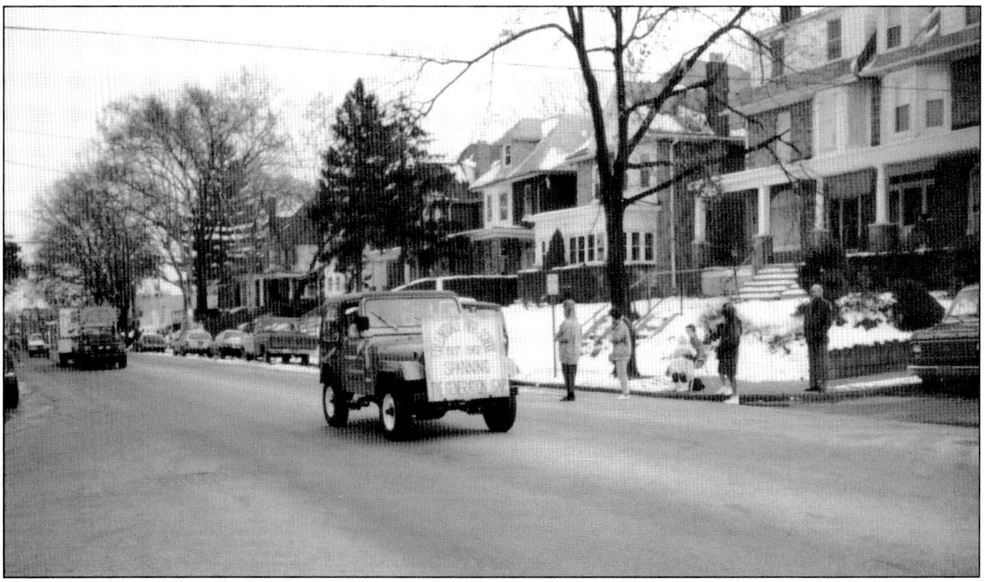

In November 1989, Collingdale held a "Welcome Home to Collingdale" celebration that included a parade that featured most of the graduating classes of Collingdale High School. "Spanning the Generation Gap" was the theme, and the leading car held a sign that indicated the dates the high school opened and closed for good (1927 and 1982, respectively). An assortment of both young and old alumni participated in the parade, which was held on November 25, 1989. (Photograph by Elizabeth MacGuire.)

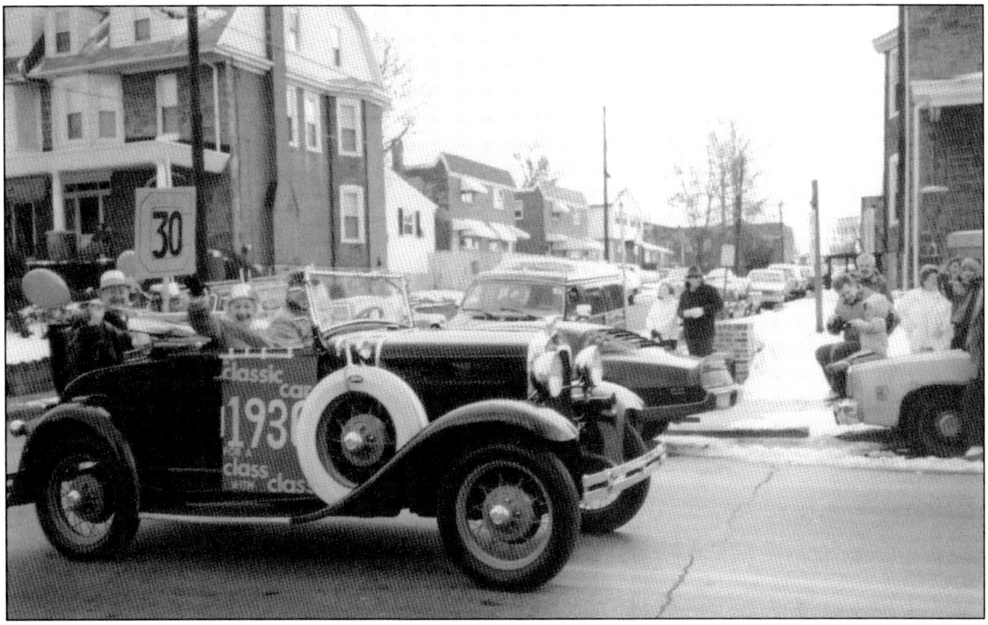

In this November 1989 photograph, members of the Collingdale High School class of 1930 ride down MacDade Boulevard in a classic Rolls-Royce automobile. Some recall, with nostalgia, riding down what was then called Parker Avenue in a similar automobile in the late 1920s and early 1930s. Others recall Sue's Sweet Shop, or the Campus Sweet Shop, which catered to high school students with milkshakes and other treats. (Photograph by Elizabeth MacGuire.)

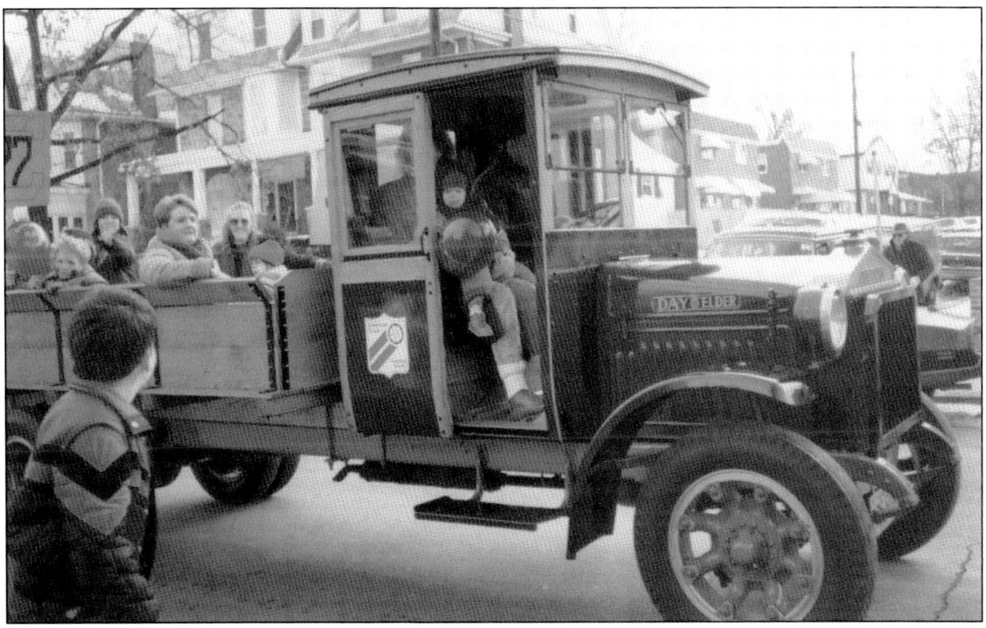

The younger classes were also represented in the 1989 parade; the CHS class of 1977 float boasted more children than alumni. Those who represented the class had a good time swapping stories and watching the children play. The children, of course, had the best time, as they got to ride on the flatbed or in the truck. Donna Mitchell (wearing glasses) rode in the back of the truck with her daughter Laura Beth. (Photograph by Elizabeth MacGuire.)

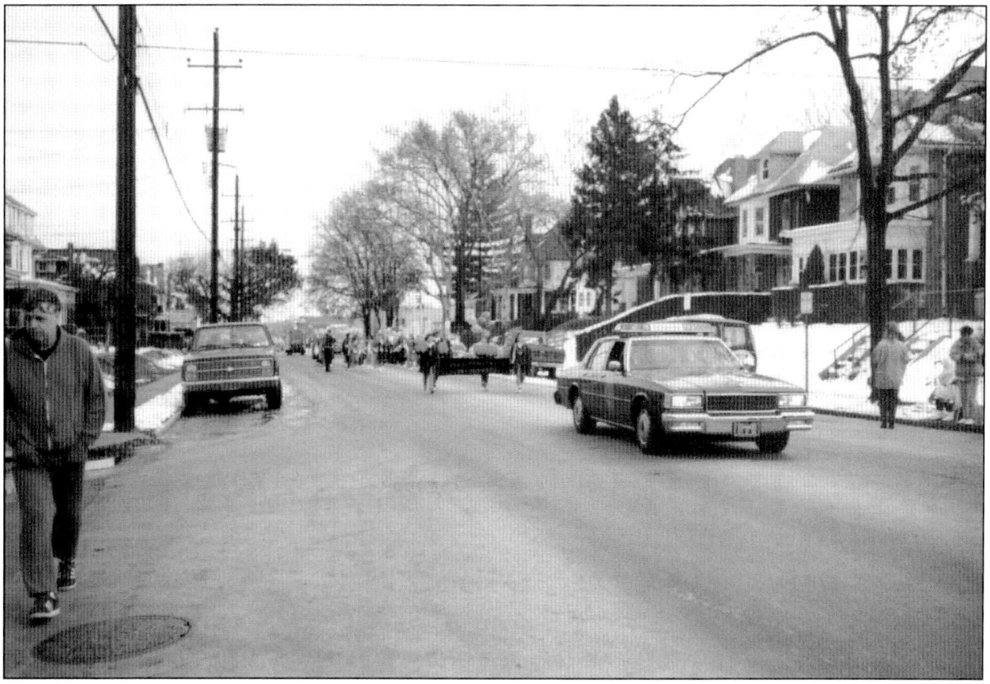

In another view of the 1989 "Welcome Home to Collingdale" parade looking down MacDade Boulevard from Lincoln Avenue, a police cruiser moves down the boulevard. Behind the police cruiser are some of the Collingdale High School cheerleaders. (Photograph by Elizabeth MacGuire.)

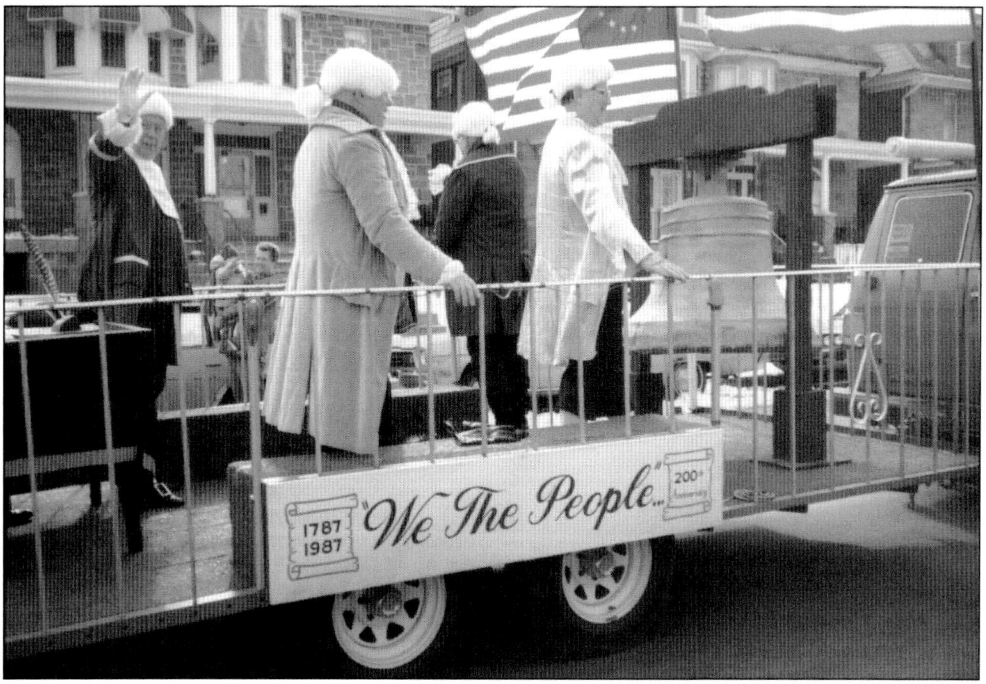

Before the 100th anniversary parade, the November 1989 "Welcome Home to Collingdale" parade also featured patriotic themes, like this one celebrating the bicentennial of the US Constitution. (Photograph by Elizabeth MacGuire.)

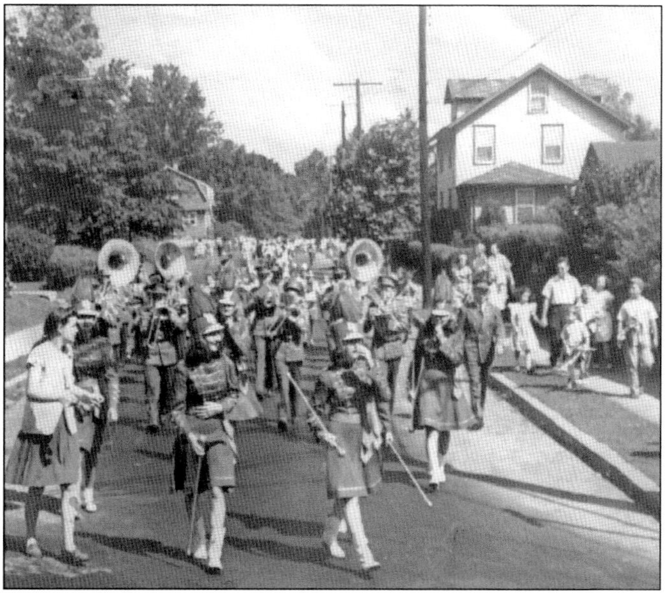

The Collingdale High School band shines in this picture from the 1946 Fourth of July parade. Many of the participants spent months practicing and participating in other parades and half times at football games. Twirlers lead the band in a rousing rendition of the "Star Spangled Banner" as a young girl follows excitedly by their side. (Courtesy of Collingdale High School Alumni Association—William Cox collection.)

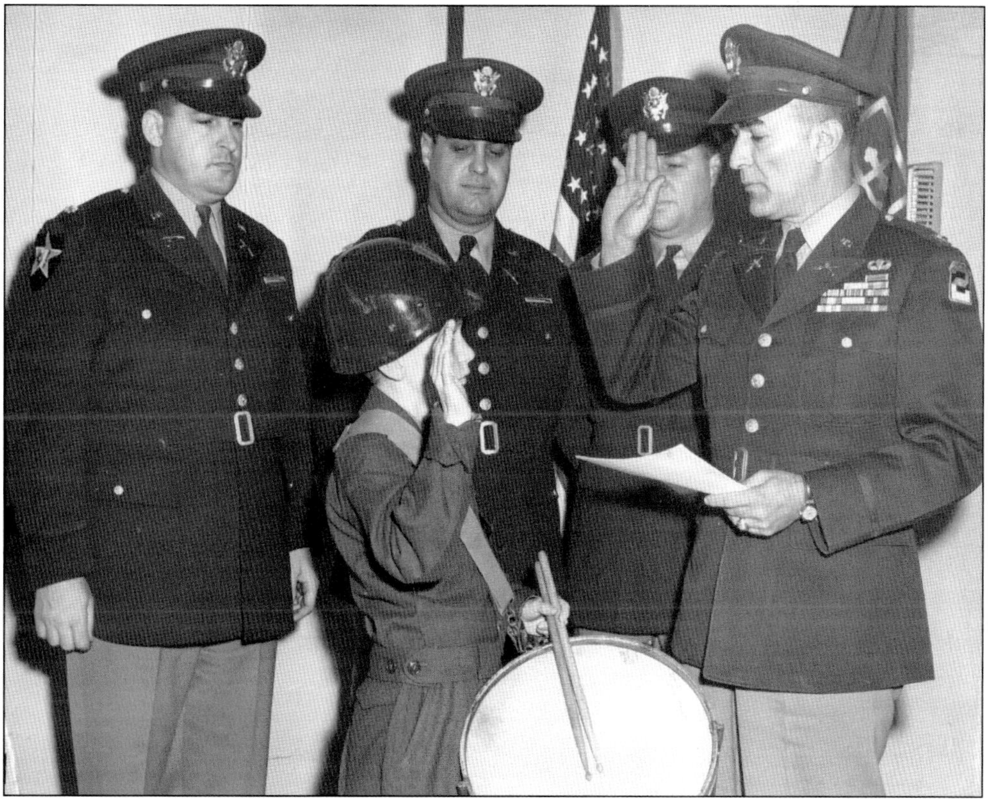

This April 22, 1956, photograph shows Peter Sullivan, age 11, assuming his duties as an honorary drummer boy for Pennsylvania's 79th Army Reserve Division by taking the oath from 79th Division Special Unit advisor Col. Rafael Konilla as other members of the division bear witness. Pictured from left to right are Maj. Norman L. Martin, Sullivan, Lt. Col. Garold E. Shick, Capt. Edgar North, and Colonel Konilla. (Courtesy of Collingdale Alumni Association.)

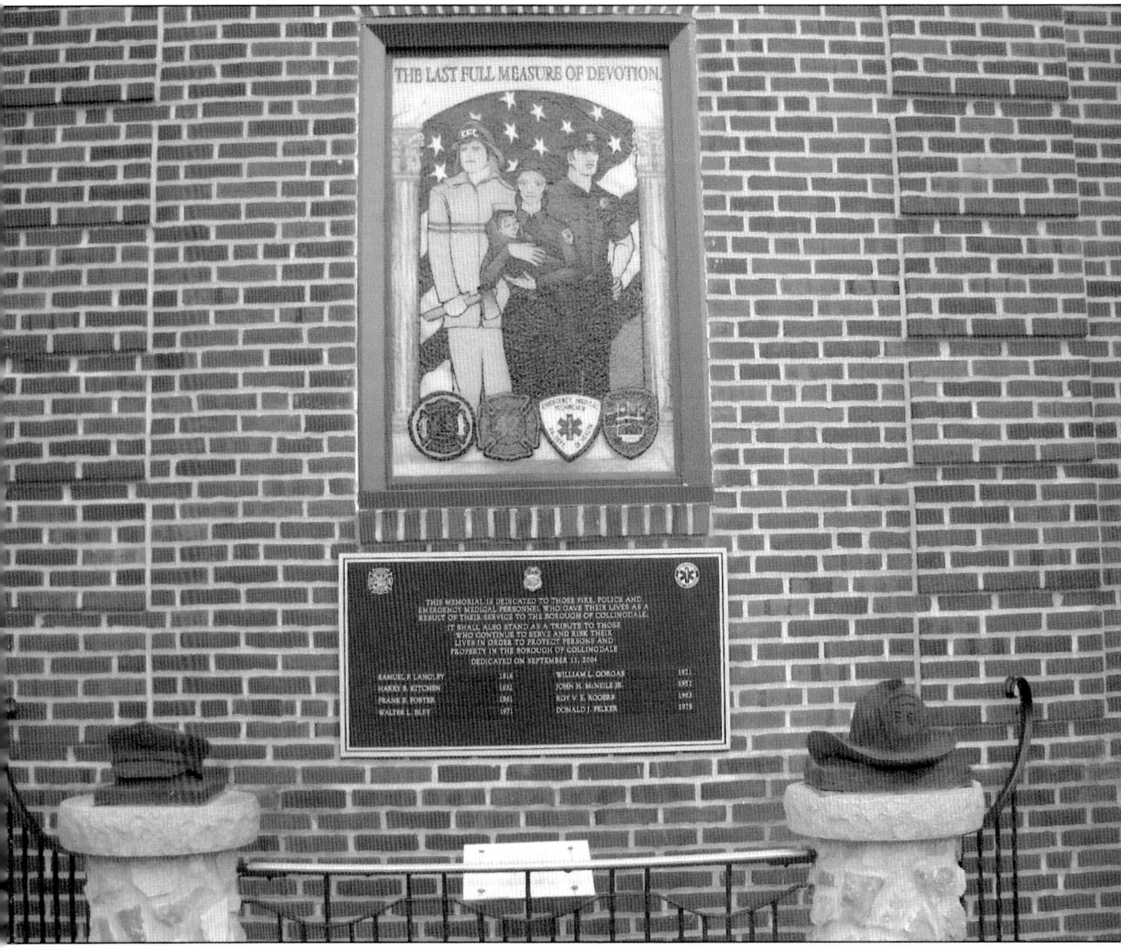

The police and fire department memorial, dedicated on September 11, 2004, and seen here in November 2011, provided a way to recognize fallen heroes from the Collingdale fire and police departments for their sacrifice and service to the community. Eight men are named on the plaque, and the glass display above it depicts a fireman, a policeman, and an emergency medical technician. (Photograph by Elizabeth MacGuire.)

Six

Family Community
Deepening Roots

A number of factors make Collingdale the family-friendly community it is today. Family was—and still is—a very important factor in the continued existence of this tiny borough. It is the connection that drives the businesses that established themselves in Collingdale, and the connection that keeps them in the borough. This connection can be seen in the firehouse and the schoolhouse as generations of families interact with each other and participate in the many activities and services the borough provides for its citizens. Frank Kelly, the longest-serving mayor in Pennsylvania, has strong family connections in Collingdale. As mayor, Kelly has experienced the highs and lows of the community at large. He and many of his family members still reside in Collingdale and are actively involved with the government and the church.

One of the oldest residents of Collingdale, Richard Kettigan, celebrated his 100th birthday on November 11, 2011. Helen Morris, age 102, lived in Collingdale for 70 years and has many fond memories of the borough. The Harris family has the deepest roots in Collingdale, having resided in the borough since 1886, when Enon Harris and his sister Margaret first settled in the area.

Collingdale has a perfect atmosphere for growth, and for some it has fostered a sense of loyalty and commitment to the borough. As a testament to this, only a small number of the older residents left to venture into other communities. Even those who eventually left the borough returned often to see how the community changed. Memories of times past linger, as many of the buildings in the borough date from its incorporation and were renovated in the 1920s and 1940s.

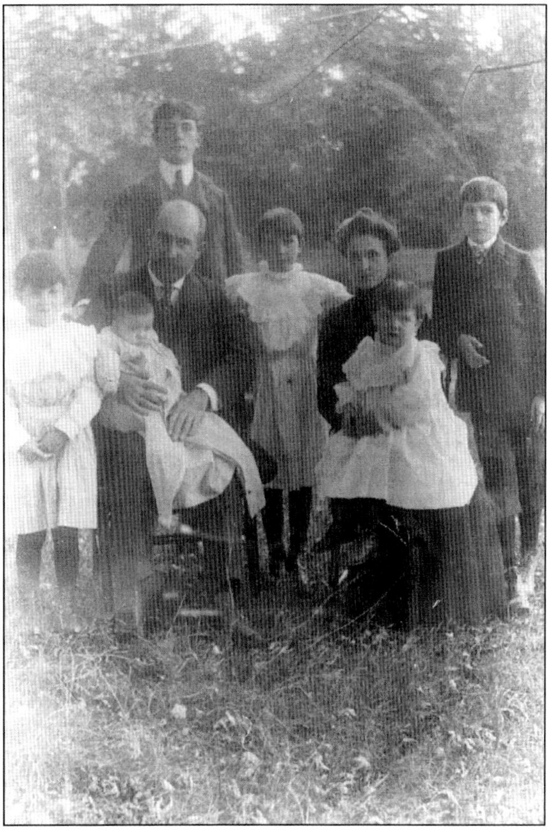

In this c. 1910 photograph, Enon Harris Jr. poses with his wife Helen and their six children at their property on Felton Avenue. Enon's potash business, as well as his surveying work, thrived in Chester. His children also thrived under the tutelage of Enon's sister, Margaret B. Harris. (Courtesy of Helen Dick Deyo Moyer.)

Pop Marsh was a beloved janitor for many years at Harris Elementary School. Many students recall how he helped and supported them, and many considered him a father figure. Marsh also served as a volunteer fireman at Collingdale Fire Company No. 1. (Courtesy of Collingdale High School Alumni Association—Ann Speer collection.)

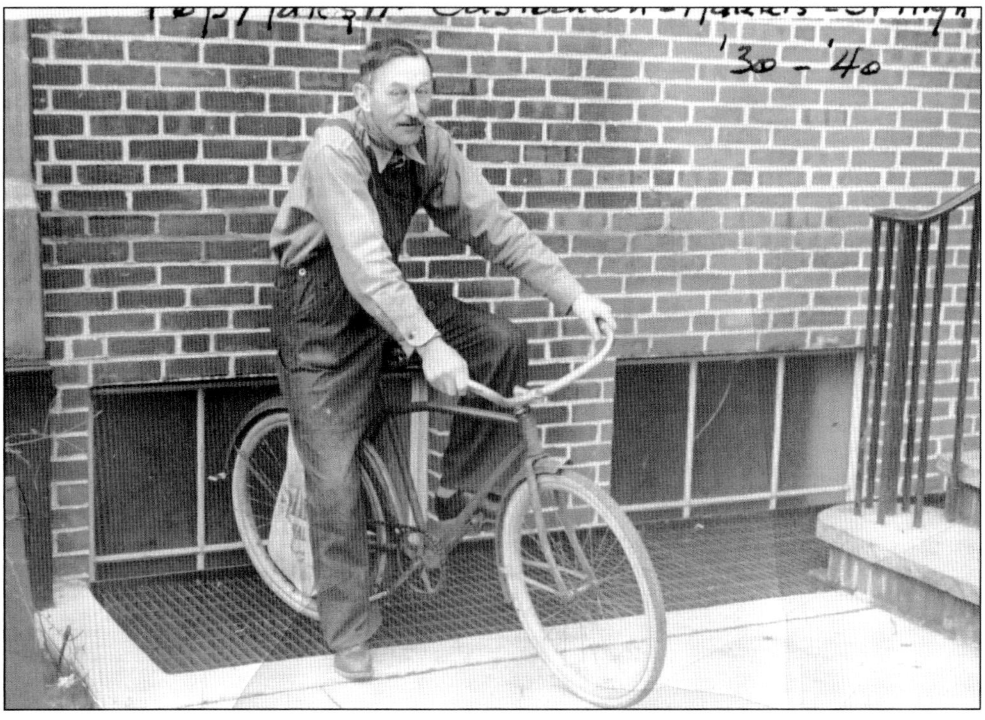

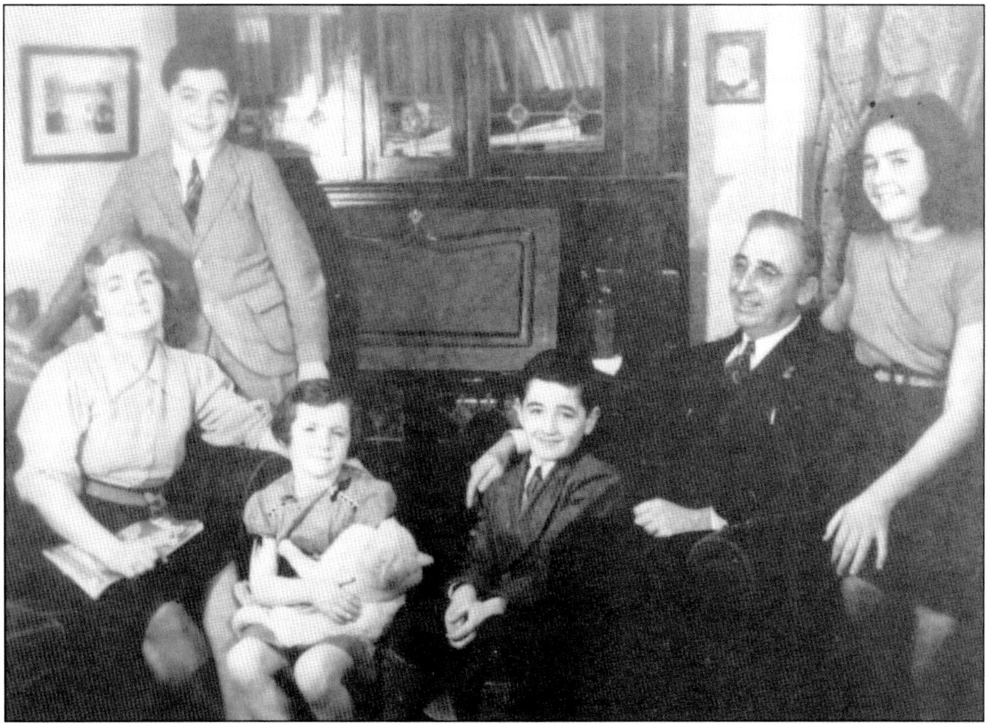

The Johnston family, pictured here in their living room in 1938, were actively involved with the borough during the 1930s and 1940s. From left to right are Florence, Paul (standing), Nancy, Joseph, Charles, and Eileen. Burgess Charles Johnston, along with his wife and daughters, worked tirelessly for the library and government associations in the borough. (Courtesy of Nancy Johnston Collier.)

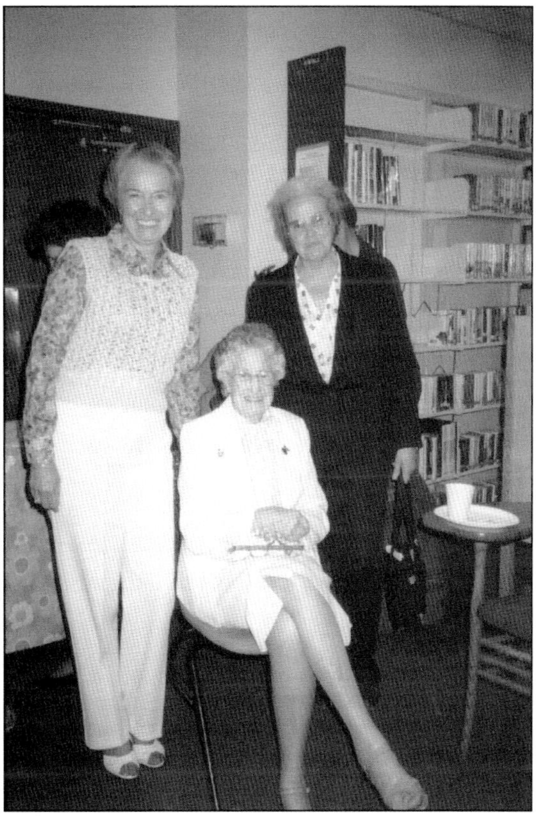

Olive Heimech, pictured here with her two daughters, Margaret (left) and Dorothy (right), served on the first library board and as president of the Collingdale library association for many years. Her contributions toward the overall improvement and viability of the library provided its many patrons with enough resources and support to maintain the library's continuing role in the community. One of her challenges was to direct young people away from the numbing influence of television and toward literature. (Courtesy of Nancy Johnston Collier.)

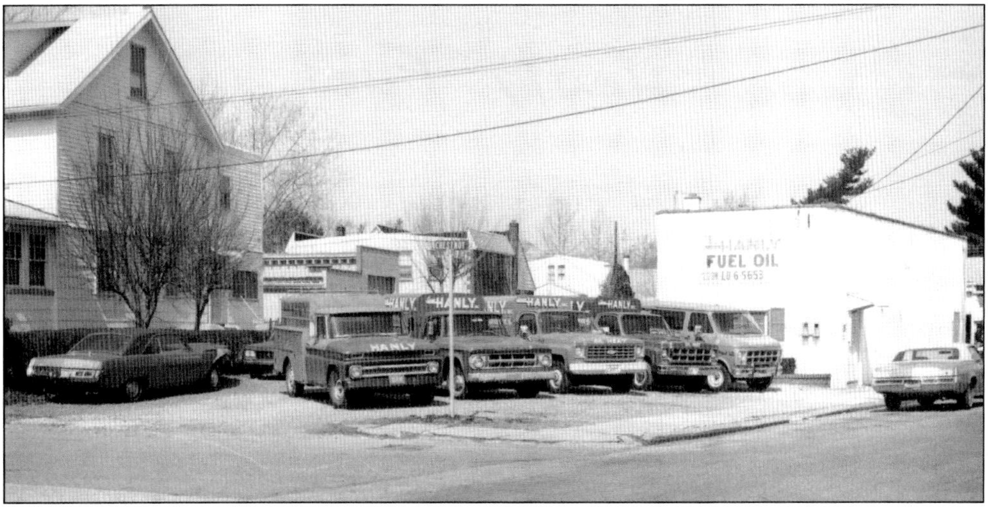

Dave Hanly started his fuel business in 1967 out of his home on Broad Street. The business grew, and it became necessary to expand into this building, located on Chestnut Street and Woodlawn Avenue, in 1973. This photograph shows Hanly Fuel Co. in 1978. Hanly's son, Dave Hanly Jr., took over the business after it moved to its current location on MacDade Boulevard in 1980. (Courtesy of Dave Hanly Jr.)

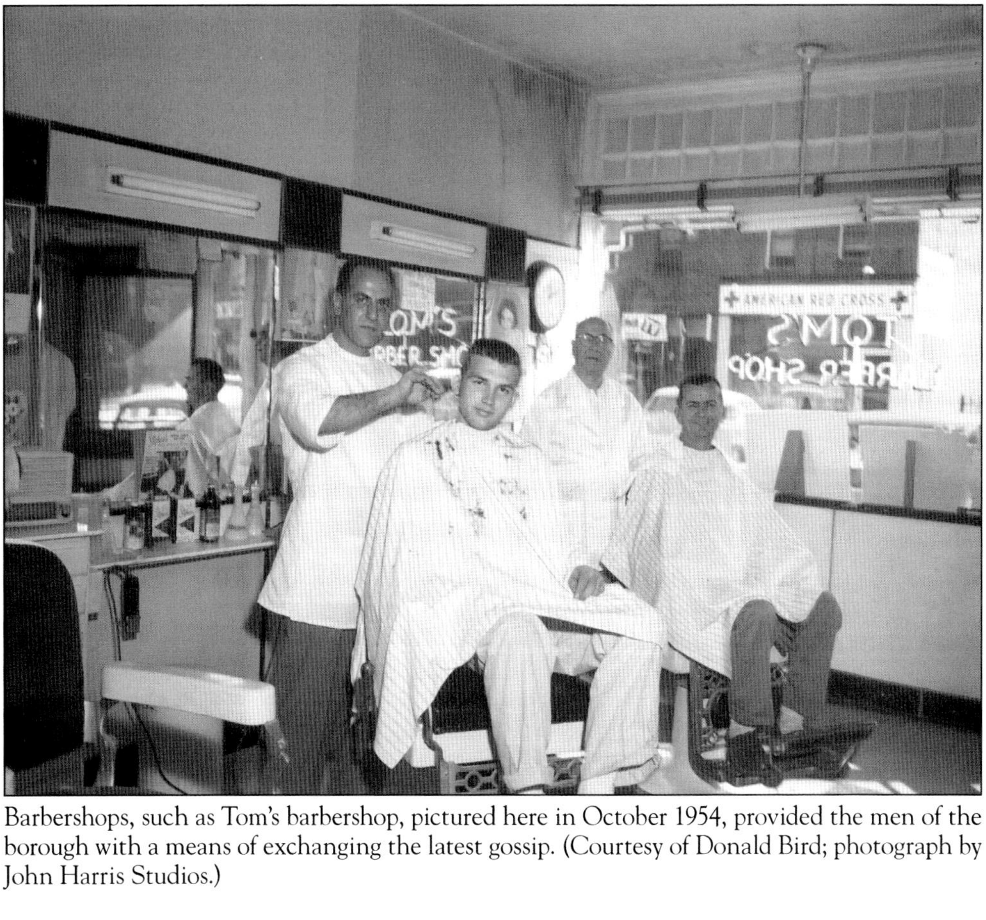

Barbershops, such as Tom's barbershop, pictured here in October 1954, provided the men of the borough with a means of exchanging the latest gossip. (Courtesy of Donald Bird; photograph by John Harris Studios.)

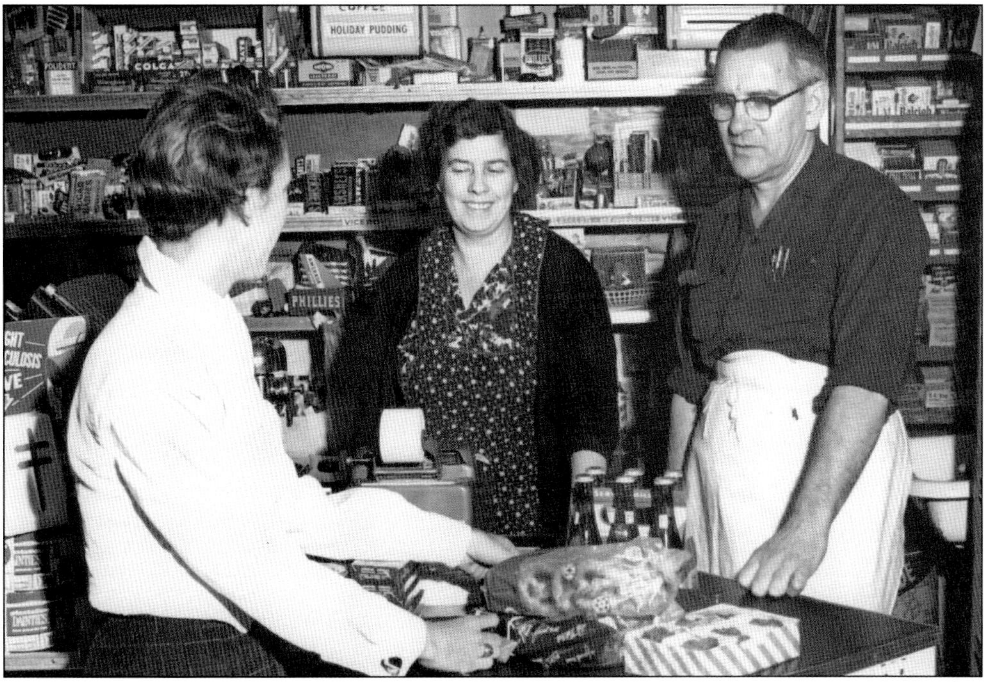

Dan McCloskey's grocery store served as both a deli and convenience store in the 1950s. Quality meats and cheeses were their hallmark, but they also supplied the community with candy. LaRosa's Market, which opened in the 1960s, followed McCloskey's lead and filled up the void left when Pop Eliskey's store closed in the late 1940s. In this 1956 image, McCloskey rings up a customer as his wife looks on. (Courtesy of Collingdale Alumni Association—Ann Speer collection.)

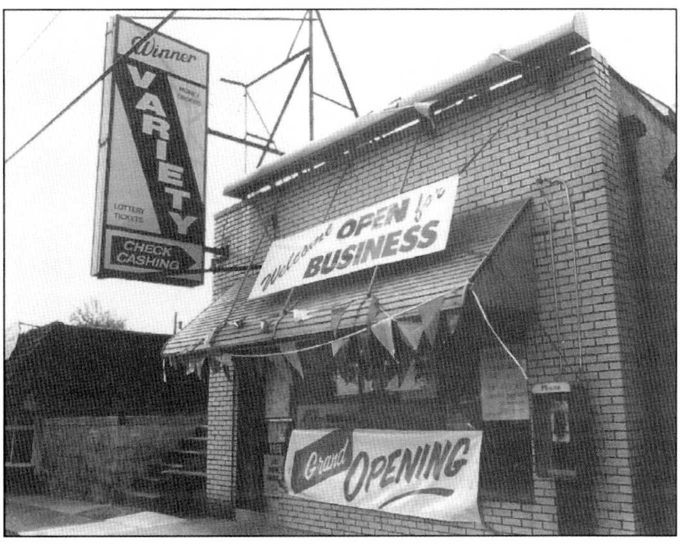

Fred and Jeanette Winner opened Winner Variety Store in September 1967 at 933 MacDade Boulevard. It was a family business that stocked everything from toilet paper to screws for the front door. Fred Winner had a motto that he stuck by: "If I do not have it, I'll find a way to get it for you." Liked by everyone he knew, Fred Winner was tragically murdered outside his shop on February 18, 1993. (Courtesy of Joy Winner-Vasaturo.)

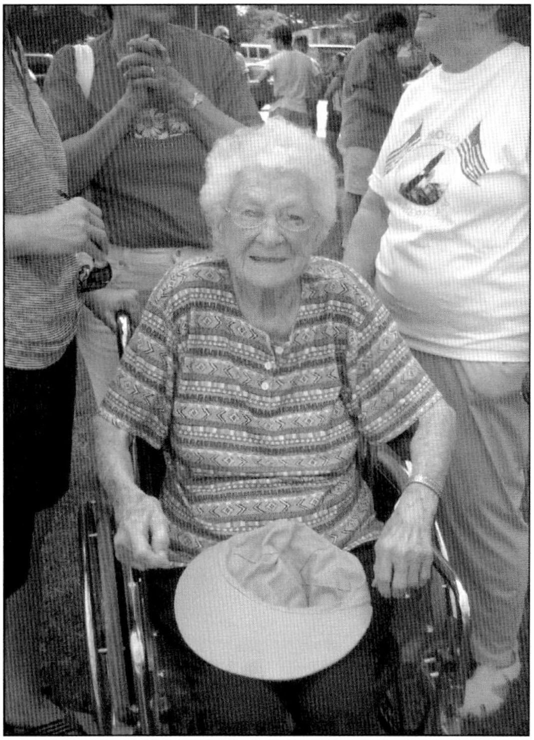

Helen M. Morris, age 102, enjoys the Memorial Day ceremony at the Collingdale Community Center on May 30, 2011. Morris lived in Collingdale with her husband, David, and raised two sons, David and Richard, in the borough. She has many memories of early Collingdale, having arrived with her husband in the early 1930s and remained in the borough for 70 years. (Photograph by Elizabeth MacGuire.)

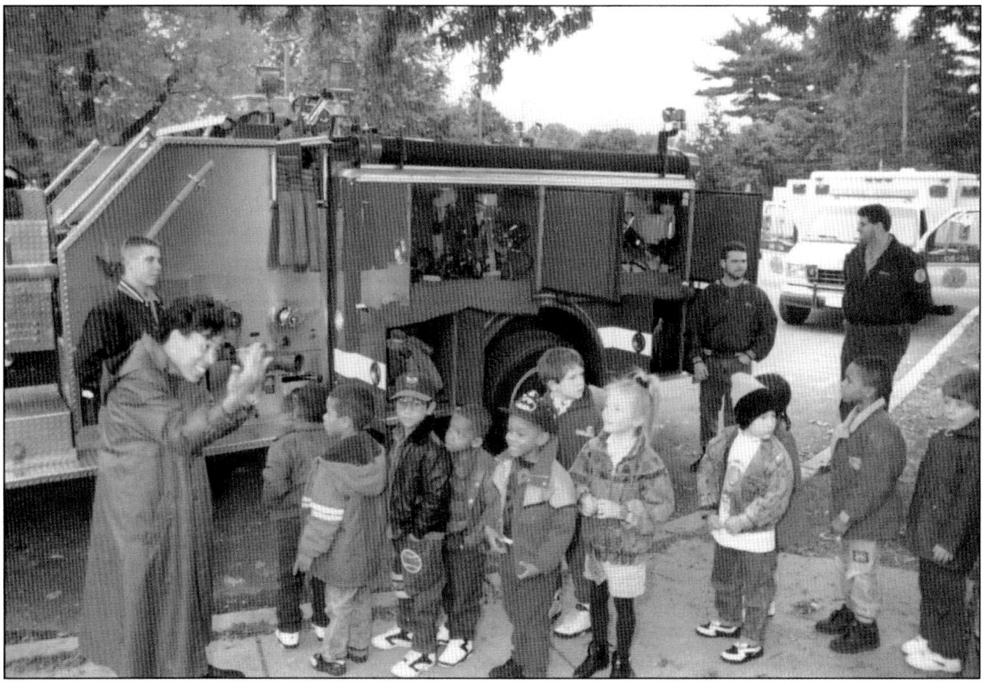

Generations of families serve the community as firemen and emergency medical personnel. The camaraderie of all the men and women cannot be matched, as they risk their lives to save others. Fire safety classes, such as this one from the 1980s, serve as reminders of how involved the firemen are in the local community. (Courtesy of Collingdale Fire Company No. 2.)

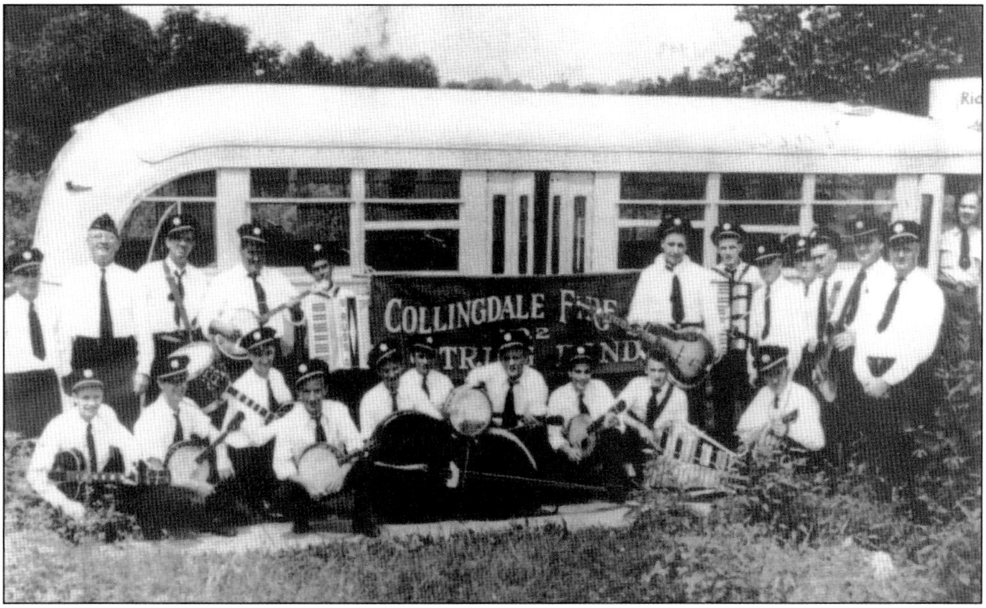

The more musically inclined firefighters of Collingdale Fire Company No. 2 established a string band in the 1940s. They routinely played at dances held in Floral Hall, which raised funds for the war effort and for the company. The Collingdale Fire Company No. 2 string band also routinely traveled throughout the tri-state area for parades and other events. (Courtesy of James Powers.)

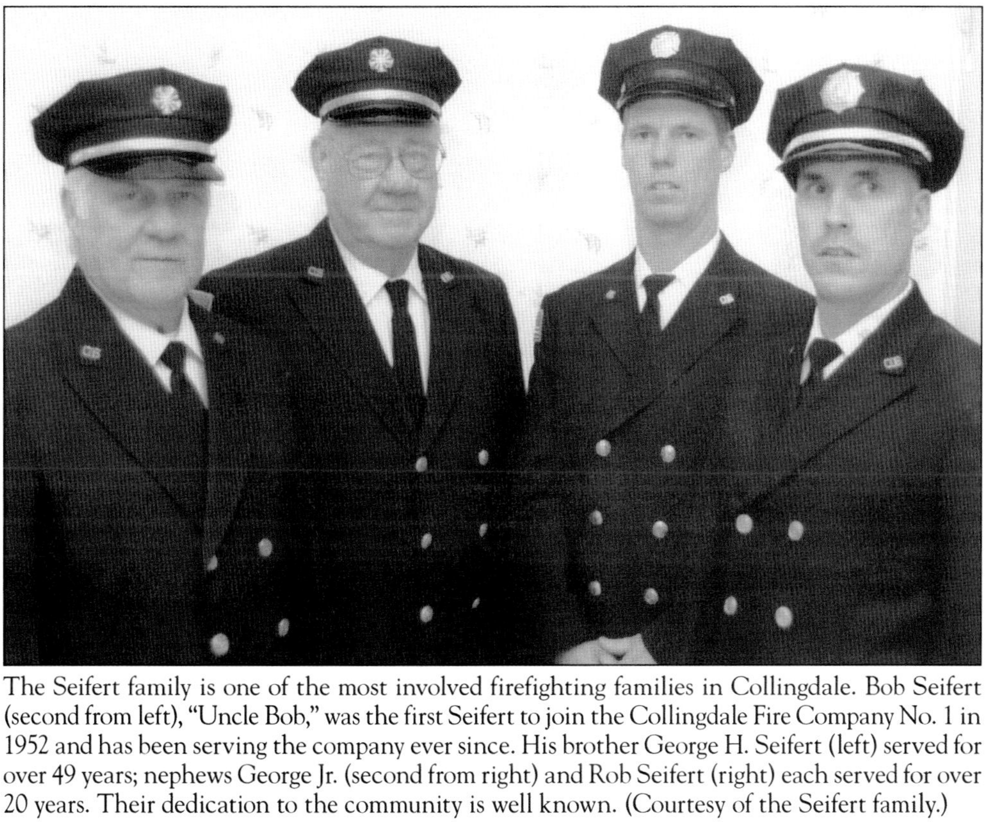

The Seifert family is one of the most involved firefighting families in Collingdale. Bob Seifert (second from left), "Uncle Bob," was the first Seifert to join the Collingdale Fire Company No. 1 in 1952 and has been serving the company ever since. His brother George H. Seifert (left) served for over 49 years; nephews George Jr. (second from right) and Rob Seifert (right) each served for over 20 years. Their dedication to the community is well known. (Courtesy of the Seifert family.)

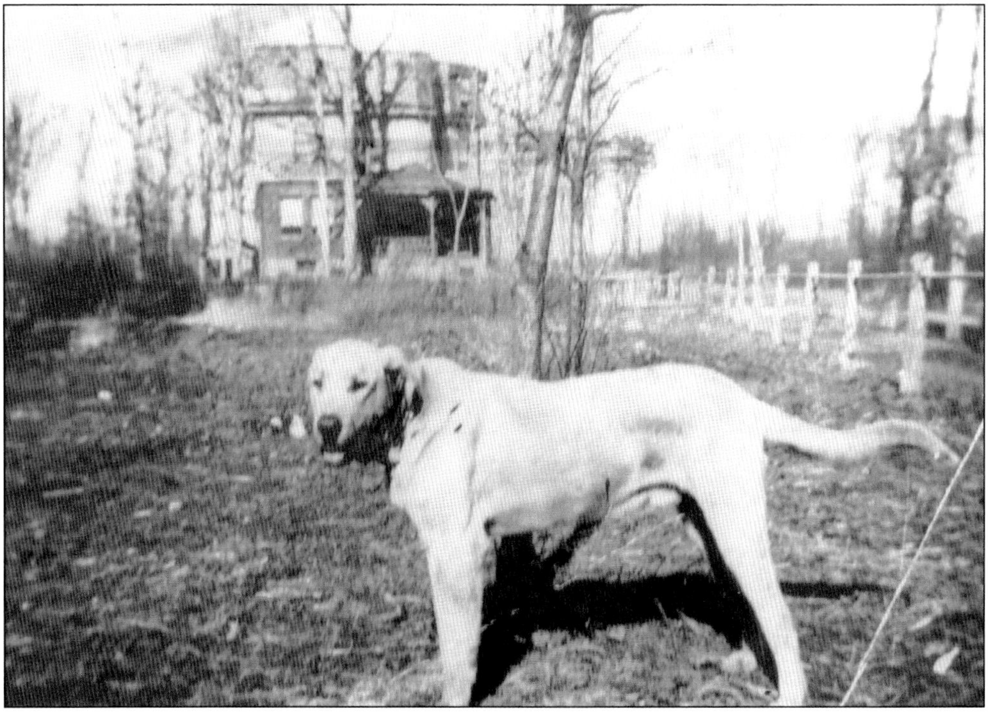

In this 1903 photograph, Burgess William Joyce's dog poses in front of the Joyce residence on Clifton Avenue. Joyce moved in when Maximilian LaRoche moved out after his tenure as justice of the peace. During Joyce's term in office, improvements continued as they had under the previous burgess, Joseph F. Beswick, who served from 1897 to 1909. (Courtesy of Keith Lockhart.)

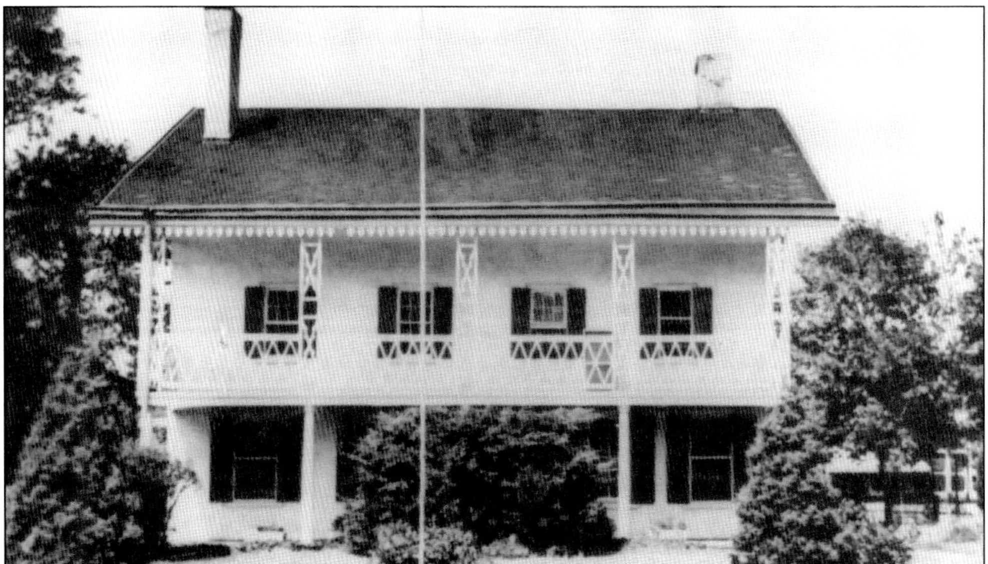

Associate Judge James Andrews lived in this farmhouse when he retired from public service after serving two terms in office from November 1858 to November 1865. Andrews was one of the first associate judges elected by the people of Pennsylvania. The office was abolished by the state constitution in 1874. (Courtesy of Keith Lockhart.)

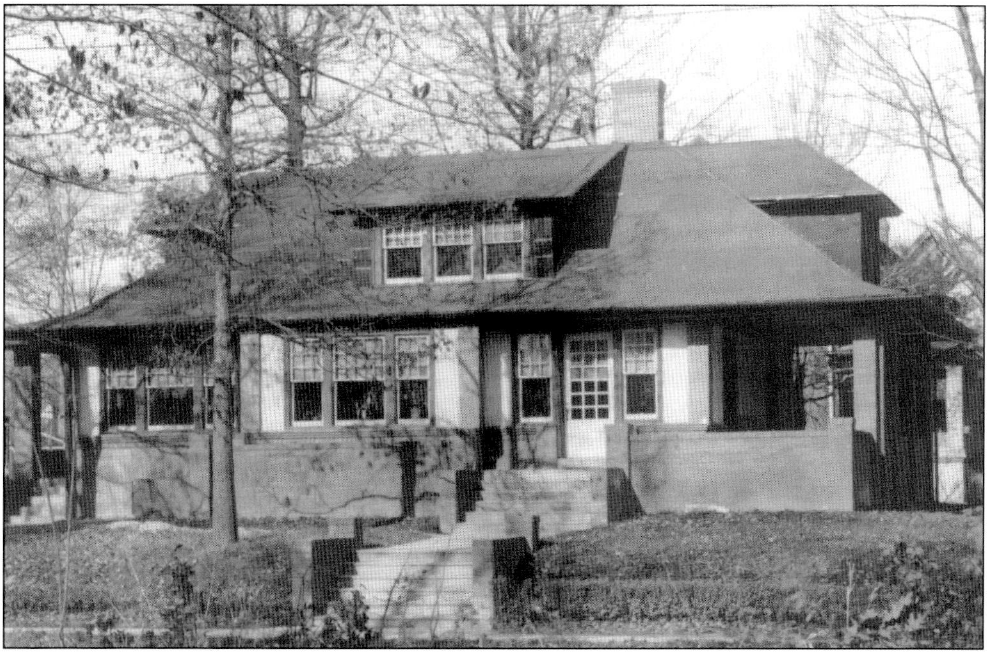

This home, owned by Earl and Kate Wilson, became the headquarters for American Legion Post 669 in the late 1950s. (Courtesy of James Powers.)

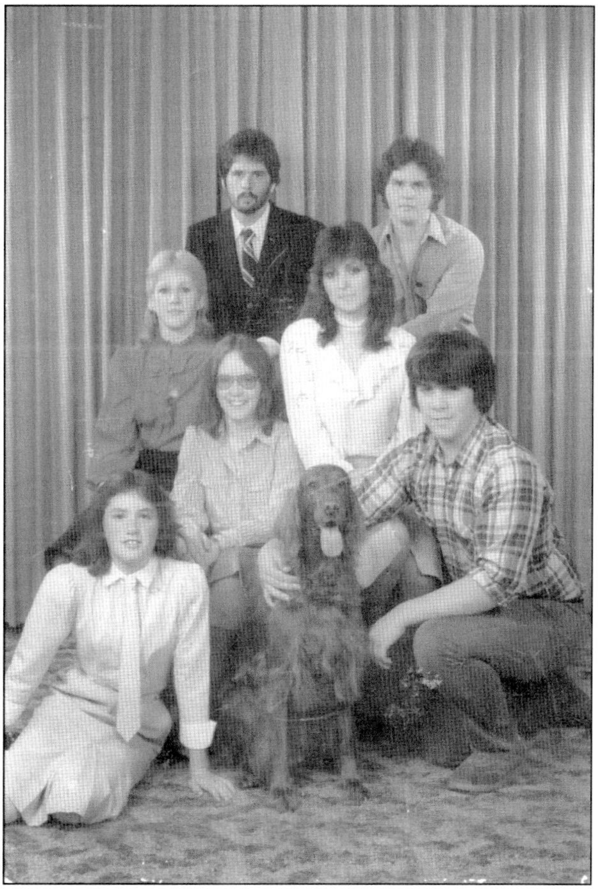

Mayor Frank Kelly embodies the spirit of Collingdale, and has raised his children to be involved with many of the activities and organizations the borough provides. This 1984 photograph shows his seven children. From left to right are (first row) Kristine, the dog Bridgett, and Patrick; (second row) Colleen, Jeanette, and Kathie; (third row) Frank and Brian. (Courtesy of the Kelly family.)

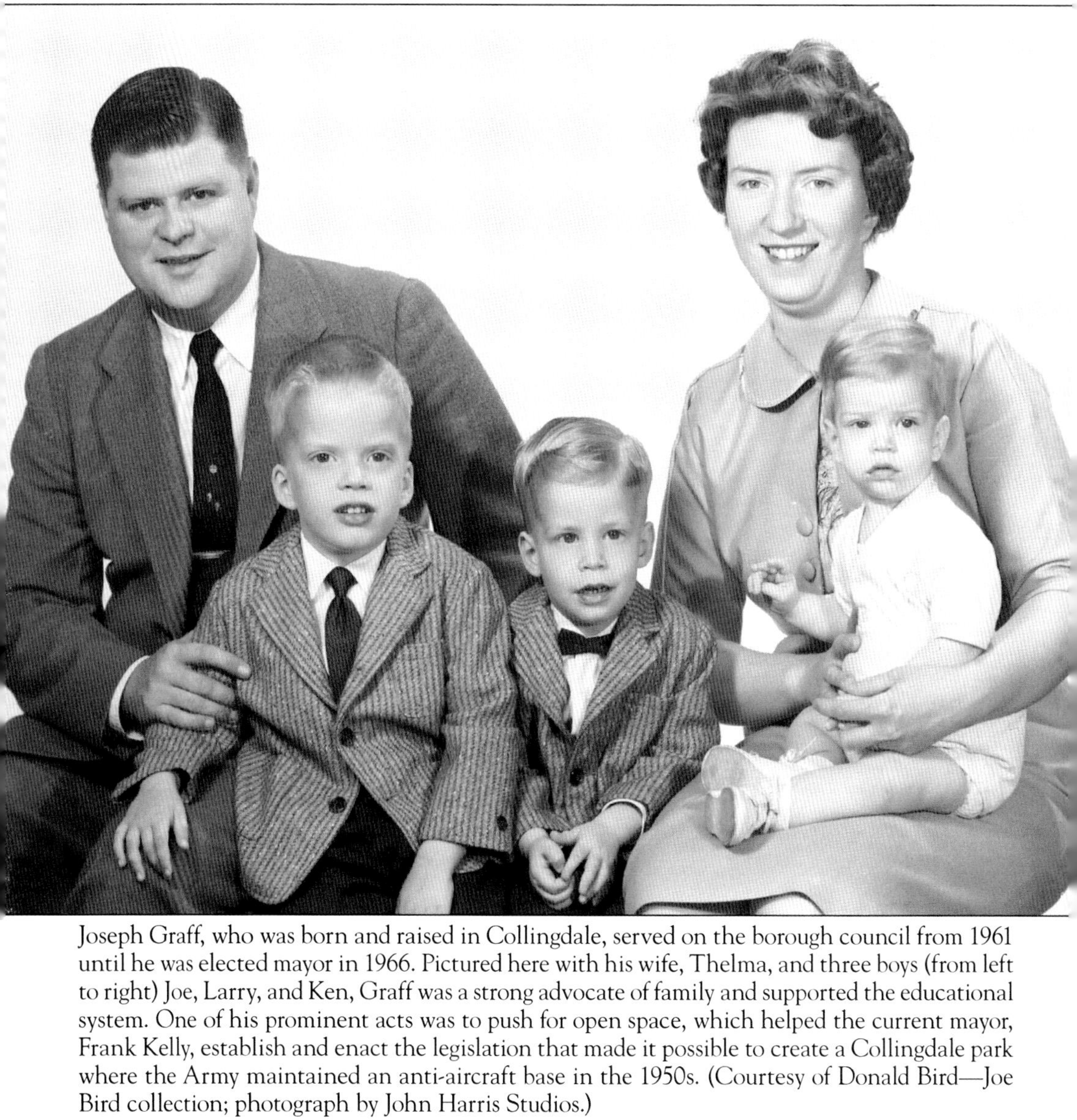

Joseph Graff, who was born and raised in Collingdale, served on the borough council from 1961 until he was elected mayor in 1966. Pictured here with his wife, Thelma, and three boys (from left to right) Joe, Larry, and Ken, Graff was a strong advocate of family and supported the educational system. One of his prominent acts was to push for open space, which helped the current mayor, Frank Kelly, establish and enact the legislation that made it possible to create a Collingdale park where the Army maintained an anti-aircraft base in the 1950s. (Courtesy of Donald Bird—Joe Bird collection; photograph by John Harris Studios.)

Seven

Athletic Community
For the Glory of the Game

Collingdale's pride in its athletic teams shows whenever a team wearing the Collingdale colors orange and blue takes the field, whether it is in a baseball, basketball, or football game. Collingdale can boast of individual athletes, including Carson Thompson, who pitched a no-hitter exhibition baseball game in the 1936 Olympics, and numerous championship teams. Collingdale baseball and swim teams were two of the first six teams inducted into the Delco League.

Other locally famous individuals include Bill Schultz, who ran 3,000 miles across the United States—from Neptune Beach, California, to Atlantic City, New Jersey—in 1991, and Scott Brown, who—despite injuries from an automobile accident—went on to become a world-class rower, providing inspiration to Collingdale's youth to achieve their dreams.

For adults, bowling teams dominated the scene in the 1930s and 1940s. John Taylor led the Collingdale Millwork five-man team in the 1935 American Bowling Congress tournament championship by toppling 2,946 pins in the highest single game of the tourney.

Until Collingdale High School closed in 1982, high school sports dominated the hearts and minds of the community. Many who attended CHS have fond memories of the pep rallies that preceded opening games. Marching in the band meant that one could catch the game *and* participate in the halftime show. The Collingdale Athletic Club took the logos, colors, and name of the CHS football team to keep its memory and spirit alive and has won many championships of its own.

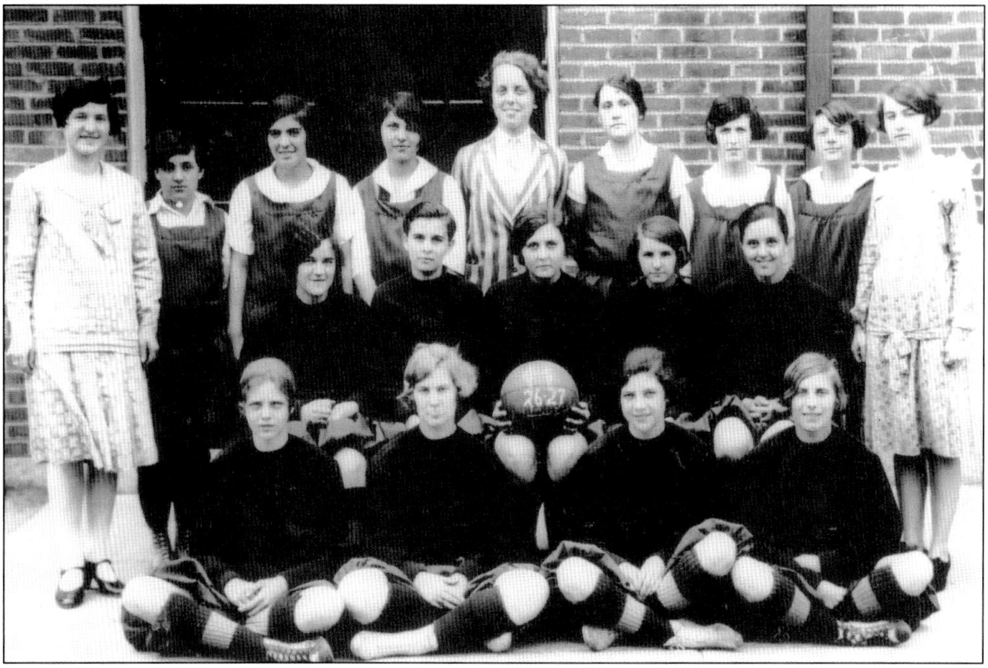

Freida Hurlbrick (third row center, in the striped jacket), Collingdale's first women's coach and physical education teacher, stands proudly in this photograph of the 1926–1927 Collingdale High School girls' basketball team. Hurlbrick was the driving force behind many great female athletes because she inspired the girls to achieve their goals and strive for perfection in everything they did. (Courtesy of Collingdale High School Alumni Association.)

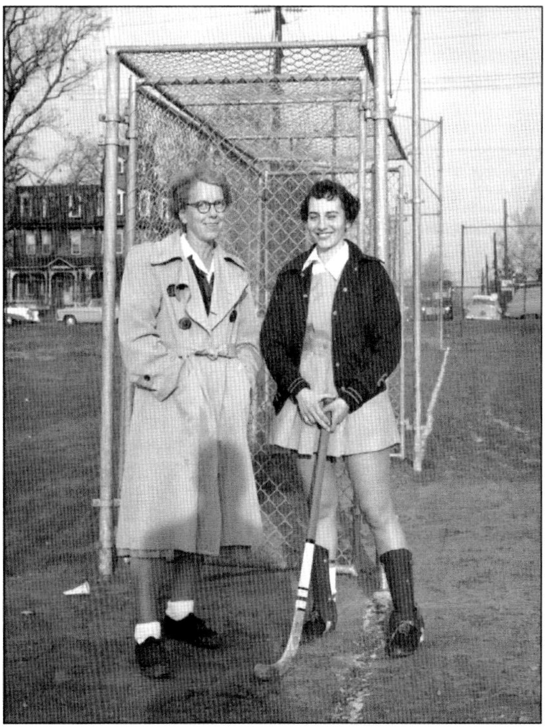

Field hockey teams were also Freida Hurlbrick's responsibility. She supported the field hockey and basketball teams during her tenure as the physical education teacher at Collingdale High School, which lasted from the school's inception in 1924 to the late 1960s. Memories abound of her leadership skills. In this 1940s photograph, she poses with a star player. (Courtesy of Collingdale High School Alumni Association.)

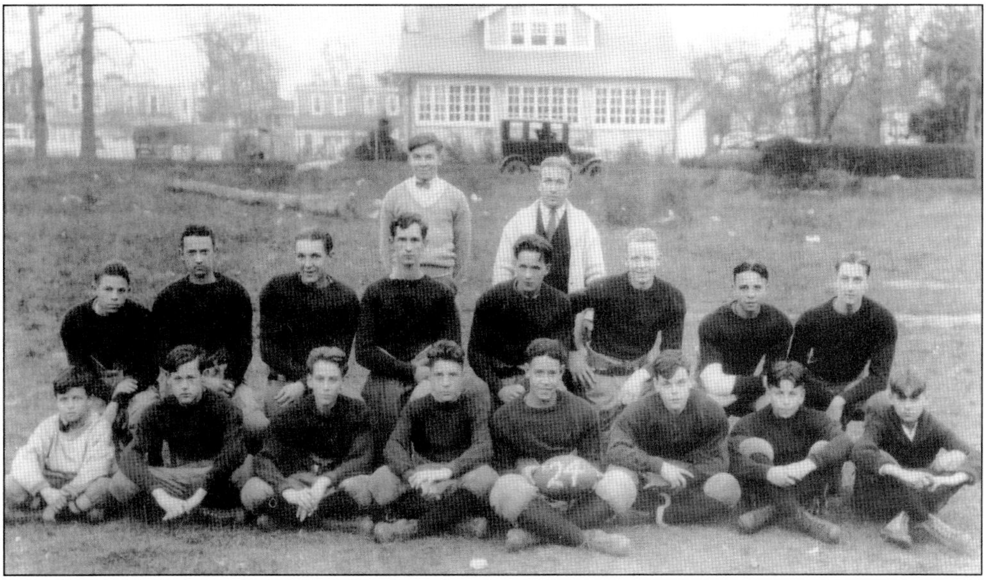

Collingdale High School football players from the 1920s and 1930s recall Coach Story (third row, right), who inspired and drove them toward success both on and off the football field. In this photograph, he poses with the first CHS football team in September 1924. (Courtesy of James Powers.)

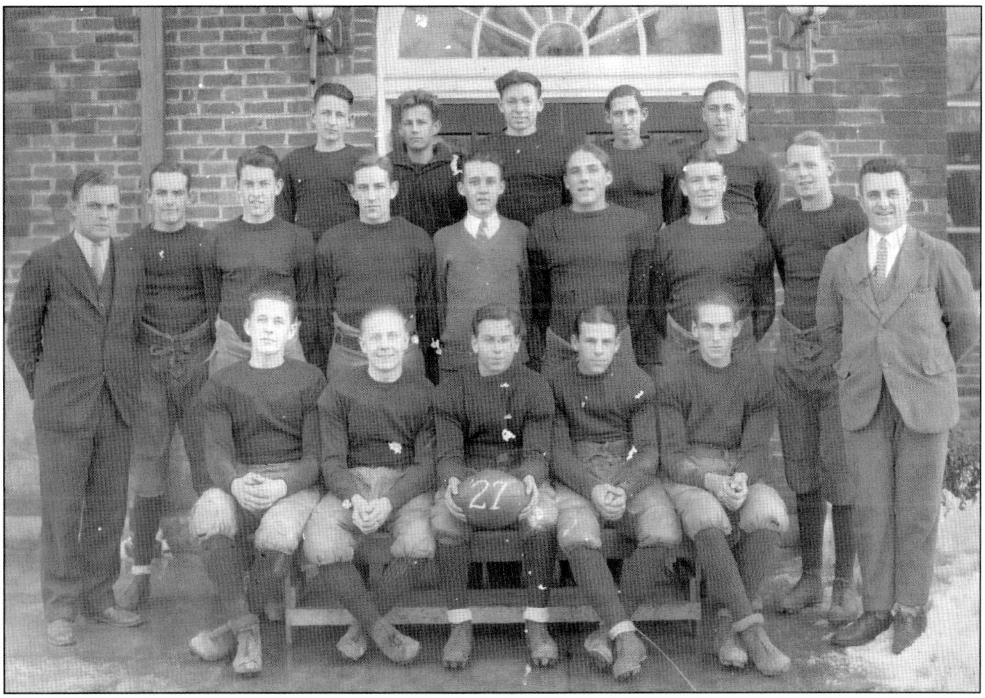

Proud seniors from the first Collingdale High School football team pose in front of the junior high building in September 1927. Most of the boys shown here joined the football team when it first started in 1924, while a few were added during the intervening years. Future Olympian Carson Thompson, third player from right in the second row, was one of the stars of the team. (Courtesy of Collingdale High School Alumni Association.)

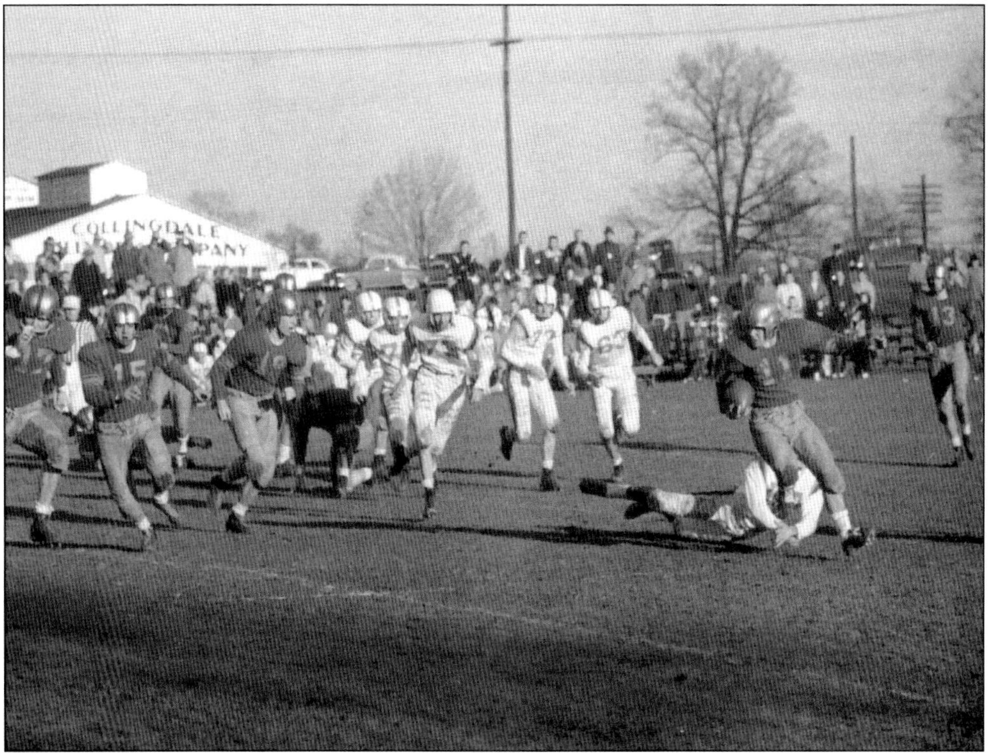

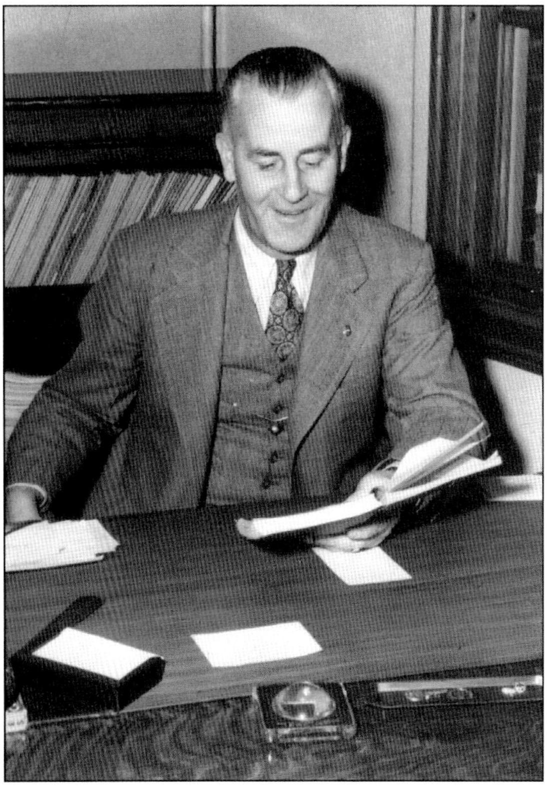

Home games, such as this one in 1942, provided students and parents with a way to cheer on and encourage the CHS football players. Many good-natured rivalries existed between area schools, such as Darby and Sharon Hill. (Courtesy of Collingdale High School Alumni Association—Ann Speer collection.)

Harry Mercer, longtime principal of Collingdale High School, also coached football and track teams from 1935 to 1940. During his tenure as the football coach for the Collingdale Bulldogs, the team reached the pinnacle of being undefeated champions in 1939. Affectionately called "Merc" by the players, Mercer tried to retire from the football team in 1940, but got called back in 1942 and remained until 1958. (Courtesy of Collingdale High School Alumni Association—Ann Speer collection.)

Ed Bowe, pictured here in his typical suit, coached football and basketball teams from the late 1950s to the late 1960s. Though he was not as personable as Harry Mercer, Bowe had a great rapport with other coaches and utilized his resources to ensure that he gained the teams' confidence and support. (Courtesy of Collingdale High School Alumni Association—Ann Speer collection.)

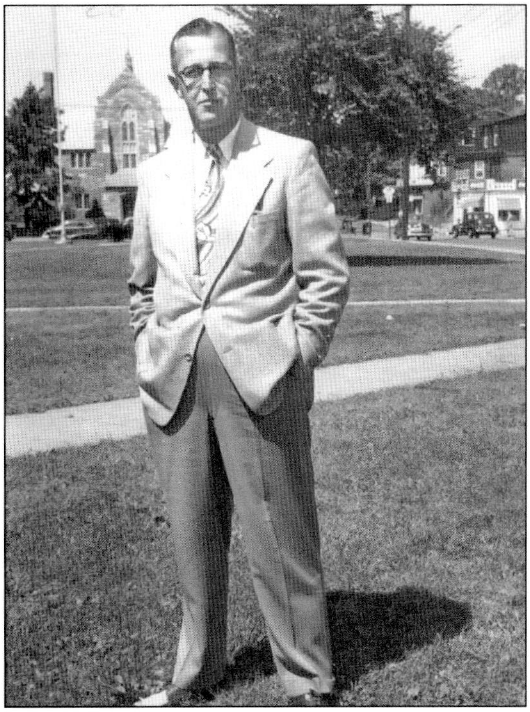

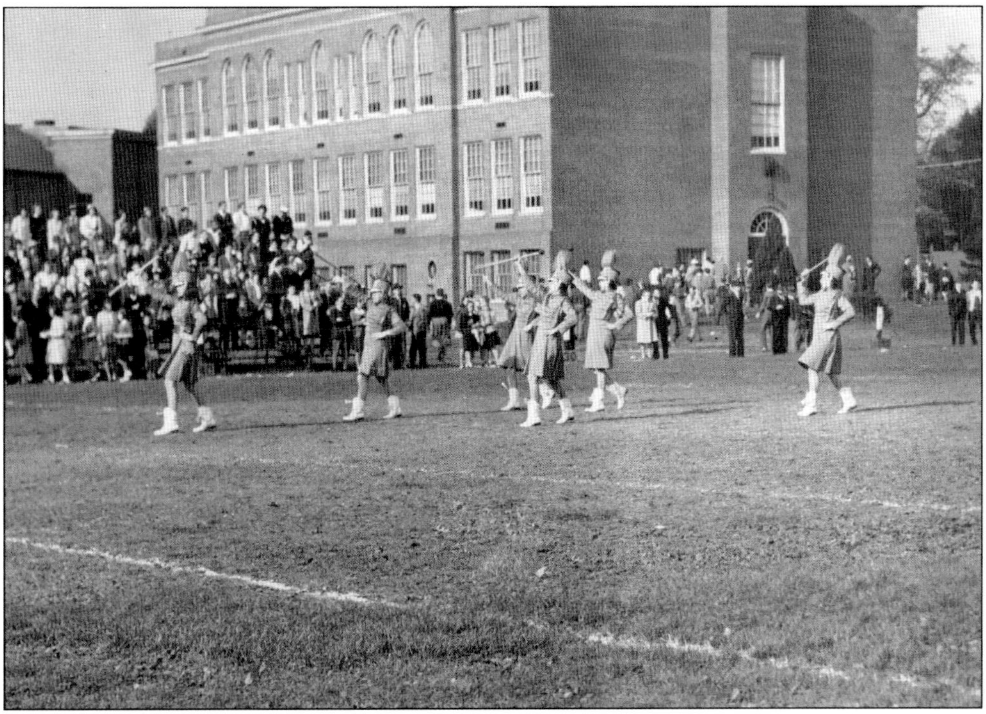

Baton twirlers strut onto the field at halftime in this photograph from 1948. Uniforms with shiny brass buttons shone in the sun as the girls lifted their heads high and moved down the football field as the fans cheered. (Courtesy of Collingdale High School Alumni Association—William Cox collection.)

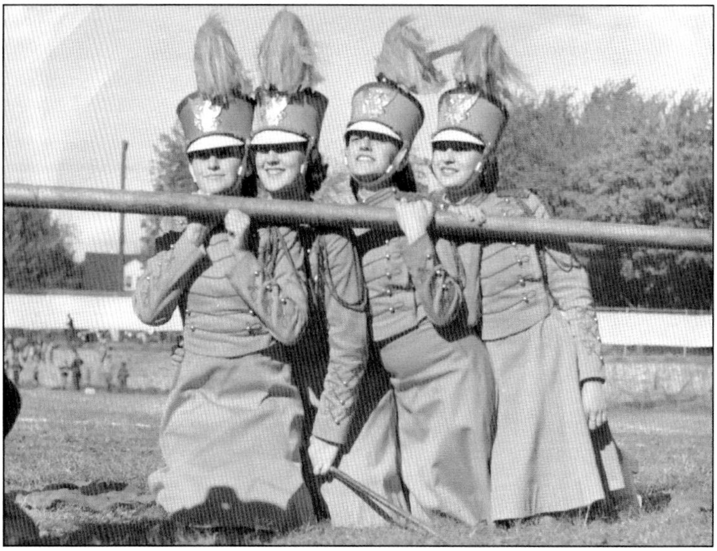

From left to right, Violet Naice, Jean Puitz, Anna Essef, and Mizzie Balbevin pose in this 1941 photograph in their baton-twirler uniforms. The girls became fast friends, as they relied on each other to carry the banner that was prominently displayed in front of the band. (Courtesy of Collingdale High School Alumni Association—William R. Cox collection.)

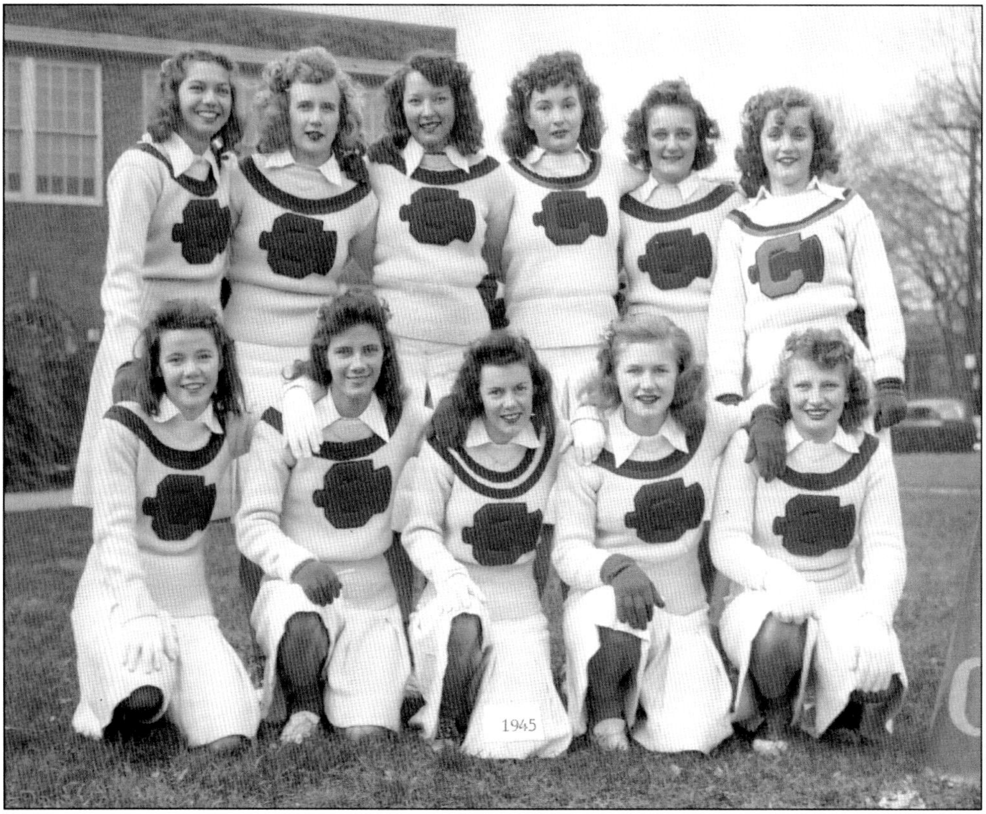

Cheerleaders were the heart of the game, as they encouraged both the fans and the players toward victory. The 1945 Collingdale High School cheerleading squad was adept at performing routines that entertained and provided incentive to younger girls eager to join them. From left to right are (first row) Lorraine Sharkey, Ruth Ann Saxton, Elaine Sharkey, unidentified, and Mildred Baumann; (second row) Elaine McBride, Mary Monaghan, unidentified, Elizabeth Fry, Jeanne Johnson, and unidentified. (Courtesy of Collingdale High School Alumni Association—William R. Cox collection.)

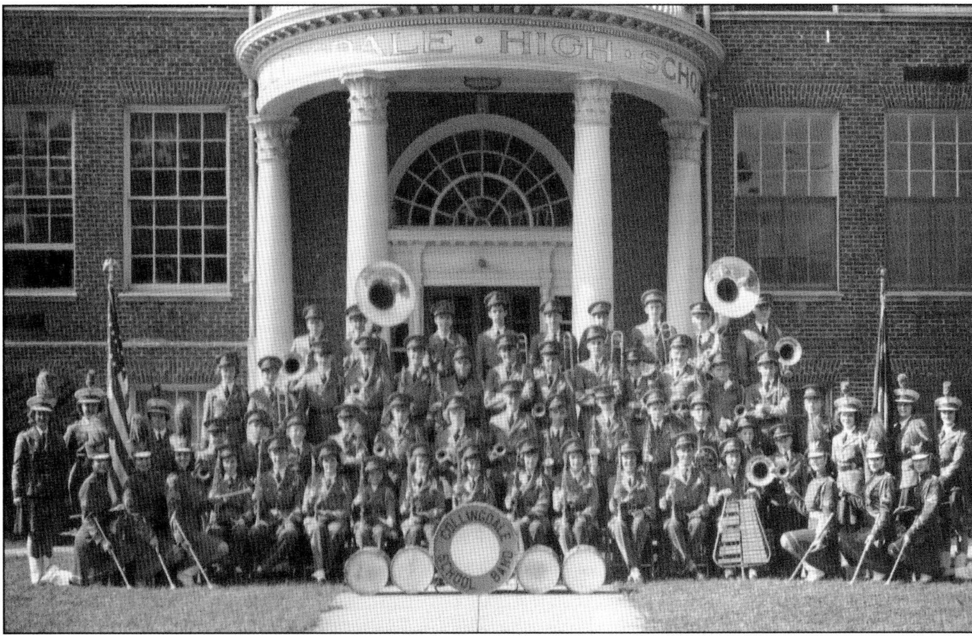

Members of the Collingdale High School band proudly pose in front of the columns of the senior high school in this 1951 photograph. After the popularity of the Collingdale "Scotties" in the 1940s, membership in the marching band grew to about 200. The band performed in many competitions during the 1940s and through the 1960s. After the school joined the Southeast Delco School District in the early 1970s, band membership dropped off. (Courtesy of Collingdale High School Alumni Association.)

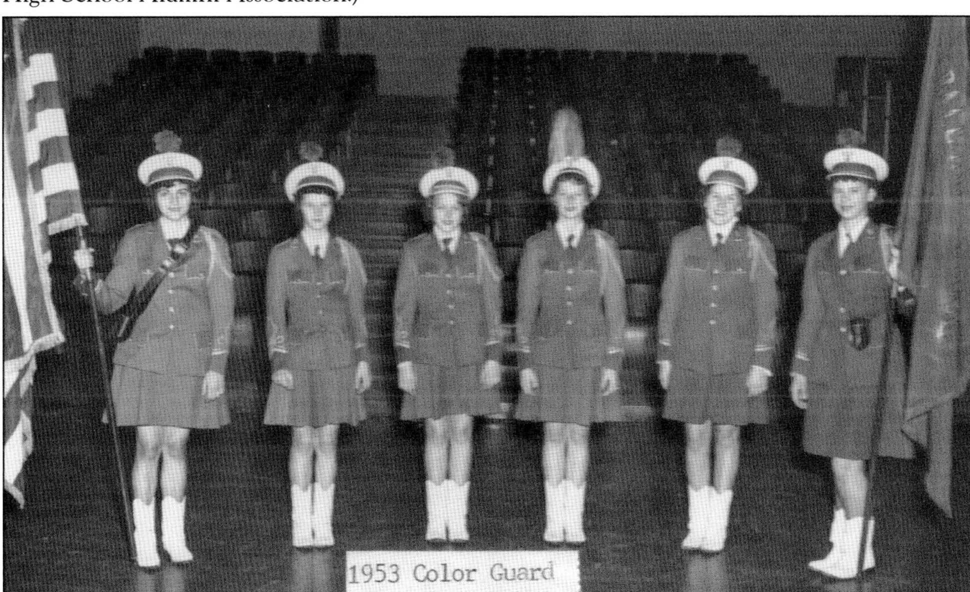

Color guards sometimes accompanied the band when they played at halftime during football season. After football season was over, the color guard usually participated in various parades and competitions with the band. During Veteran's Day ceremonies, they added a patriotic touch. (Courtesy of Collingdale High School Alumni Association—Ann Speer collection.)

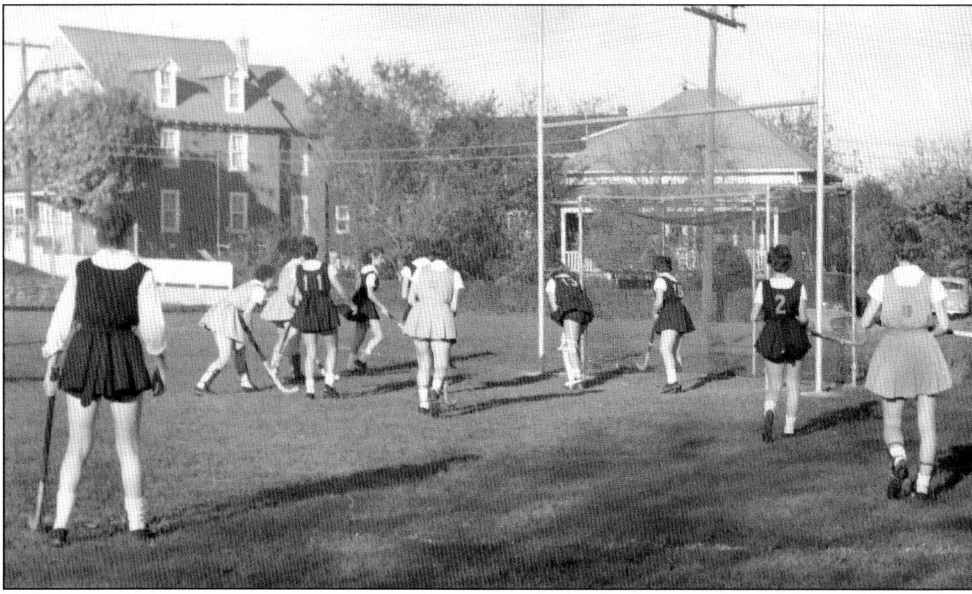

During autumn, while the boys played football, the girls played field hockey. In this mid-1940s photograph, girls from both teams fight to get the ball. (Courtesy of Collingdale High School Alumni Association—Ann Speer collection.)

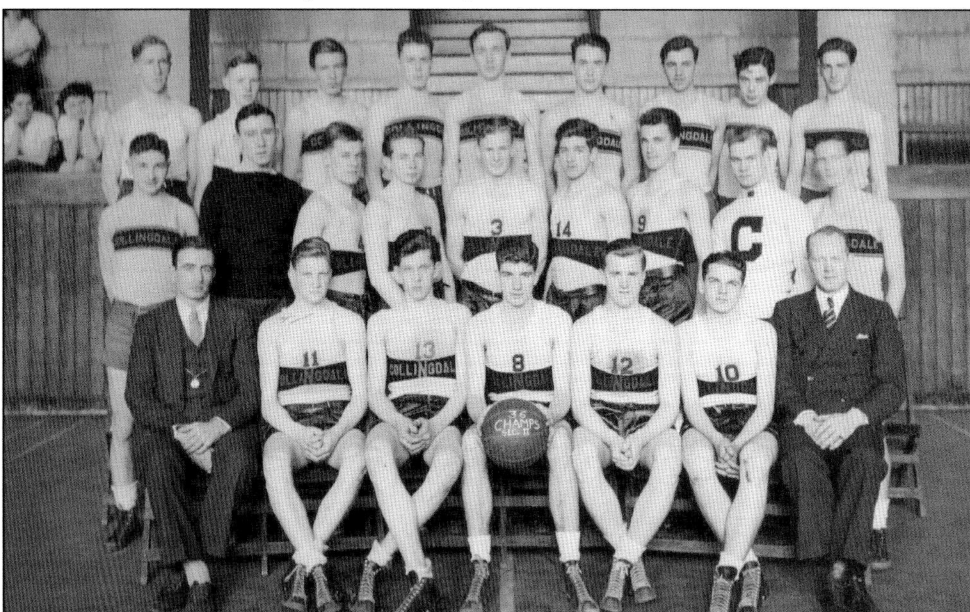

One of the first Collingdale High School championship basketball teams was the 1936 Section II division champions pictured here. From left to right are (first row) Assistant Coach Lawson Earl, Harry Hayes, Andy Speer, Ed Meell, Harold Rowces, Lou Elko, and Coach Carson Thompson; (second row) Abe Elitsky, student manager Sam Hoffman, Frank McMcMullin, Irv Betterman, Herb Gobrecht, George Lincoln, Paul Donnelly, George Smith, and Herb Wright; (third row) Gus Collins, Andy Bromelt, Clarence Smith, Herb Scholcross, Ernest Bromer, Dunbar Pauline, Eugene Scotti, Joe Connors, and Ed Stoebe. (Courtesy of Collingdale High School Alumni Association—Carson Thompson collection.)

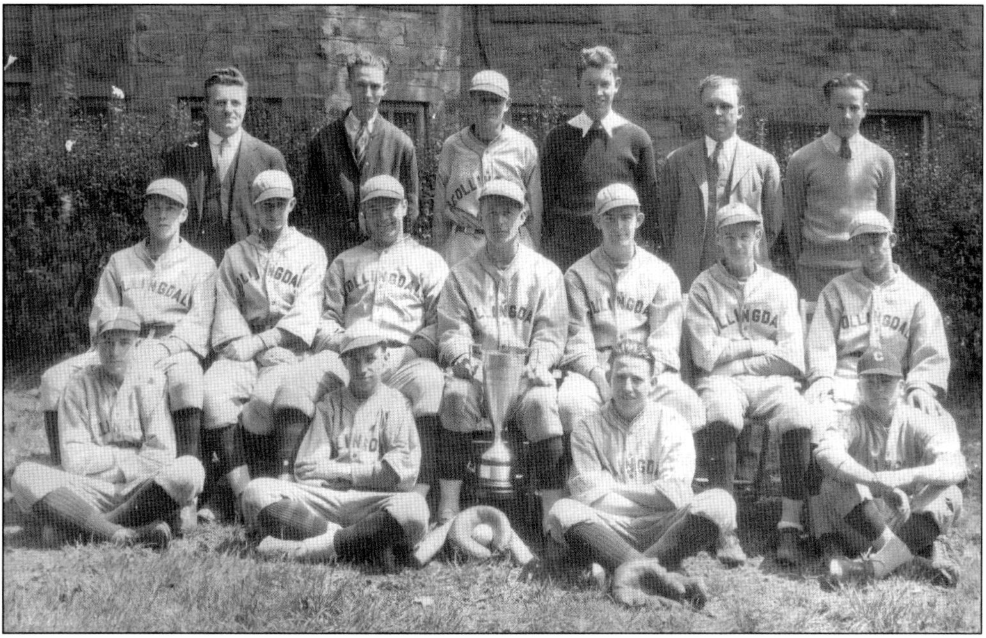

After a winter of basketball games, baseball season beckons. Besides the Collingdale High School team (pictured here in 1929), another Collingdale baseball team formed—the Collingdale Cubs. (Courtesy of Collingdale High School Alumni Association.)

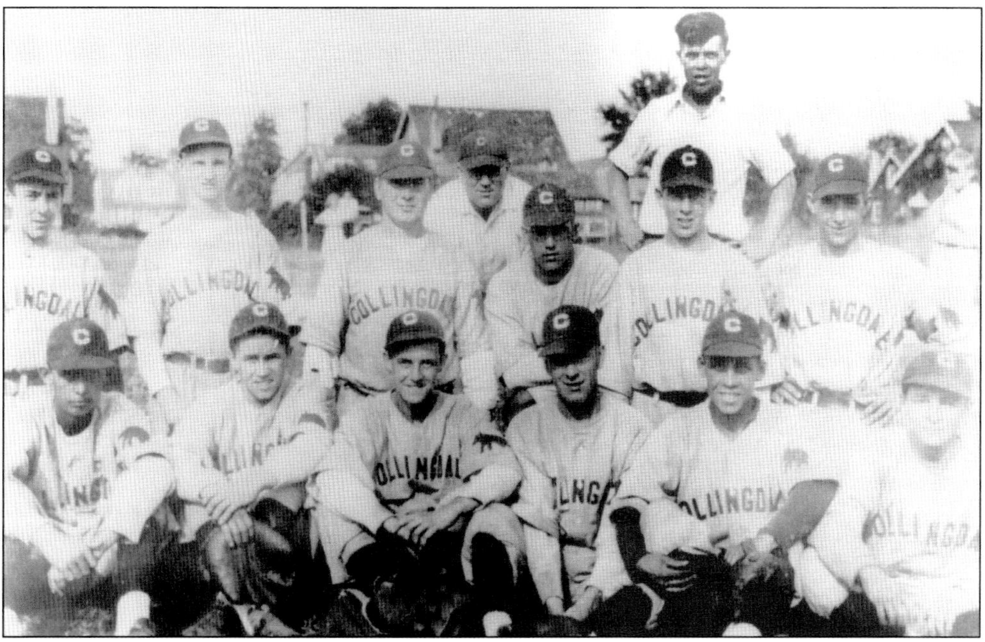

The Collingdale Cubs, Collingdale's second semipro baseball team and the borough's first chartered athletic club, was formed in 1931 by Sam Neville, who became burgess of Collingdale in 1934 and served for almost 20 years. Neville bought the first uniforms when he noticed that the team was playing in street clothes. The team was inducted into the Delco League soon afterwards, filling a gap that formed when Collingdale withdrew from the league in 1910 due to club disputes and changing league rules. (Courtesy of James Powers.)

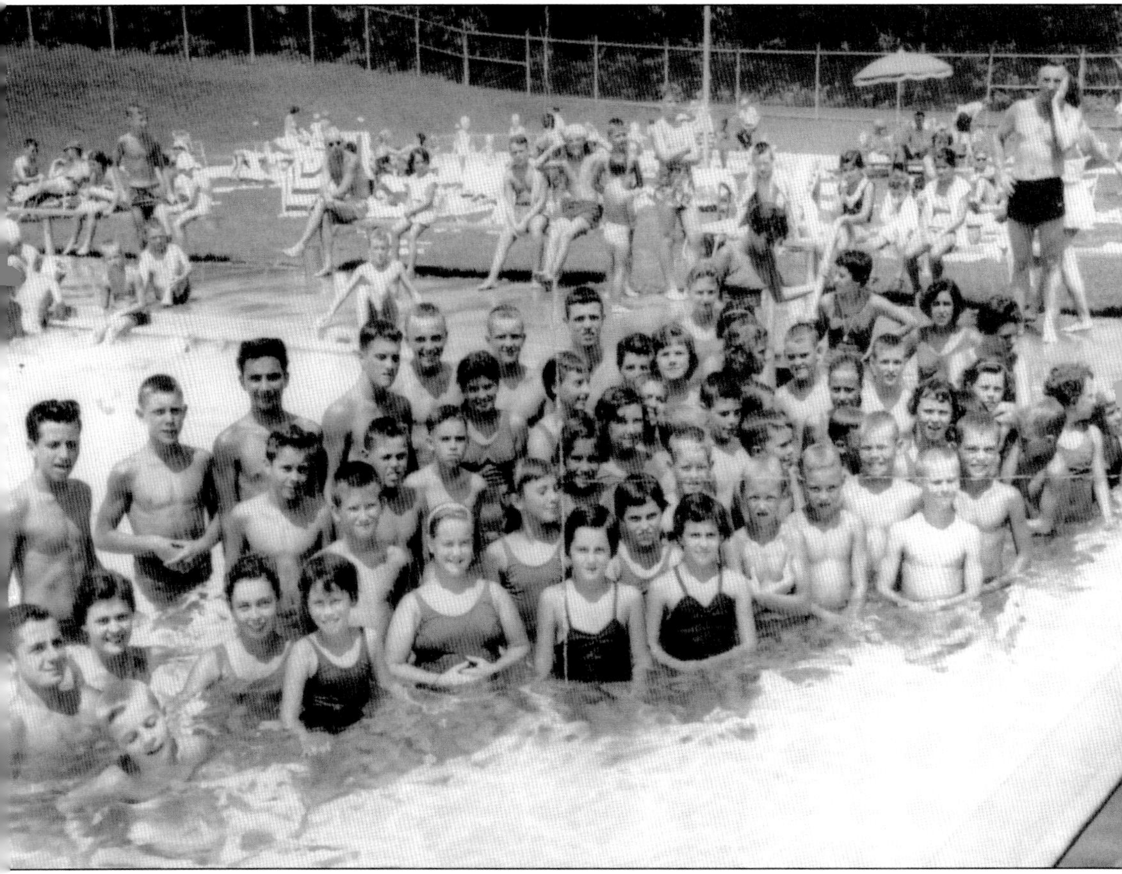

When Jack Saling formed the Collingdale swim club in 1957, his vision was to make the pool a family-friendly place. His vision was fulfilled in the 20 years that followed. Collingdale swim teams such as the Collingdale Dolphins won championship meets, and various contests, such as the Miss Collingdale contest, were held yearly. Around 550 families signed up for memberships that first summer. This 1957 photograph shows many of the families enjoying the pool. The club officially closed in September 2011. (Courtesy of James Powers.)

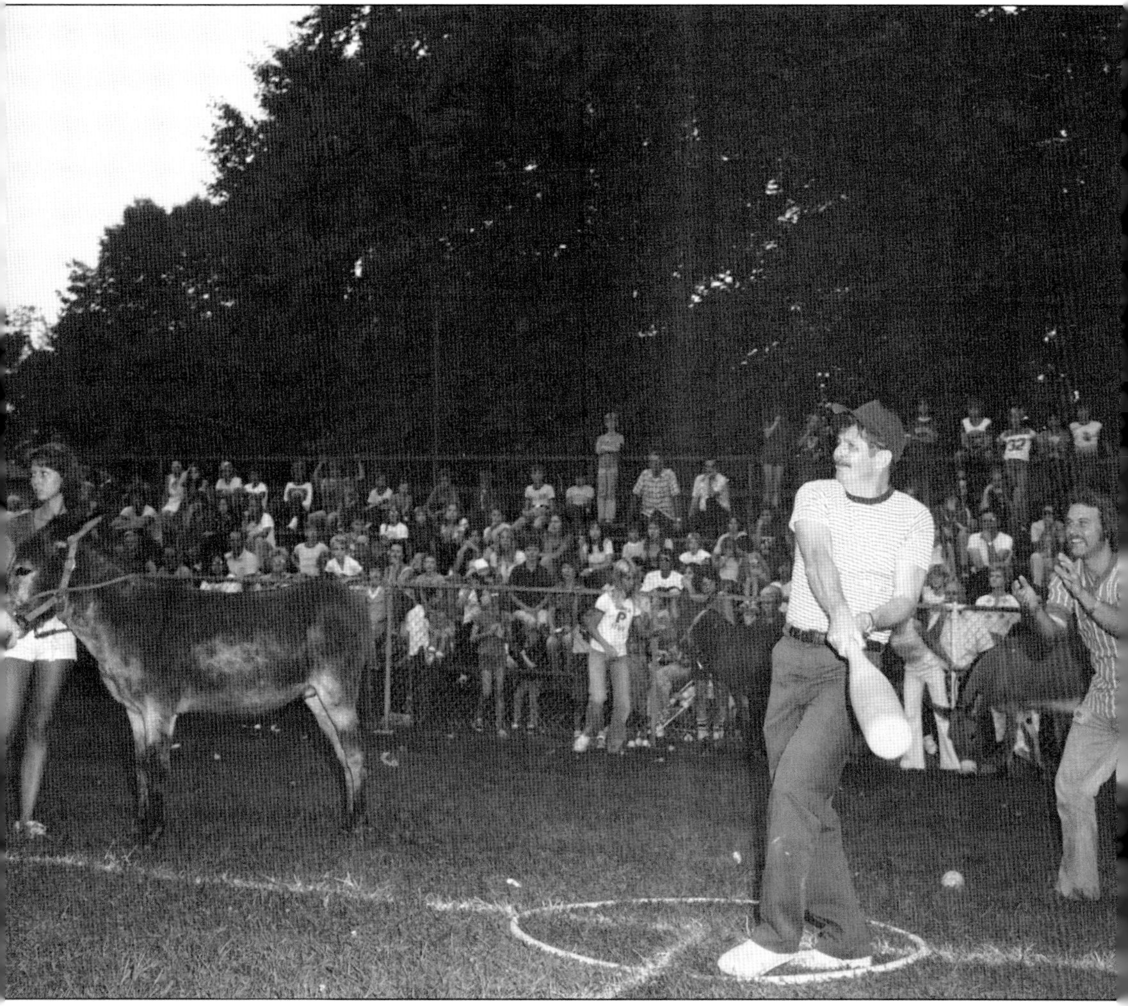

As part of the bicentennial celebration, the Collingdale Athletic Club put together a mule baseball game in September 1976. Getting the mules to cooperate made for moments of hilarity and fun for all. As a result of the success of this endeavor, a donkey basketball game was also put together as a way to raise funds for sport programs. (Courtesy of Donald Bird—Joe Bird collection; photograph by John Harris Studios.)

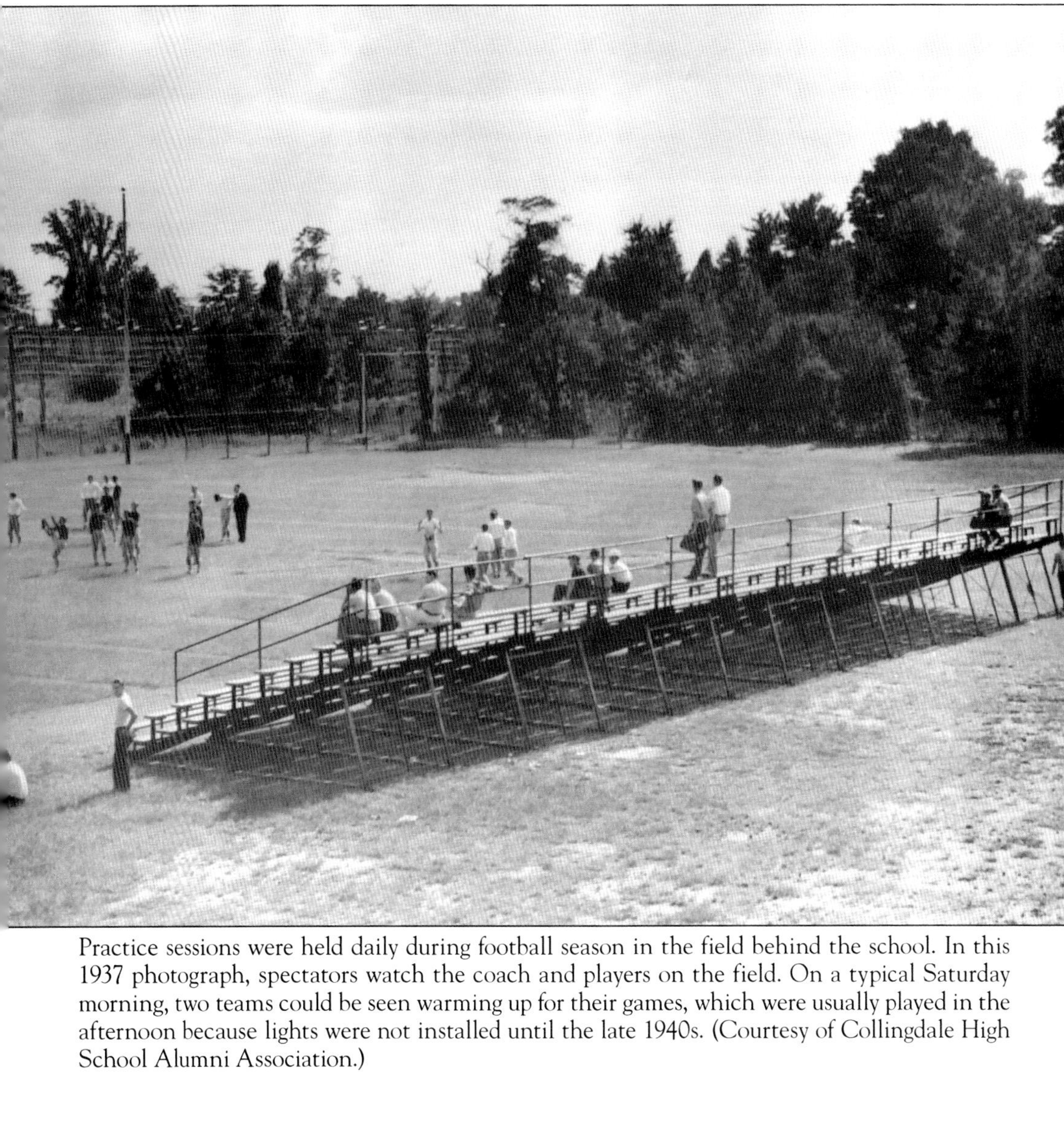

Practice sessions were held daily during football season in the field behind the school. In this 1937 photograph, spectators watch the coach and players on the field. On a typical Saturday morning, two teams could be seen warming up for their games, which were usually played in the afternoon because lights were not installed until the late 1940s. (Courtesy of Collingdale High School Alumni Association.)

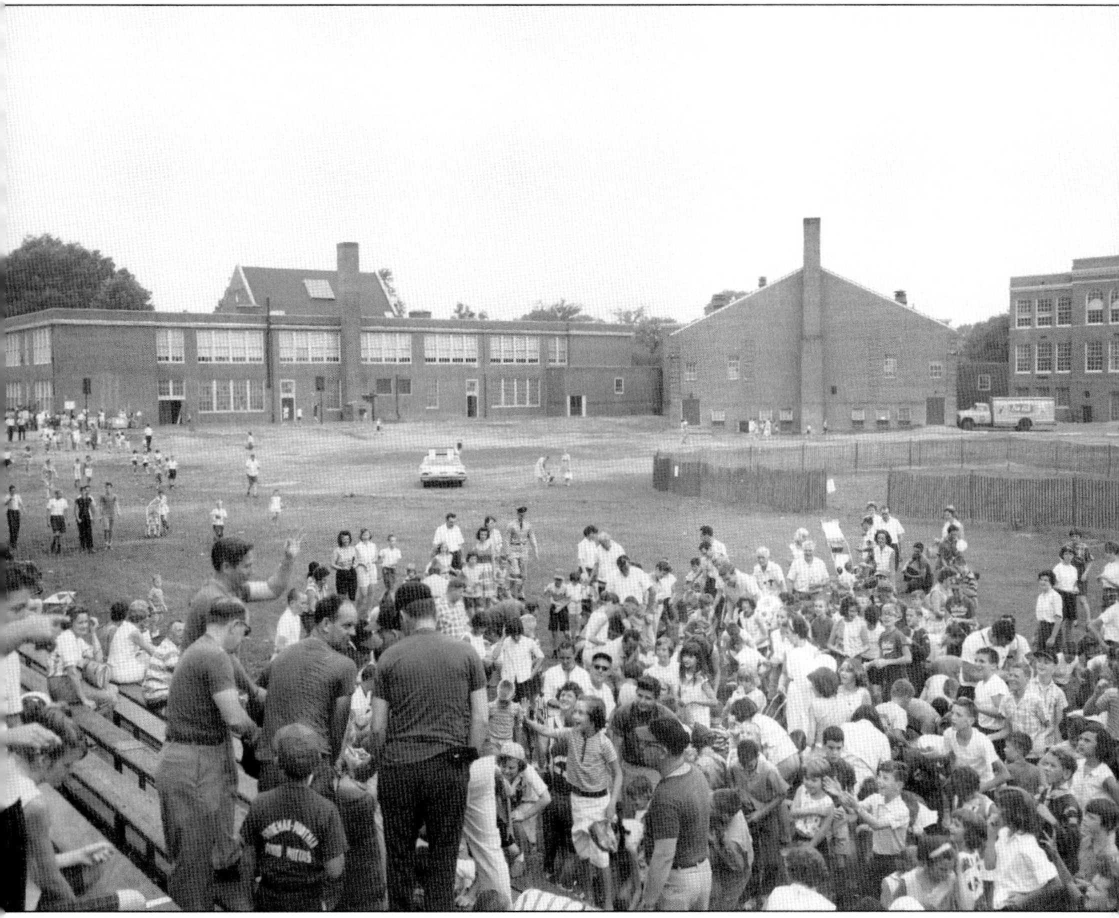

High school sports were a community affair and were usually well attended until Collingdale merged with its former rivals into the Southeast Delco School District in 1972. After that, the games were not as well attended, as the rivalry was gone. In this 1960s photograph, kids participate in a Peanut Scramble during the Fourth of July festivities on the field where most of these games were played. Jimmy Cox, all-star football player for Collingdale in 1958, is at left with his hand raised. (Courtesy of Don Bird—Joe Bird collection; photograph by John Harris Studios.)

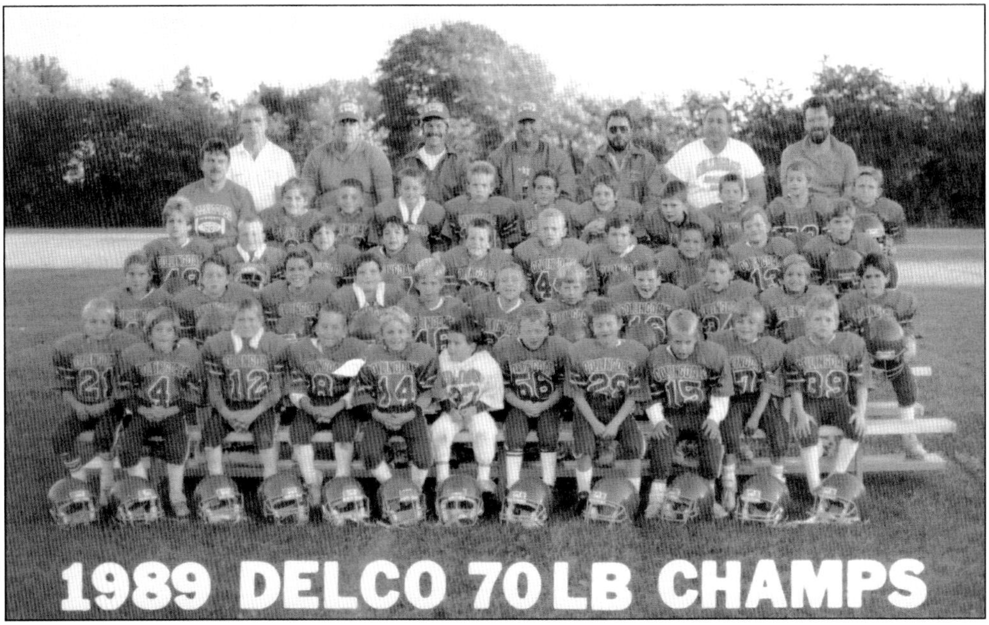

Collingdale's Athletic Club began as an alternative to school sports and did not require a person to be enrolled in one of the schools to join. The only criteria were that the person needed to be a resident of Collingdale. The Collingdale Athletic Club was established in 1968 when the Big Brothers, Lansdowne Park Athletic Association, and the Collingdale Chargers (a boys' football team formed in 1962) merged. Since its inception, it has included teams for both adults and children. The 1989 70-pound championship football team seen here would be considered a children's team. (Courtesy of James Powers.)

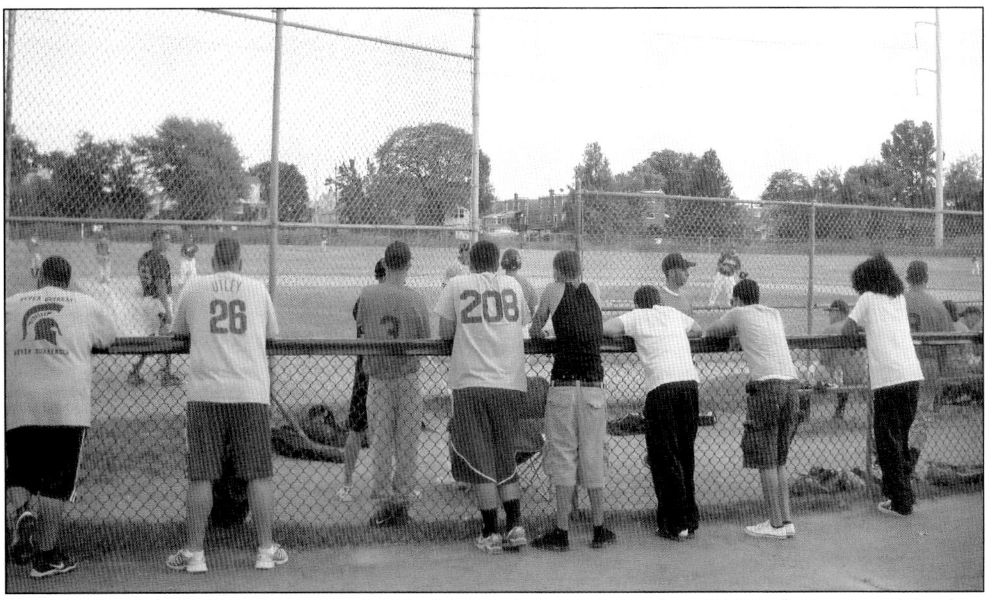

The Collingdale Colts is a semi-pro baseball team that was formed in 1908 and was part of the first six teams in the Delco League, the oldest semi-pro baseball league in the United States. Back then, they were just called Collingdale—the "Colts" name came much later. This is the young adults' team from Collingdale Athletic Club in May 2011. (Photograph by Elizabeth MacGuire.)

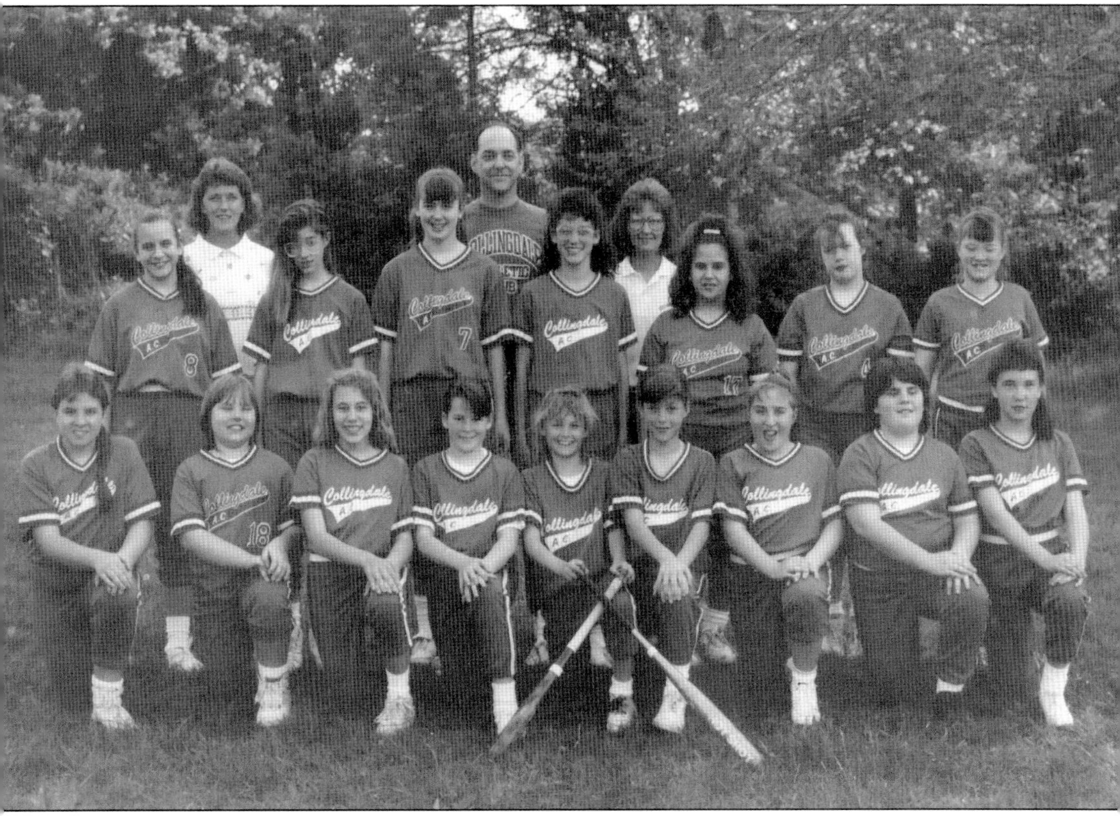

Both boys and girls had softball teams in the Collingdale Athletic Club. It was not until the early 1970s that girls participated in this sport regularly enough to establish a team for them. Once teams were established, the girls did just as well as the boys, as seen in this photograph of the 1990 midget "C" softball championship team. From left to right are (first row) Theresa Wiegand, Sara Swayngim, Kim Rodenbaugh, Denise Gannon, Jackie Norbeck, Erica Keenan, Kelli Laurie, Ann Swayngim, and Kristy Fisher; (second row) Maria Pologruto, Lauri Rowe, Kelly Gaughan, Lea Anne Hudecheck, Dana Radico, Jennifer DePietro, and Stacey Capstick; (third row) Coaches Susan Fisher, Charley Rowe, and Pat Gaughan. (Courtesy of Keith Lockhart.)

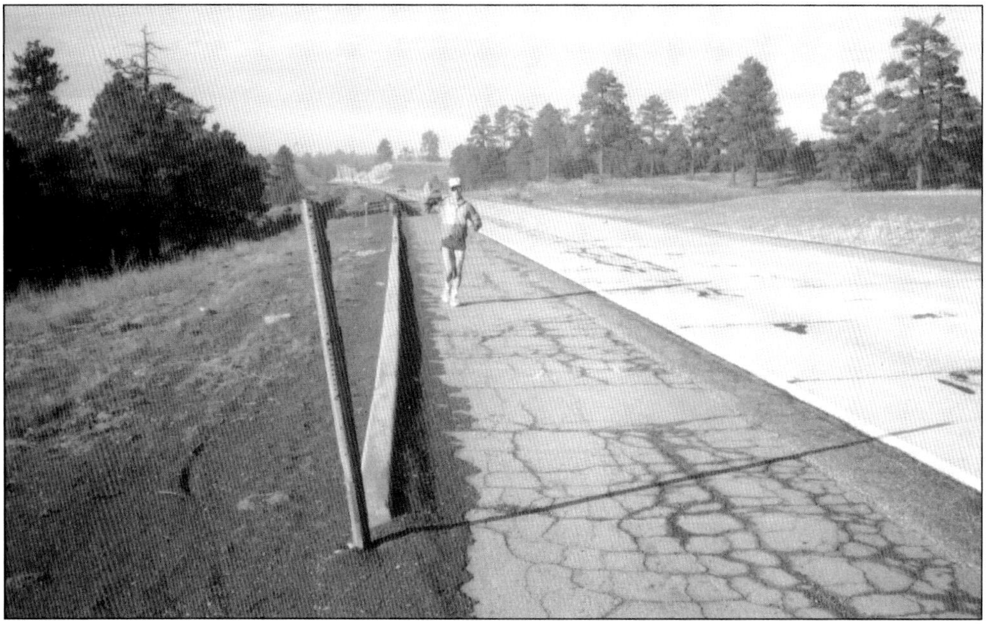

Bill Schultz, a fifth-grade science teacher from Harris Elementary School, had an idea to get his students involved in a geography lesson that would incorporate his love of running. He decided that he would run from the West Coast to the East Coast. Along the way, he would check in with his students every Wednesday, and they, in turn, would map his journey. In this photograph taken in Tucson, Arizona, on March 18, 1990, he is about a quarter of the way through his journey. (Courtesy of Collingdale High School Alumni Association; photograph by Fran McCoy.)

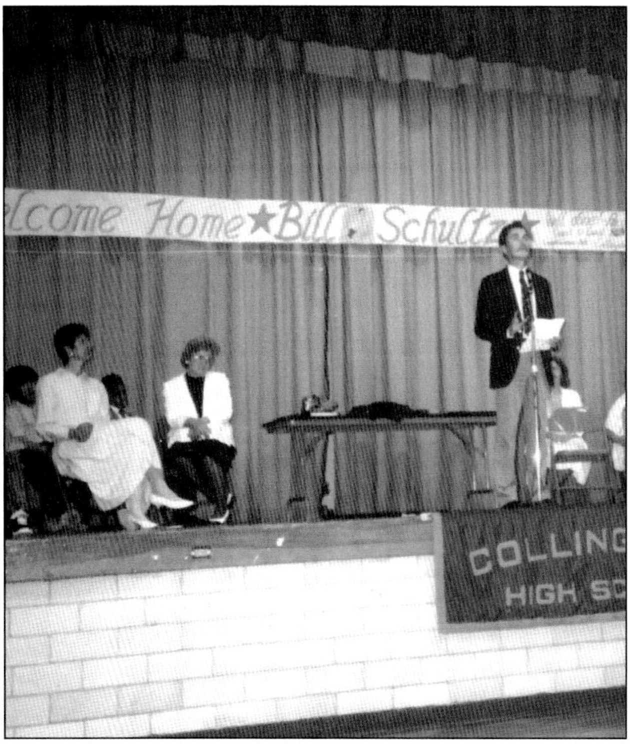

June 8, 1990, was declared "Bill Schultz Day" in Collingdale. Ceremonies at Collingdale High School included giving Schultz a key to the borough and a certificate of appreciation. (Courtesy of Collingdale High School Alumni Association)

Eight

Death in the Community
Lasting Legacies

Eden Cemetery is probably the most famous of the four cemeteries that border Collingdale on three sides. Established on August 12, 1902, after what appeared to be some irregularities over the possession of the land in question, Eden Cemetery became the oldest African American–owned and unified cemetery in the nation. Interred in its grounds are civil rights leaders, famous athletes, and world-class singers from a bygone era.

Mount Zion Methodist Meeting Cemetery, the oldest cemetery in Collingdale, was established when the church was built in 1808. A typical rural cemetery from 1800 to 1830, it is the resting place of soldiers from the Revolutionary War, the War of 1812, and more than 100 documented Civil War veterans. Mount Zion's immigrant families used their skills to develop mills and to build homes, schools, churches, and businesses. Their names grace streets and institutions in recognition of their contributions to their new country.

Two Jewish cemeteries, Har Zion and Mount Lebanon (actually in Darby Township), serve as final resting places for the Jewish communities in the surrounding area. Mount Lebanon has both an old section—which could be considered another cemetery—called Brith Achim Memorial Park, and a new section that is still being used to this day.

In the 1890s, funerals were usually held in a person's home with the loved one laid out as if they were still alive. Funeral photography, especially of children, was popular. Loved ones would then be buried in one of the surrounding church cemeteries. It was not until the early 1900s that funeral homes, which prepared the body for burial, came into vogue, and transportation was required to move a body to the cemetery. Concerns about disease kept most communities wary about letting nearby land be used as a cemetery.

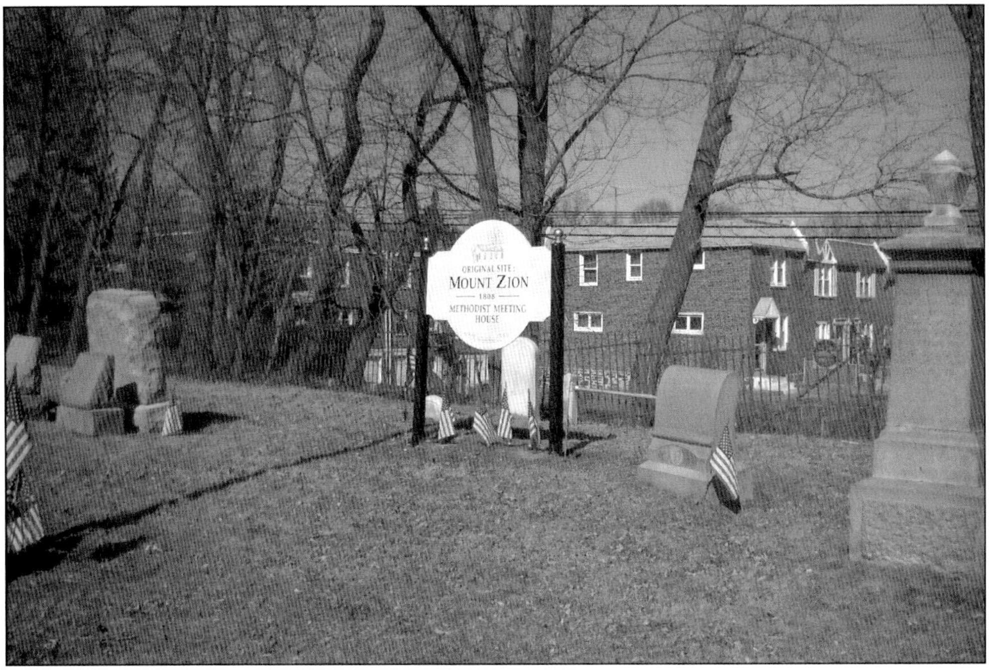

Mount Zion Methodist Meeting Cemetery, seen here in February 2012, is the site of one of the first subscription schools (1735) in Delaware County. The first temperance society in Pennsylvania (and perhaps the country) formed there in 1816. British general William Howe's troops crept stealthily here, and War of 1812 soldiers, as well as Civil War soldiers, camped on the grounds and used the church for shelter. (Photograph by Elizabeth MacGuire.)

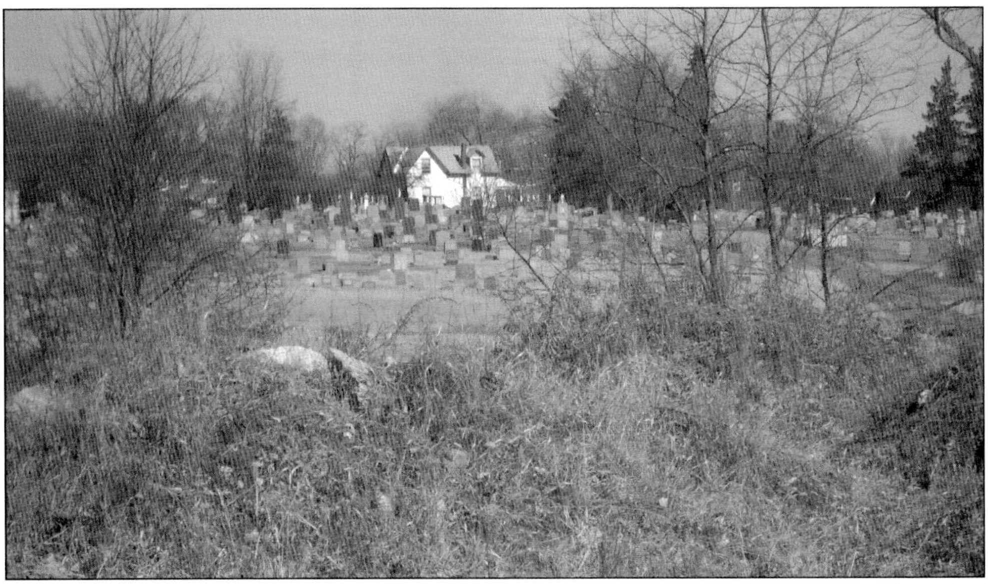

Mount Zion Methodist Meeting cemetery holds over 330 years of history. The Minquas Indian Trail came through this property. Mount Zion Methodist Meeting members were active abolitionists and welcomed black families into their church and homes, and families from all ethnic, religious, and racial backgrounds are buried here. Church members sold burial plots to local residents of all denominations and provided many for free to families in need. (Photograph by Elizabeth MacGuire.)

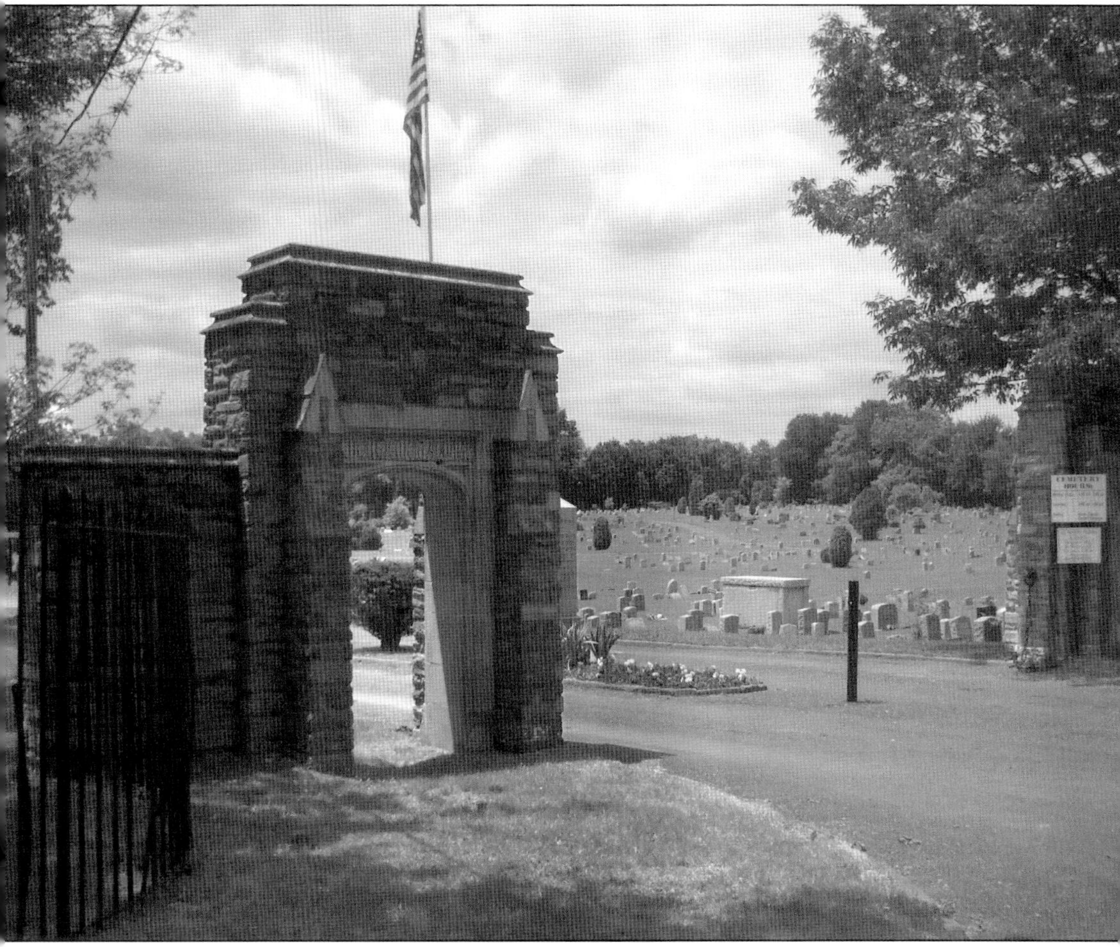

This is the entrance to Eden Cemetery, burial place of famous civil rights activists, singers, and athletes. Eden Cemetery, established on June 20, 1902 and seen here in June 2011, is listed in the National Register of Historic Places and the National Park Service's Network to Freedom. Eden Cemetery has 23 sections named either to honor the cemeteries where the deceased were first interred or after famous people such as Frederick Douglass. (Photograph by Elizabeth MacGuire.)

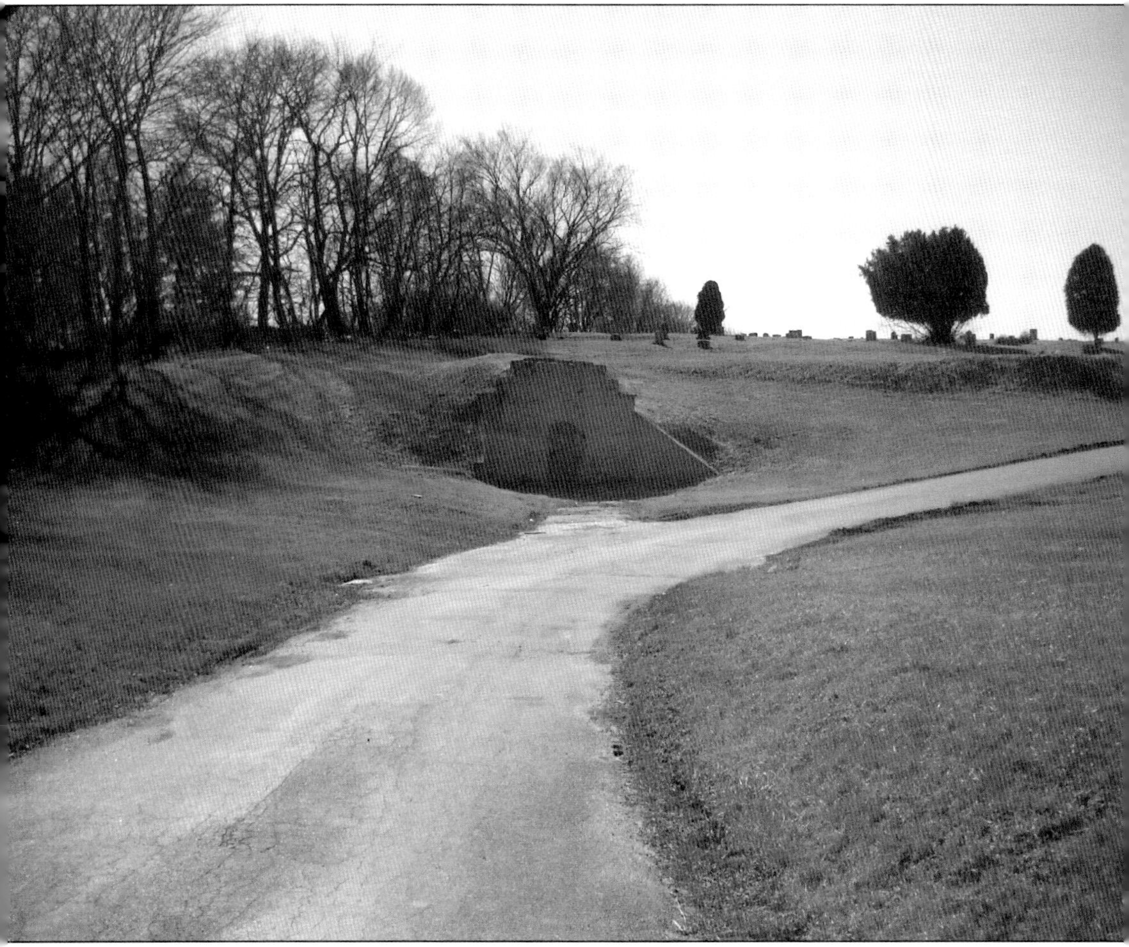

Eden Cemetery has a typical receiving vault (pictured in February 2012) dating from its establishment in 1902. Receiving vaults housed the deceased during the winter months when the ground was frozen, making it too difficult to dig graves by hand. When the ground thawed enough, the deceased were given a proper burial. (Photograph by Elizabeth MacGuire.)

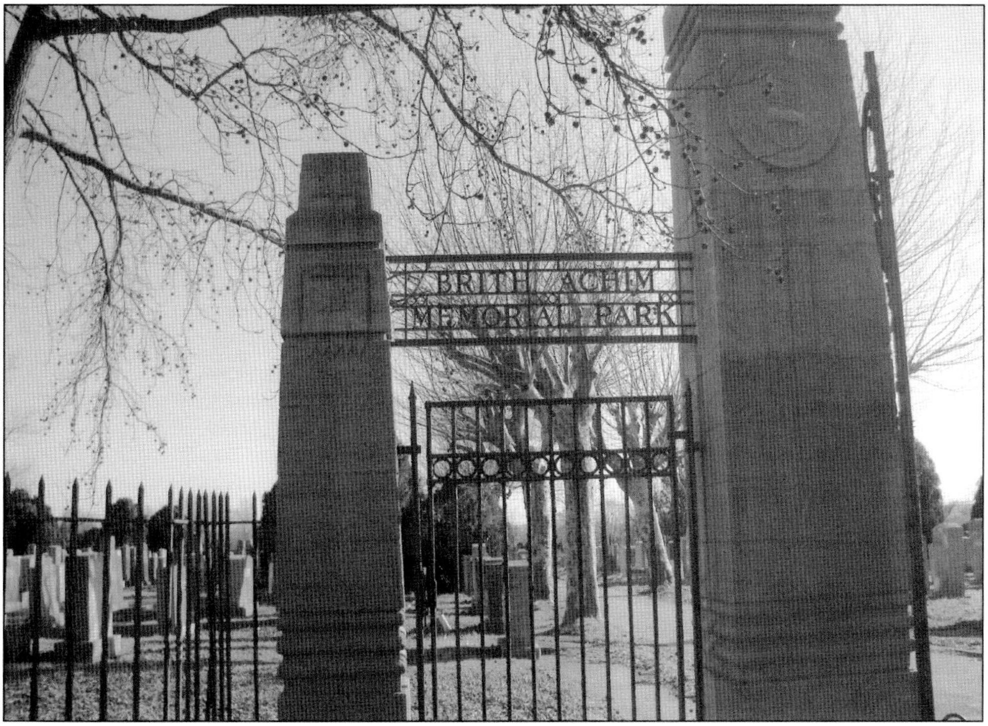

Brith Achim Memorial Park dates from 1889, according to the arch leading to the cemetery pictured here in February 2012. As part of Mount Lebanon cemetery, which dates to 1910, the Brith Achim part of the cemetery presents an example of early 19th century Jewish burial practices that faded in the early part of the 20th century. (Photograph by Elizabeth MacGuire.)

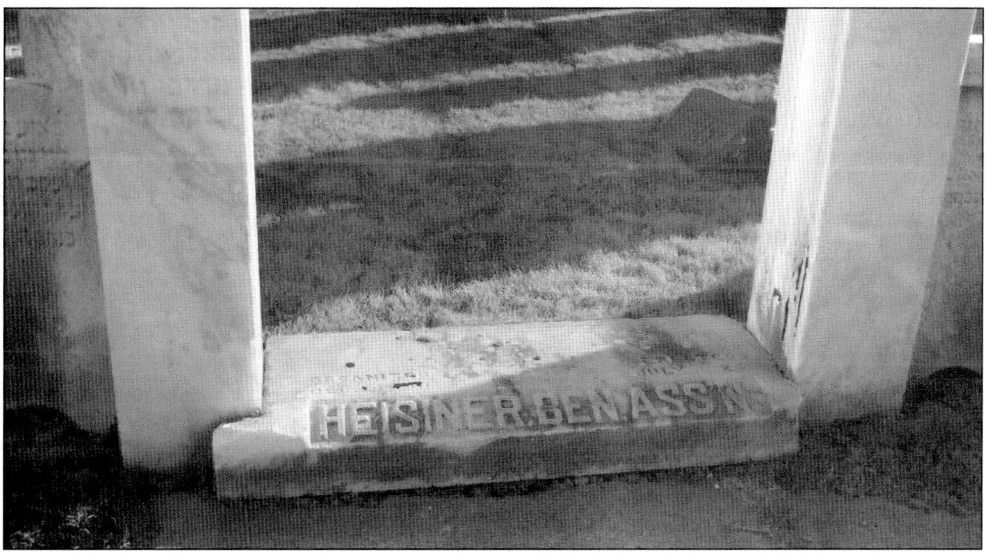

Unlike Eden Cemetery or its nearest neighbor, Har Zion Cemetery, Mount Lebanon is not sectioned off via letter, personage, or a combination of both, except in the newer sections. Instead, various civic and benevolent associations would purchase markers like this that would, until the stone etchings rubbed away, announce who was buried nearby and/or what the organization represented. (Photograph by Elizabeth MacGuire.)

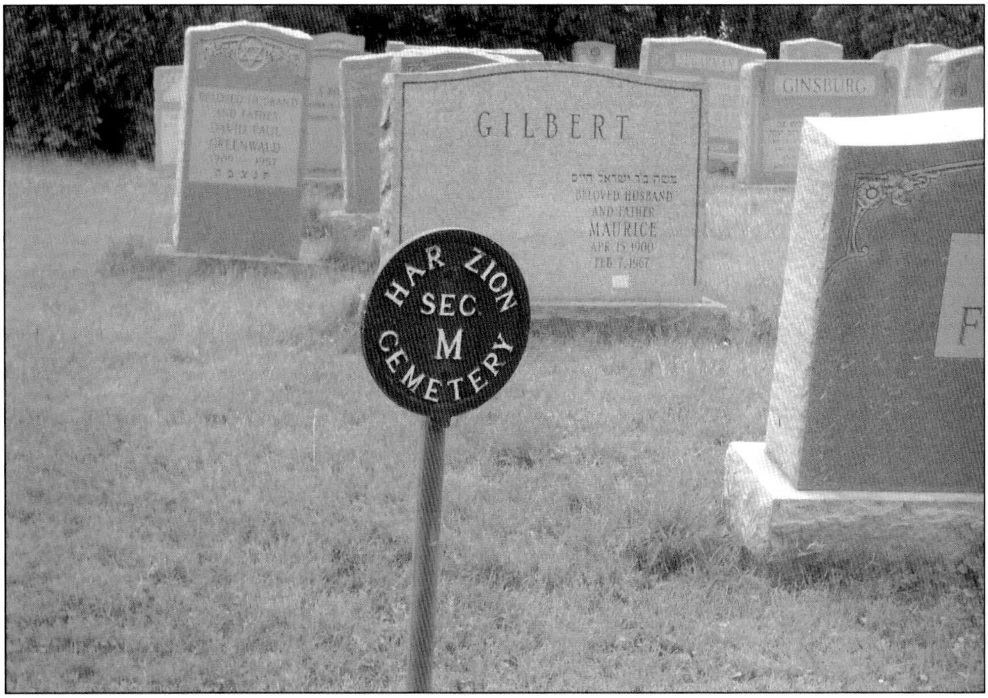

Har Zion Cemetery, established in 1936, is the newest cemetery in the borough. More modern than its neighbor Mount Lebanon, Har Zion, pictured in June 2011, uses a modern method of marking off sections of the cemetery, except for the very oldest section, which it shares with Mount Lebanon's Brith Achim Memorial Park. (Photograph by Elizabeth MacGuire.)

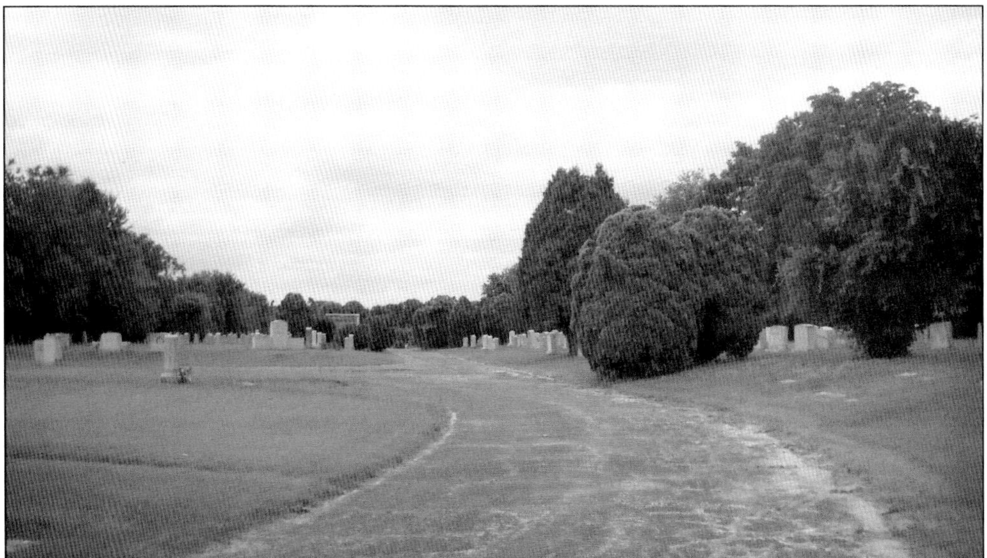

Another view of Har Zion Cemetery shows a tranquil, open, and inviting scene that allows contemplation and reflection on the brevity of life. Har Zion Cemetery is a perfect example of the transition from traditional Jewish burial practices into more modern burial practices. (Photograph by Elizabeth MacGuire.)

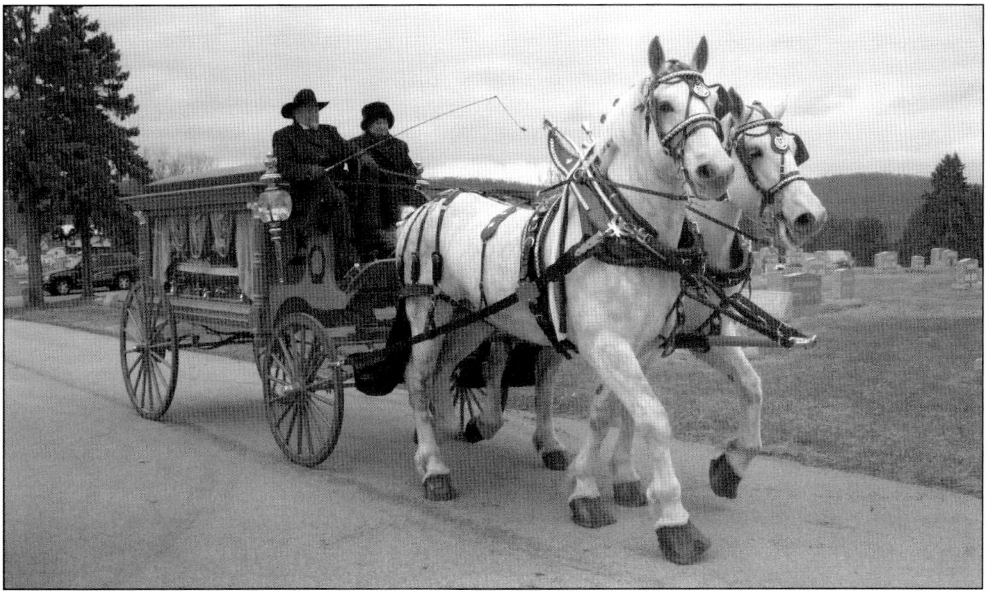

When Collingdale was incorporated in 1891, there were only three places in the county where a person could be buried outside the churches. Changes from that social norm were long in coming, as most still either buried family members in their yard or, if they belonged to the church, in the churchyard. Transporting the dead was an undertaking; one of the earliest conveyances was a horse-drawn carriage like this one belonging to Bee Tree Trail Carriage & Wagon Tours. (Courtesy of Dave Rohrach.)

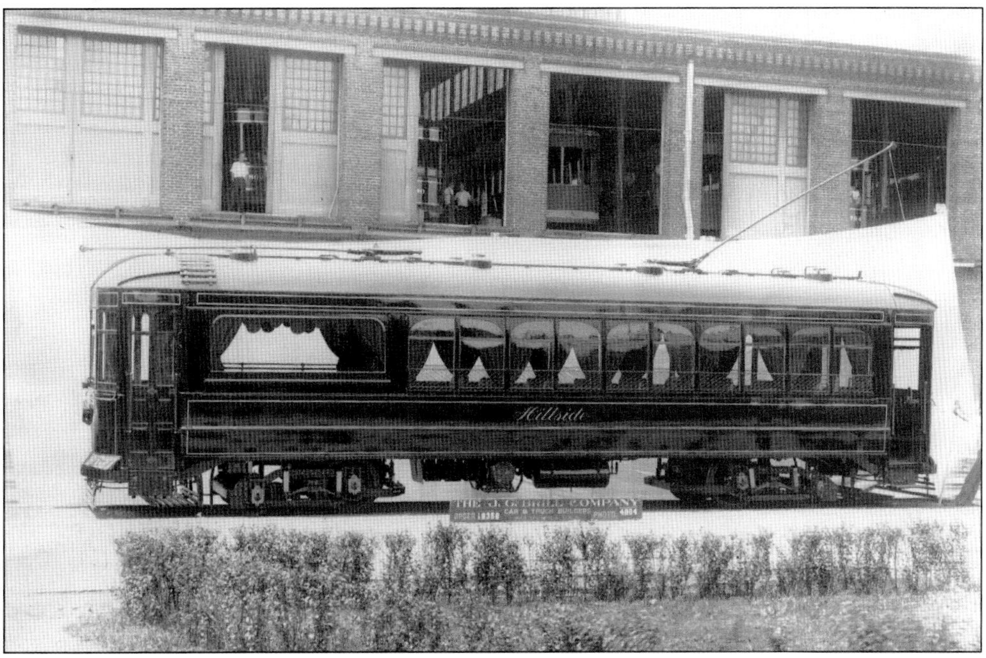

Around 1909, two trolley lines ran funeral cars to the area cemeteries. One of the trolley cars used was the J.G. Brill Company's "Hillside," which had a compartment for the deceased and seats for the bereaved to travel in comfort to the cemetery. (Courtesy of the Free Library of Philadelphia; photograph by John Gibb Smith.)

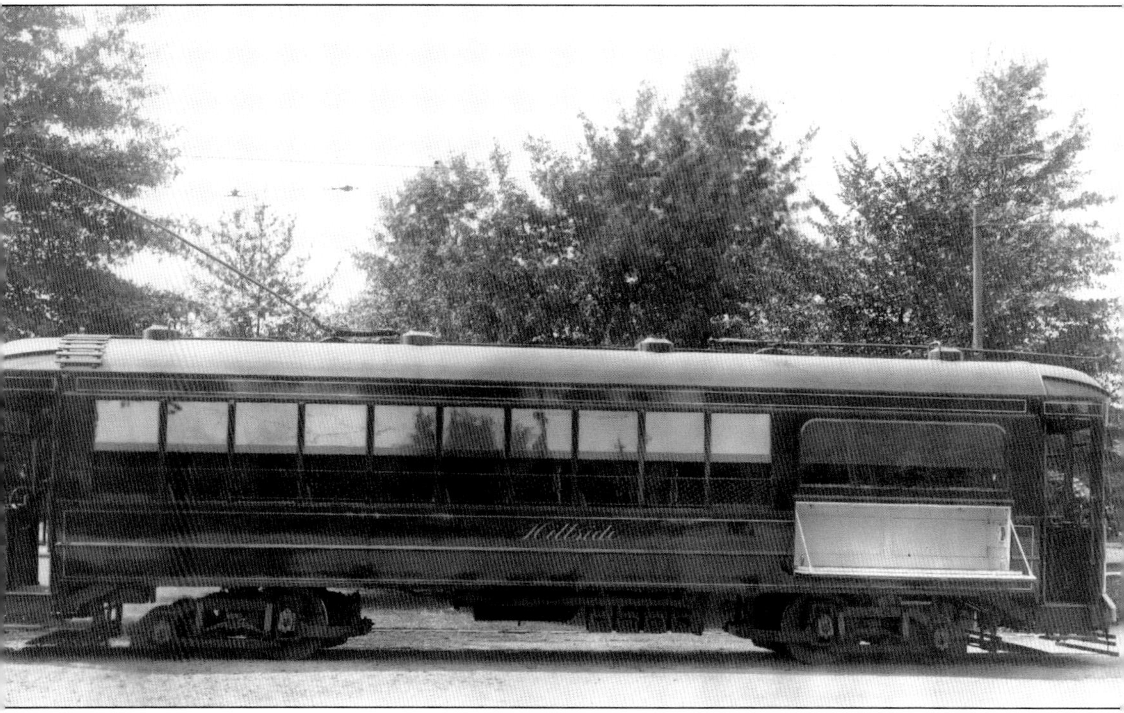

Another view of the "Hillside," with its compartment open, shows the ease with which coffins could be placed in the back. In the 1890s, when travel by trolley grew in popularity, the notion of transporting the deceased that way was still in its infancy. However, because it soon became apparent that older church cemeteries were becoming too overcrowded and unsanitary, it was necessary to find a convenient and quick way to transport bodies over a long distance. (Photograph by John Gibb Smith; Courtesy of the Free Library of Philadelphia.)

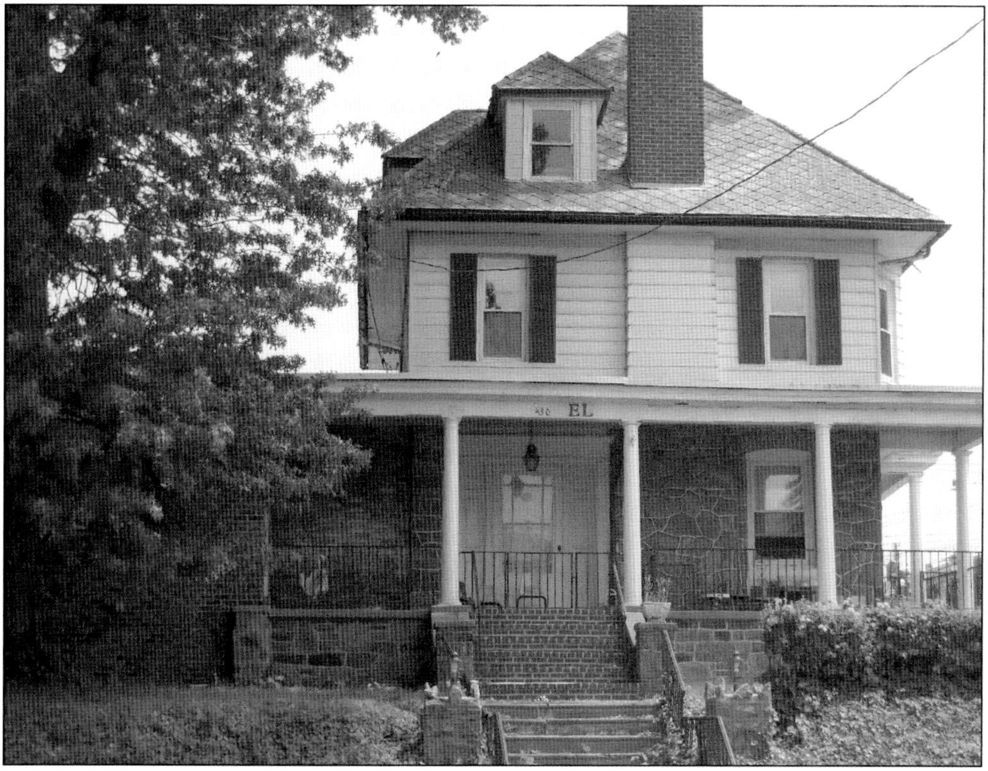

Funeral homes dotted neighborhoods during the early days of the 20th century in response to requests for elaborate funerals that included makeup, clothes, caskets, and other funereal necessities. ELF Childcare, seen here in June 2011, was once Milligan funeral home. (Photograph by Elizabeth MacGuire.)

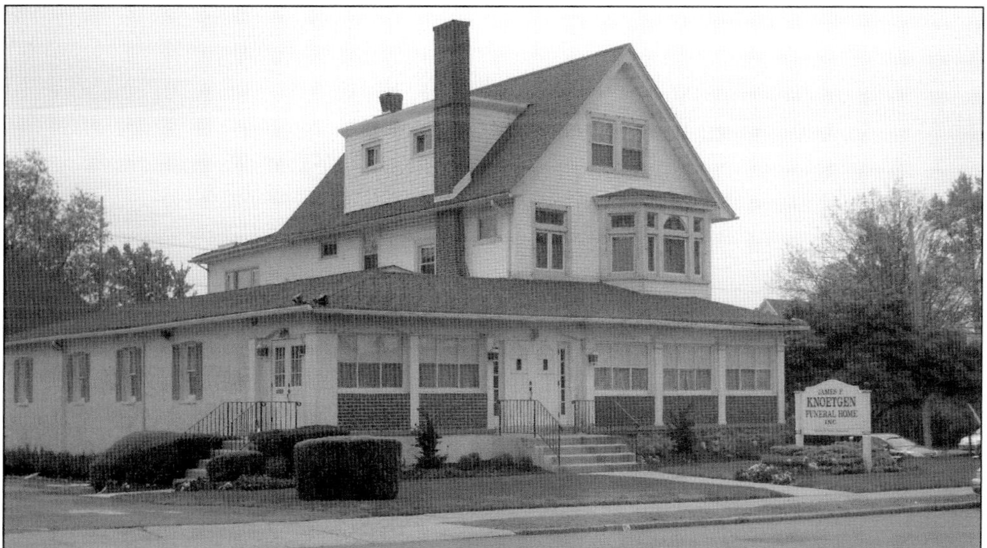

James F. Knoetgen Funeral Home, a second-generation business, replaced the funeral home next to Collingdale High School on MacDade Boulevard. Originally called Phillips Funeral Home, it was first established in the 1920s. It is seen here in May 2012. (Photograph by Elizabeth MacGuire.)

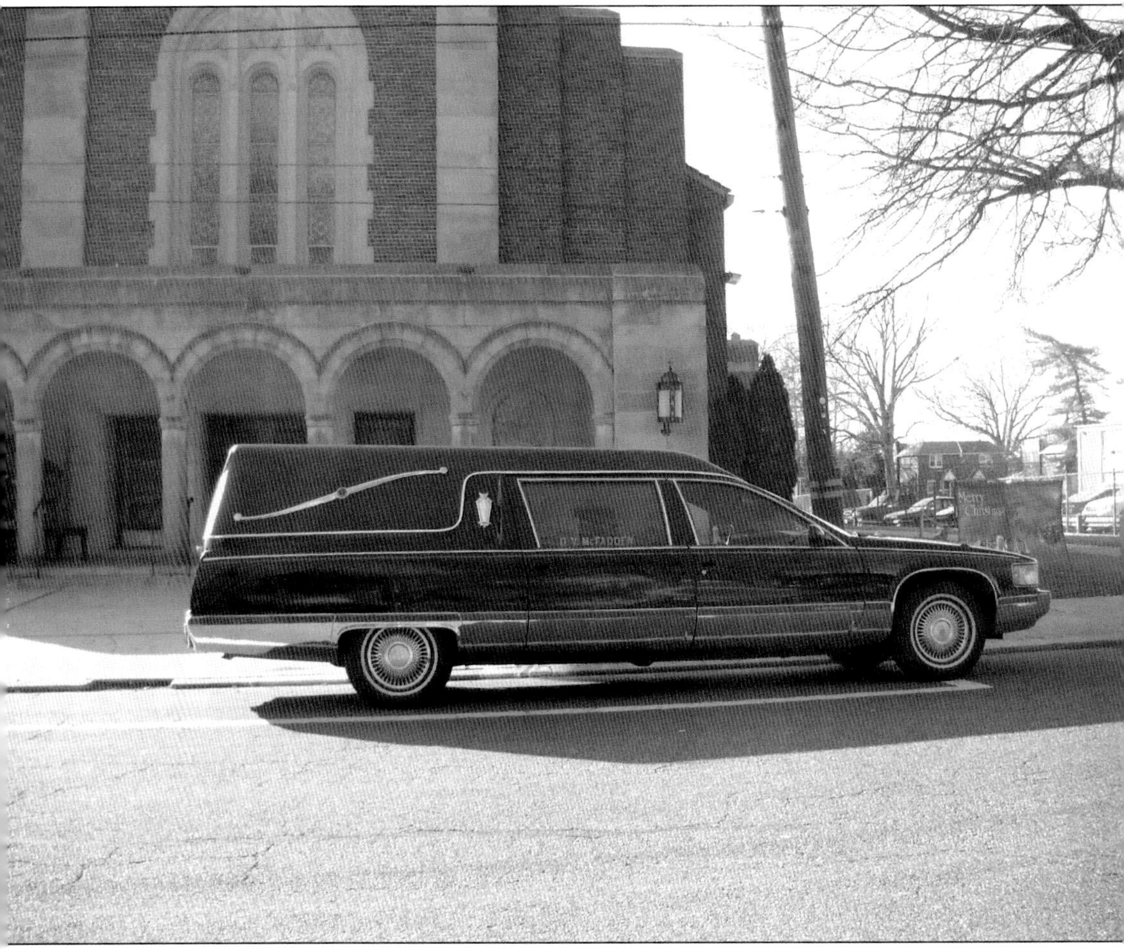

Hearses, such as this one in front of St. Joseph's church in December 2011, now serve as the primary vehicle used for transporting the deceased to the cemetery. Many former ambulances served as hearses or were models for future hearses. (Photograph by Elizabeth MacGuire.)

Nine

Religious Community
Roots in Faith

The underpinning of any community is its religious roots—without them, most communities falter and wither away—and Collingdale's came from the founders of the small borough. Both Maximilian LaRoche and William McCausland had deep religious connections. Not much is known about LaRoche's church affiliations except that he was involved in the choir and had a great singing voice. McCausland was one of the cofounders of Grace Reformed Episcopal Church in 1897. His family continued to attend, and his son was on hand when the church was renovated in 1949.

The First Baptist Church of Collingdale has been serving the community since 1882, when Mrs. E.H. Royal started a Sunday school in her home. Originally called Collingdale Baptist and established in 1887, it was the first church in Collingdale. Four members met regularly in Pop Eliskey's store, and when word spread that a former mission church was available to be purchased, they acted. Land at the corner of Andrews and Clifton Avenues was obtained, and the church was moved from Philadelphia to Collingdale. When it was shipped to Collingdale, it needed to be reassembled. The official charter for the church was not granted until May 6, 1889. Until the church was available in April 1889, services were held at Floral Hall, which could hold 75 people comfortably.

Community service was and still is the core element of all the Collingdale churches, which started soup kitchens, sports teams, family activities, and community programs. Church members got involved with various projects, such as establishing a public park, educating their children, and providing support for needy families.

From its conception in 1891, Collingdale has been open, for the most part, to various religious affiliations. There are five long-established church buildings in Collingdale and about six churches that meet in homes or various businesses in the borough. Each brings a unique flavor to the religious experience. Collingdale's diverse religious offerings reflect the current cultural shift in the country.

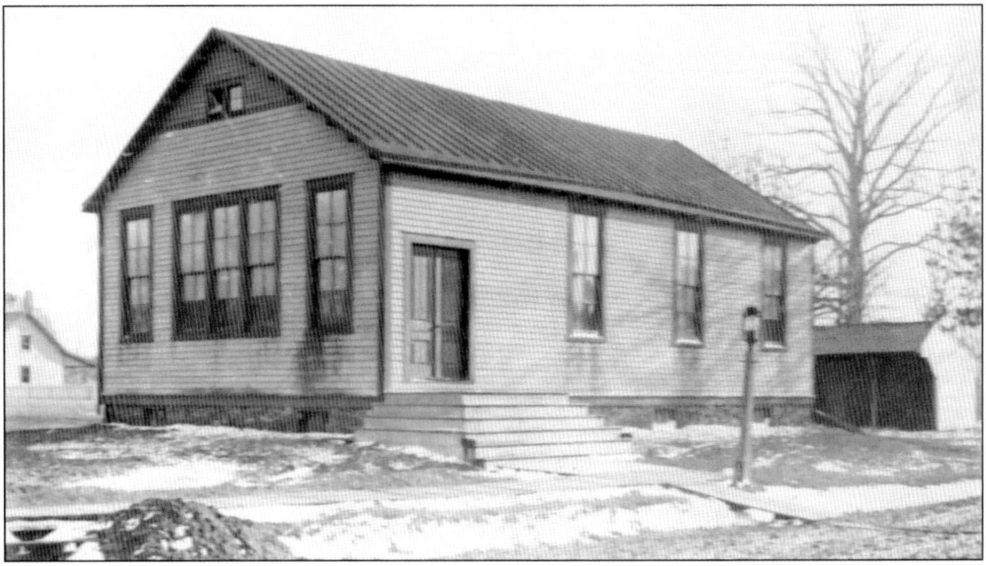

Collingdale Baptist's original church building had to be moved in two pieces due to a bridge obstruction. After it was reassembled after the move from Philadelphia, the congregation was able to move in. The original building is pictured here in 1889. (Courtesy of Pastor Perry Messick, First Baptist Church of Collingdale; photograph by H.J. Chan.)

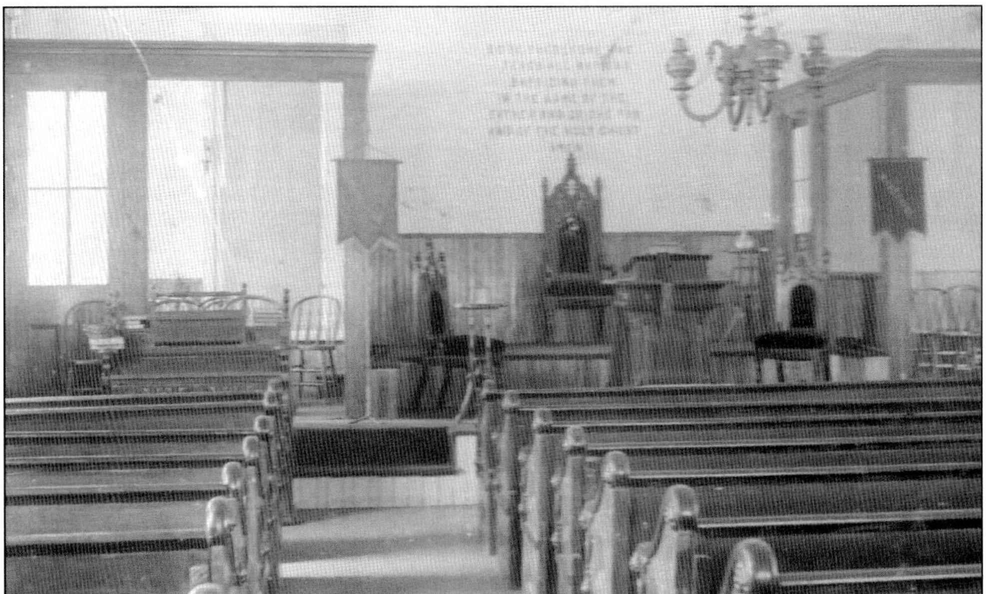

This photograph was taken inside the old church on May 6, 1889, when it received its charter. It shows the elaborate settings on the altar as it stood ready for its 75 parishioners to enter. Rev. Milton Lutz officiated at the opening, and under his guidance and leadership, 10 more members joined the church. A fire completely destroyed the church on October 31, 1898; it took two years for the congregation to raise the $3,000 needed to rebuild. During that time, the church met at Floral Hall, as it did before the original building was moved. On April 12, 1900, a ground-breaking ceremony occurred at the church's current site at the corner of Clifton and Andrews Avenues. (Courtesy of Pastor Perry Messick, First Baptist Church of Collingdale.)

In this 1950s photograph, some improvements to the outside of the church are visible, but most of the changes, like an addition to the Sunday school building, are not visible. (Courtesy of First Baptist Church of Collingdale; photograph by Frank B. Johnston Jr.)

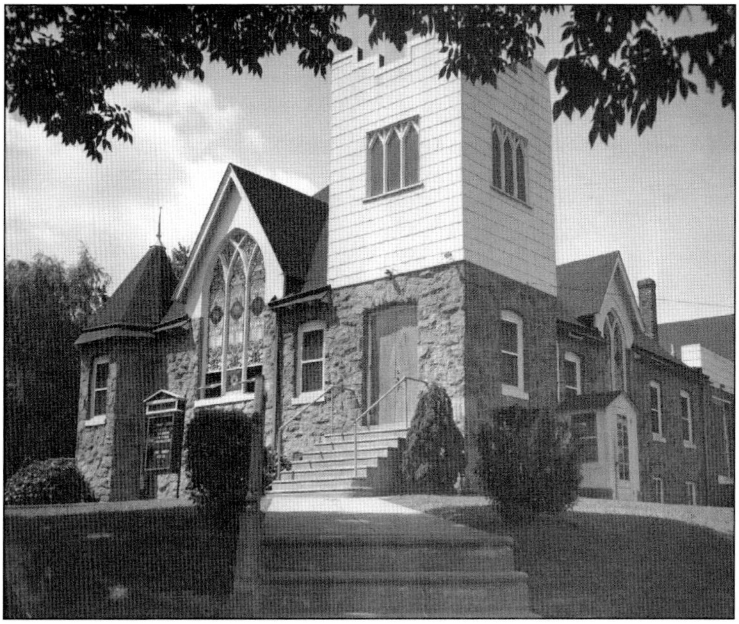

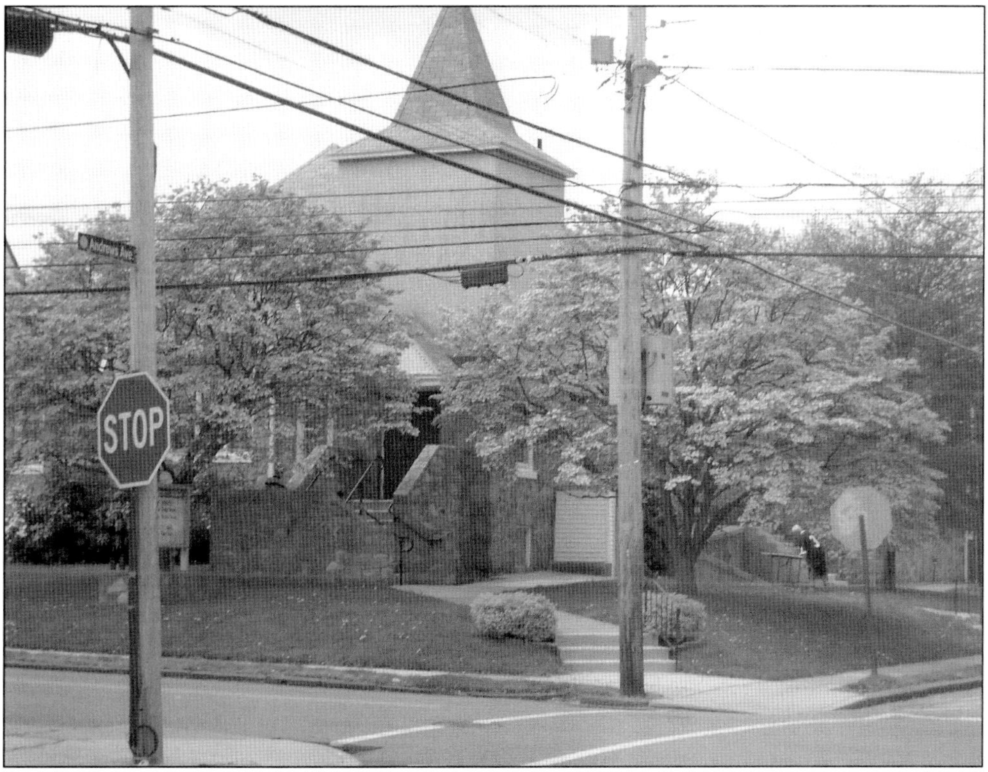

As First Baptist Church of Collingdale celebrates its 125th anniversary in 2012, there is much for the congregation to be proud of and thankful for. Most of the pastors have been active in the community, clean-up days are well attended, and support is given to the grief-stricken. Missions also are a strong component of First Baptist's ministry. In this view, the tower seen in the above image has been modified. (Photograph by Elizabeth MacGuire.)

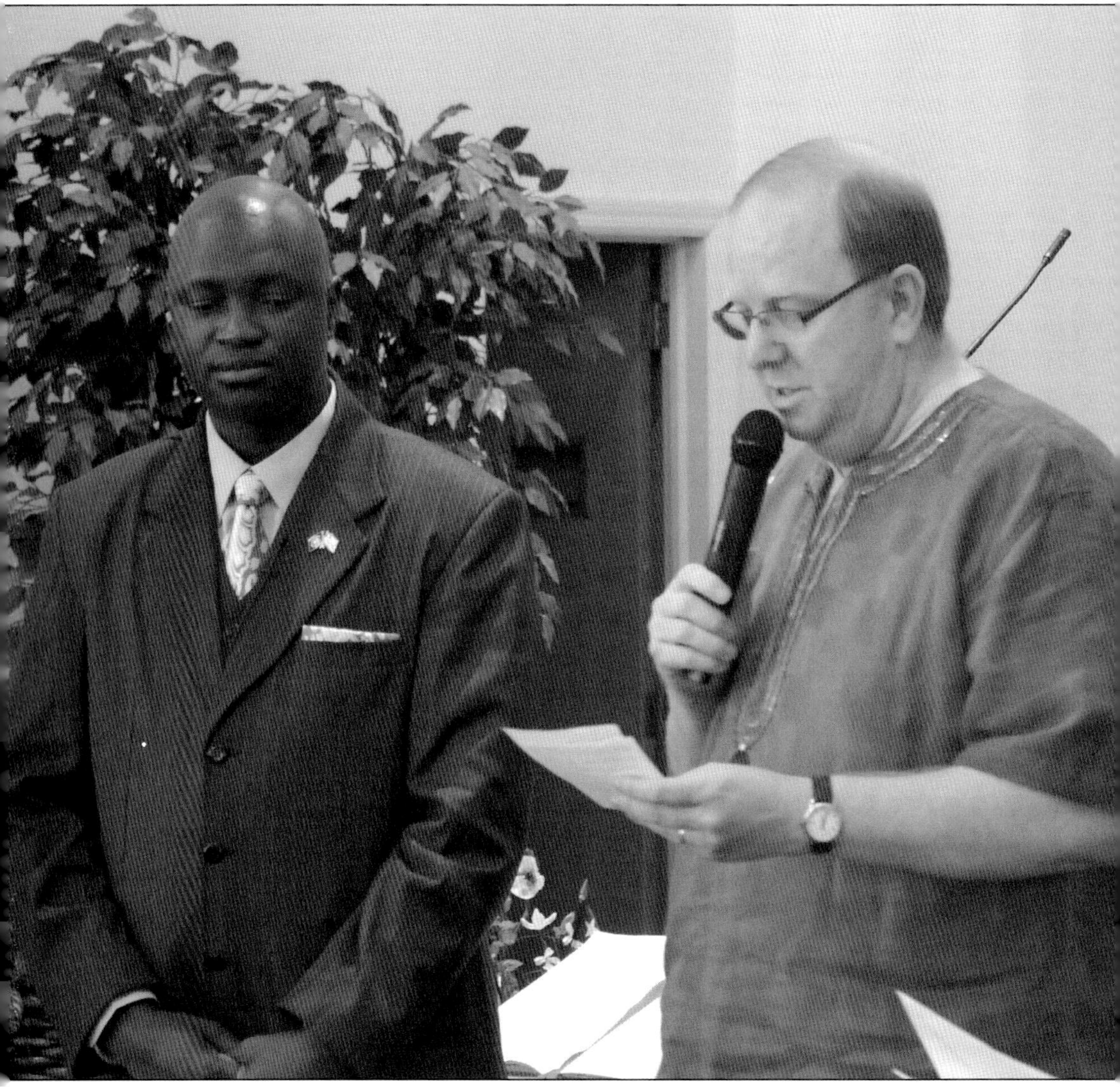

Part of the mission of First Baptist Church of Collingdale included adopting a church in Liberia in 2005. First Baptist's membership became concerned about what was currently happening in Liberia and formed a partnership with Lighthouse Baptist Church there. First Baptist sponsored Pastor Ndordor to receive training and support to return to preach in Liberia. In this picture from March 2012, Pastor John Ndordor (left) receives a certificate from Pastor Perry Messick that makes him an honorary citizen of Collingdale. (Photograph by William Regensburg.)

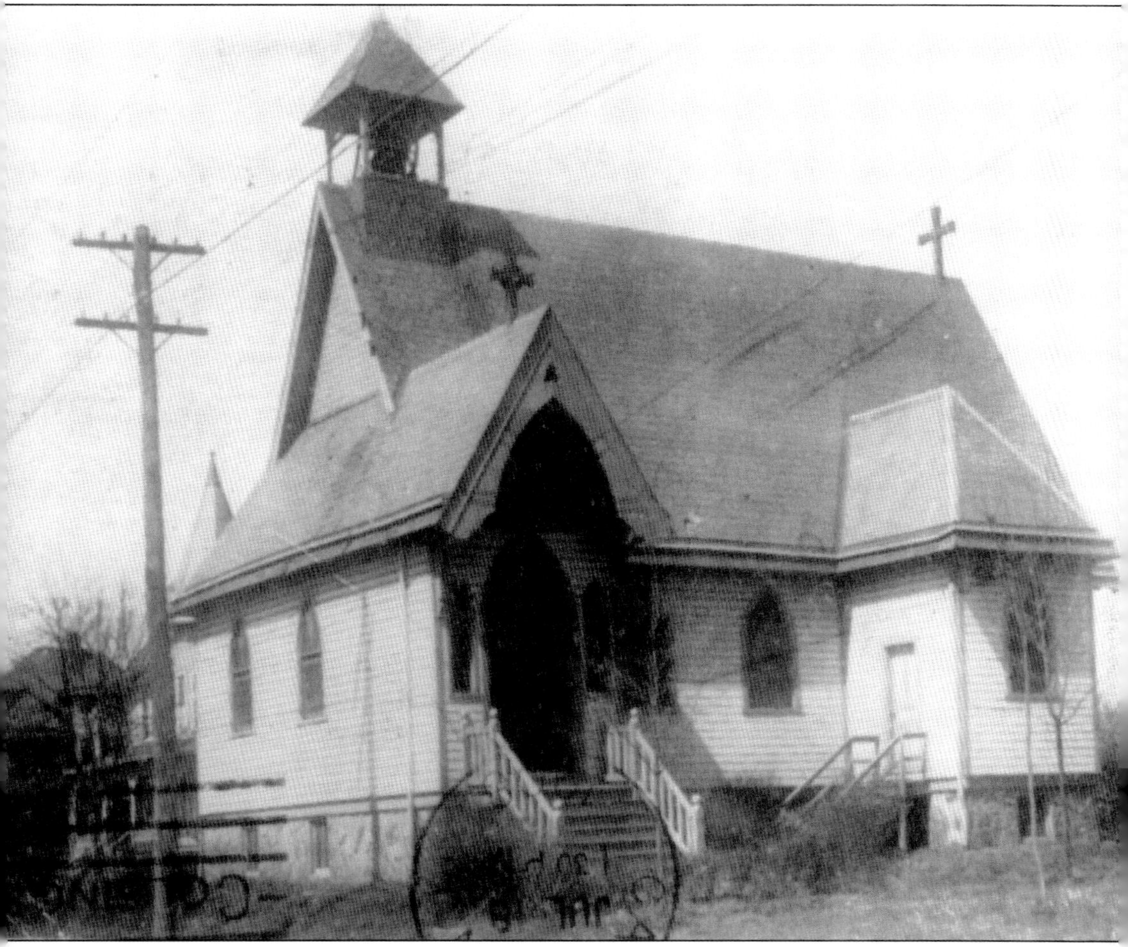

The cornerstone of Trinity Episcopal Church was laid in the spring of 1890, and the church was officially chartered on December 25 of that year. Some sources indicate that the church started in the parlor of George Perkins in January 1888, while others state that Rev. W.F.C. Morsell conducted parlor services in Collingdale in October 1888. (Courtesy of Keith Lockhart.)

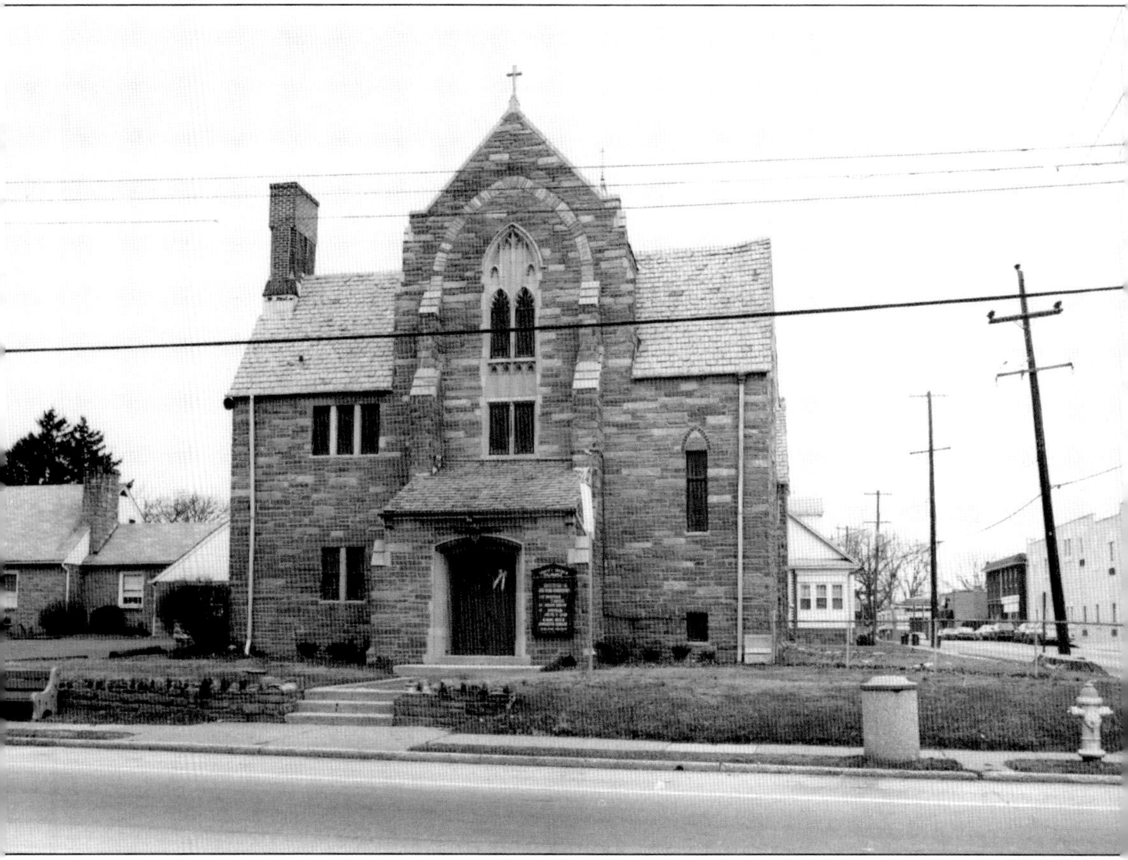

The first kindergarten and nursery schools in the borough were established in Trinity Episcopal Church by Mrs. George Holcomb around 1914 as part of the Children's Guild. A Young People's Fellowship was organized at the same time. In 1922, a Diocesan Drive conducted by Rev. Henry Davis made it possible for the current building to be built. (Courtesy of Keith Lockhart.)

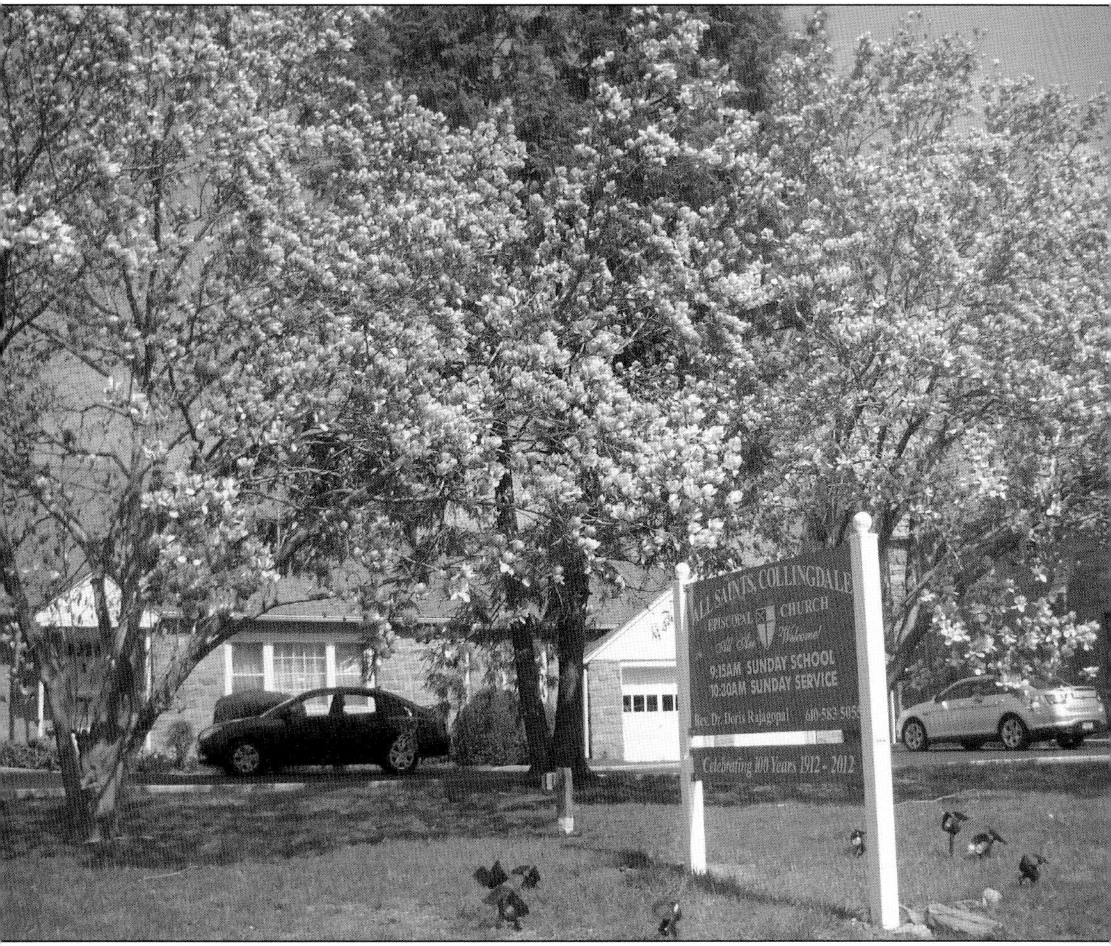

The old Trinity Episcopal rectory was donated to the Women's Club of Collingdale for $1 a year for use as the Collingdale Public Library in 1957. The new rectory, pictured here in April 2011, was home to the vicar and was used as classrooms. Trinity Episcopal Church closed its doors in July 2010 due to financial difficulties and declining attendance. It was reopened as All Saints Episcopal Church, which had a building in Darby that was rapidly deteriorating, on November 21, 2010. (Photograph by Elizabeth MacGuire.)

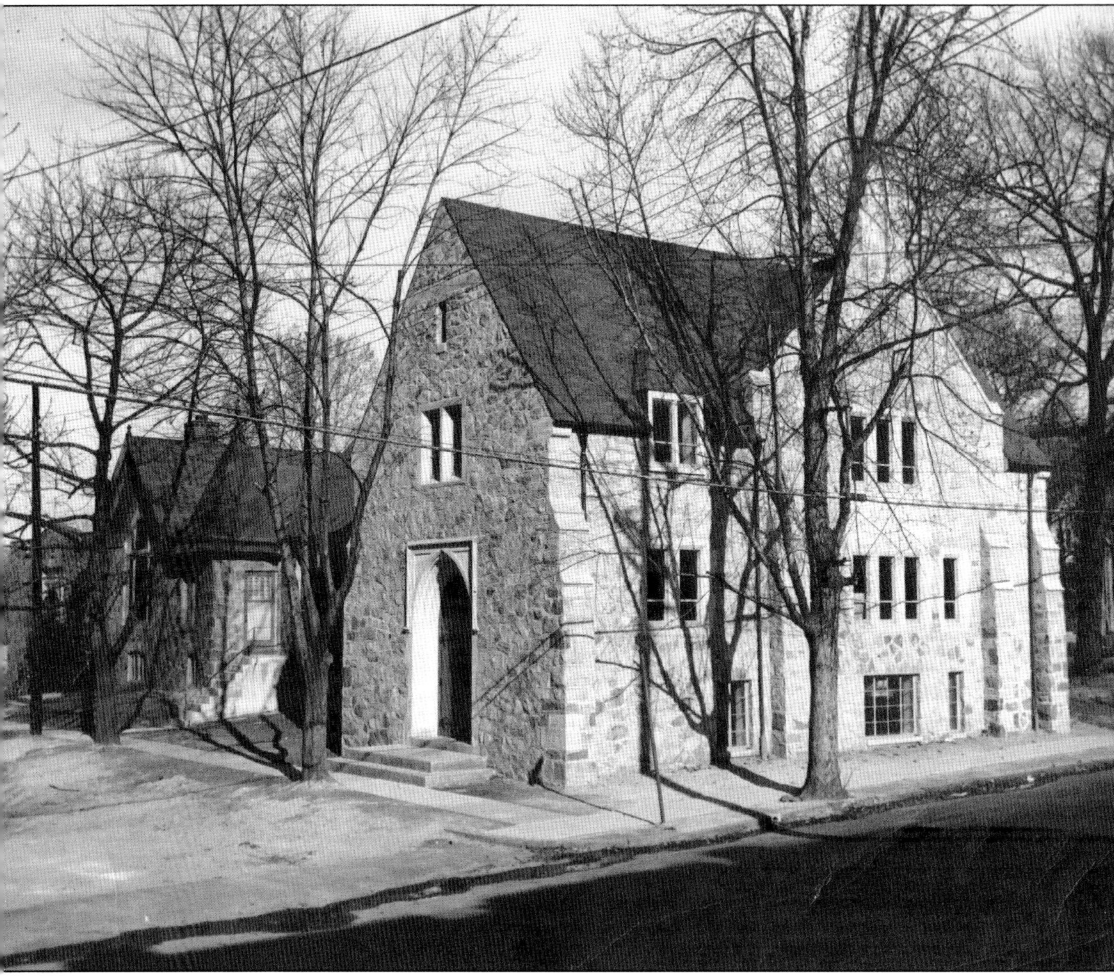

Grace Reformed Episcopal Church was first established in 1894 when members of Trinity Episcopal Church became dissatisfied with added enrichments to the worship proceedings. Services were held at various locations in the borough until a lot was purchased in 1897. The church is pictured after renovations in 1949. (Courtesy of Jim Smith and Rev. Michael Fitzpatrick.)

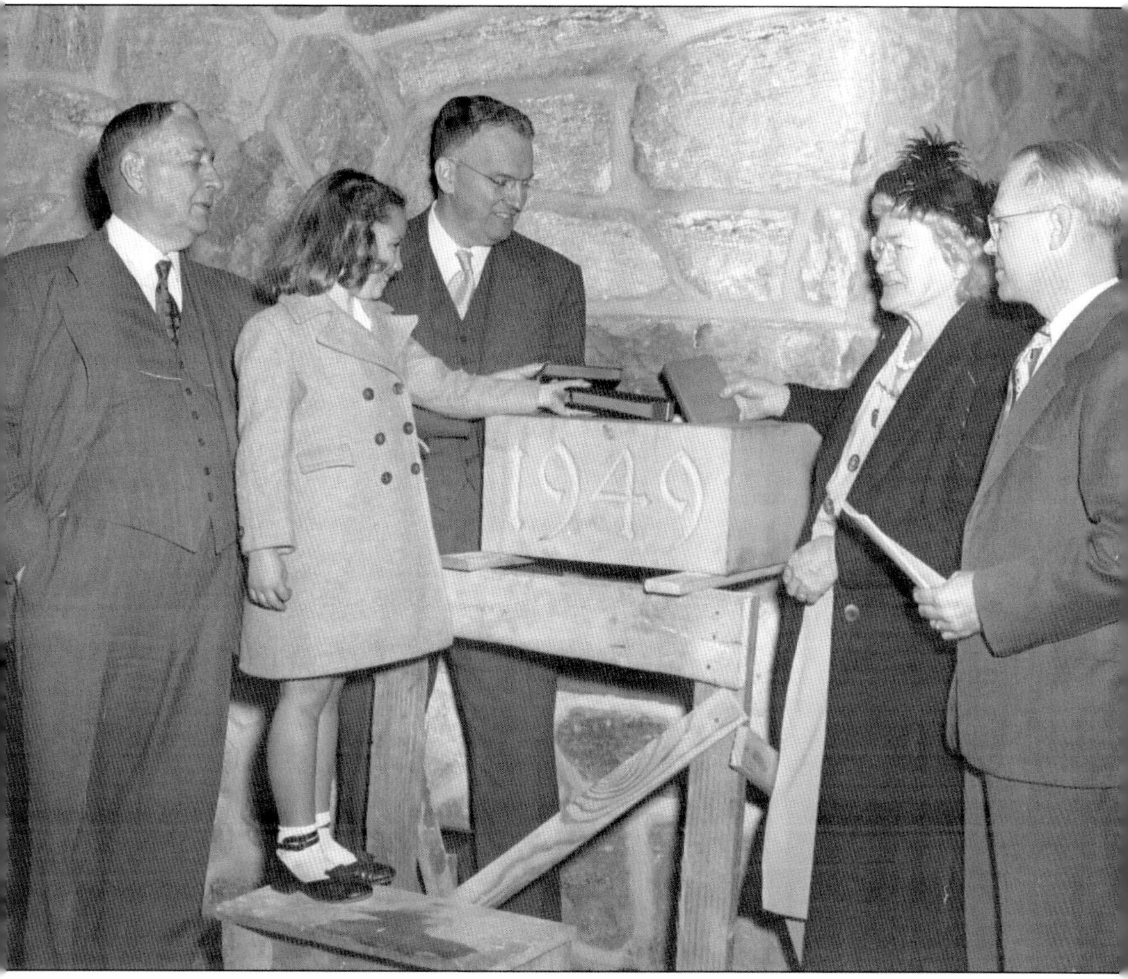

In 1949, Grace Reformed Episcopal Church decided to begin major renovations to its building. A new cornerstone was laid by Norman McCausland, son of William McCausland, one of the cofounders of the church. (Courtesy of Jim Smith and Rev. Michael Fitzpatrick.)

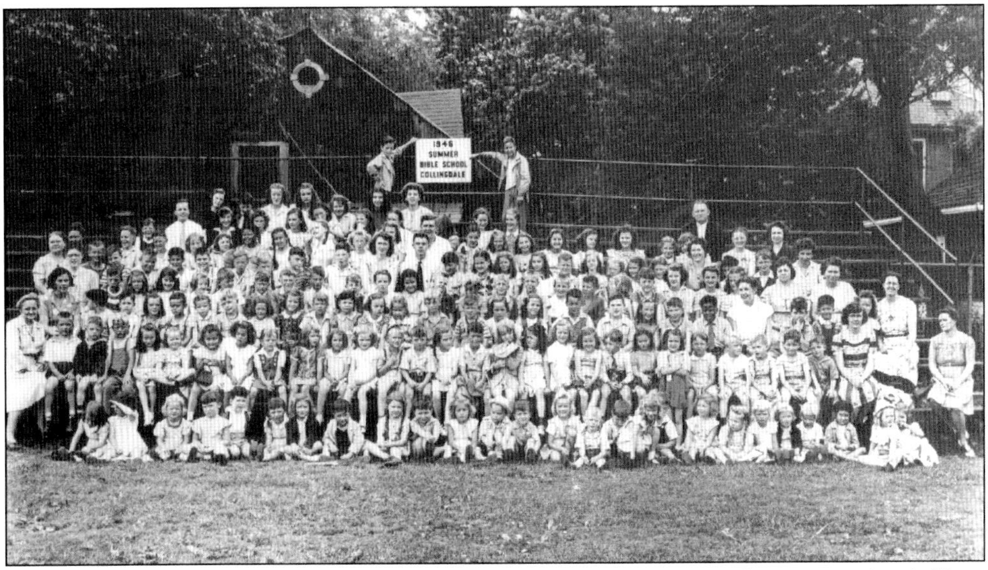

Summer bible school, now known as vacation bible school, was a popular pastime for children in the mid-1940s. Geared mostly toward younger children, it provided a venue for them to have fun and connect with others in a safe environment. Grace Reformed Episcopal Church offered a variety of activities in its summer bible school, which became a blueprint for other churches in the borough to emulate. (Courtesy of Jim Smith and Rev. Michael Fitzpatrick.)

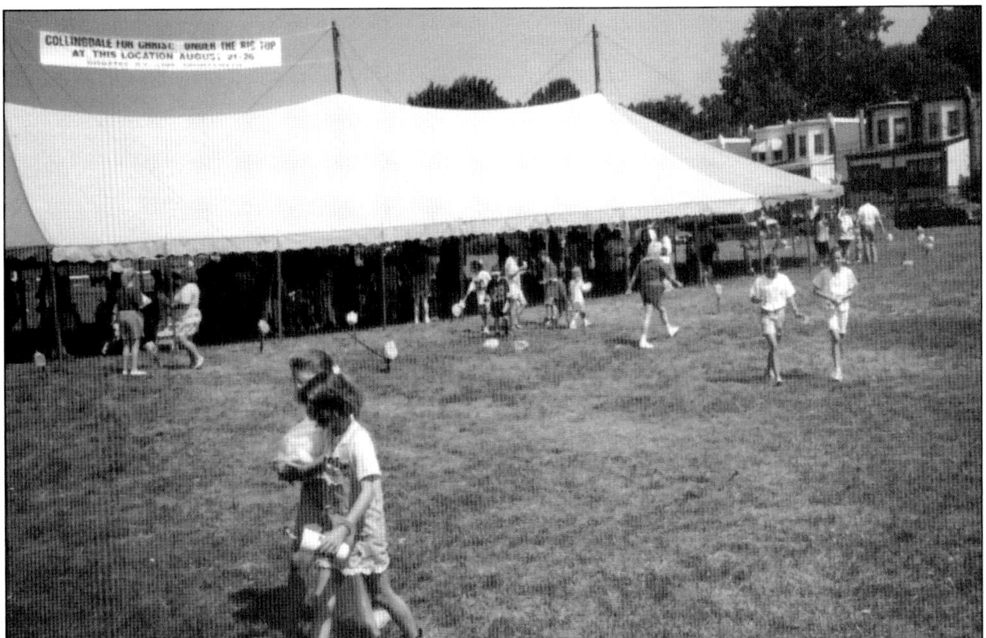

First Baptist Church of Collingdale also holds vacation bible school every summer; Collingdale For Christ, held in August 1995, was one of the most successful. Children crowded under the big top set up in the parking lot across from Collingdale Fire Company No. 2. (Courtesy of First Baptist Church of Collingdale.)

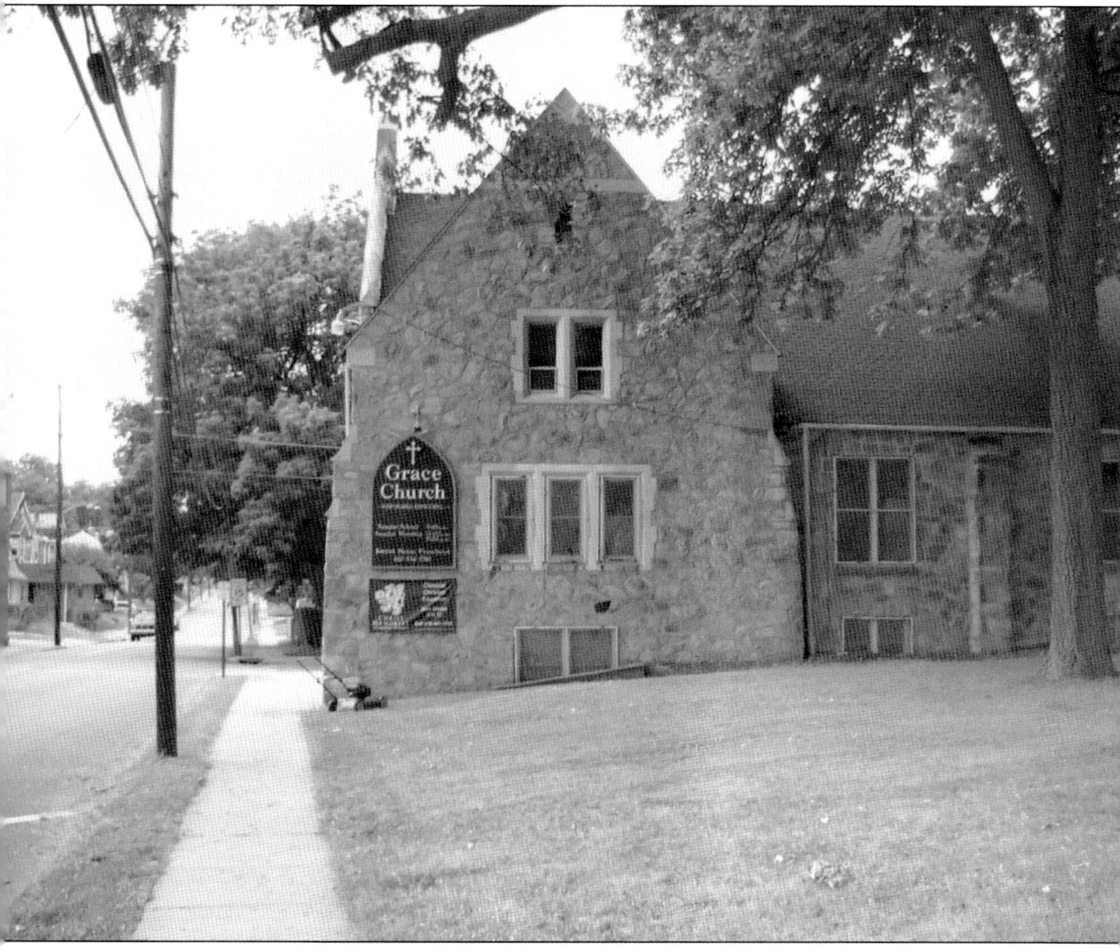

Today, Grace Reformed Episcopal Church shares its building with two schools, The Joyful Noise and Christian Academy. The Joyful Noise is for preschool children, and the Christian Academy enrolls boys in grades eight through twelve. Grace Church, pictured in April 2011, currently works with various charitable organizations, such as the Tree of Life, and helps other churches in crisis. (Photograph by Elizabeth MacGuire.)

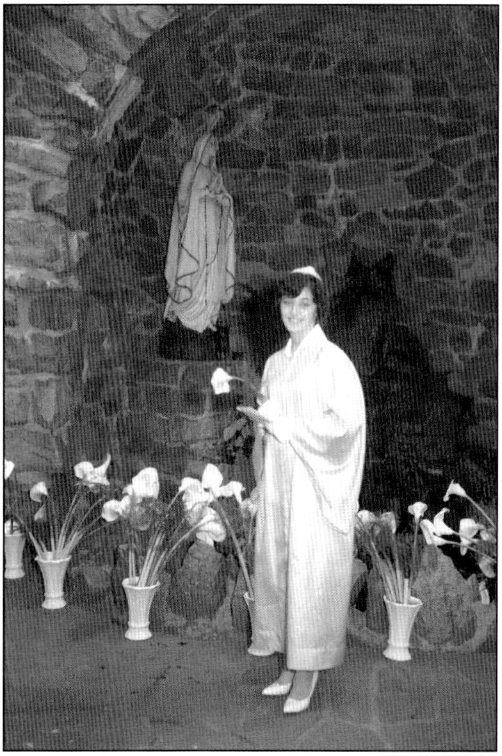

Fr. Otho C. Gromoll, the first pastor of Saint Joseph Church, organized and established the church and school in Collingdale. His tireless devotion to and love for the patron saint Our Lady of Lourdes showed in the pageantry he attached to the ceremonies of holy seasons and holy days. As a sign of his devotion, he commissioned the building of the grotto pictured here and marked his complete conversion from the Episcopal faith. (Courtesy of Donald Bird—Joe Bird collection; photograph by John Harris Studio.)

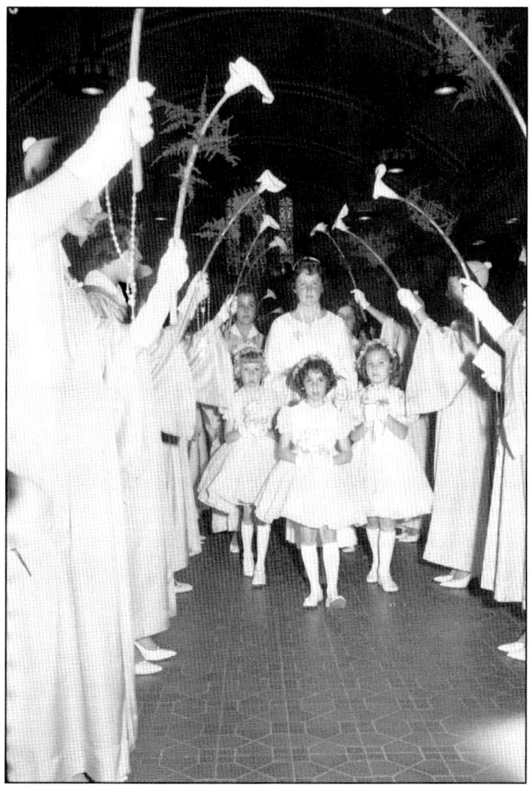

One of the many celebrations of the church, the May procession, took place in the grotto. As part of the ceremony, the girl who ranked at the top of her class crowned Our Lady of Lourdes with spring flowers. She and her court then proceeded inside and walked down the aisle as palm branches waved overhead. Each girl would then be given religious instruction and commissioned to follow the example of Our Lady of Lourdes. (Courtesy of Donald Bird—Joe Bird collection.)

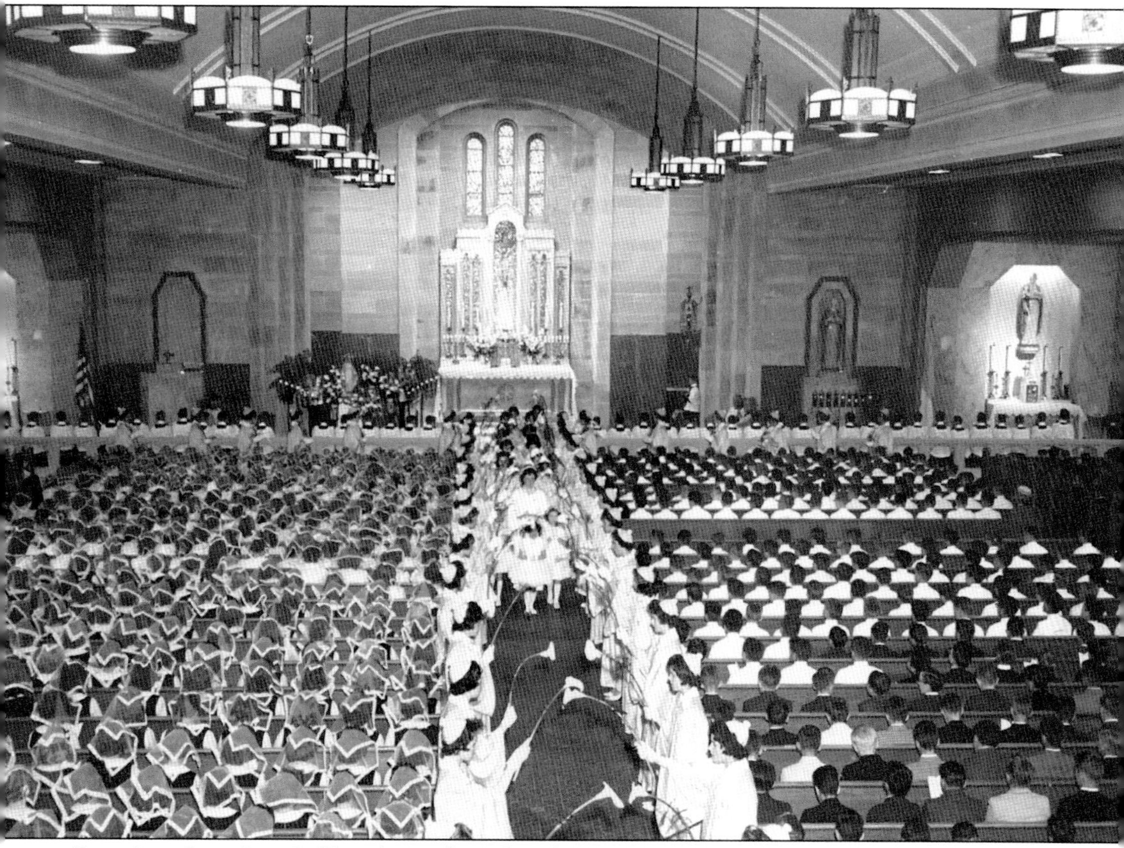

Growth in Saint Joseph Church is reflected in this May 13, 1962, photograph of the annual May procession. During the 1920s and 1930s, the parish grew to the point where two curates were appointed to handle the crowd. Community events such as minstrel shows, and programs such as the Dorcas Society (now part of the St. Vincent DePaul Society), which was formed in the early 1930s, contributed to this growth. (Courtesy of Donald Bird—Joe Bird collection.)

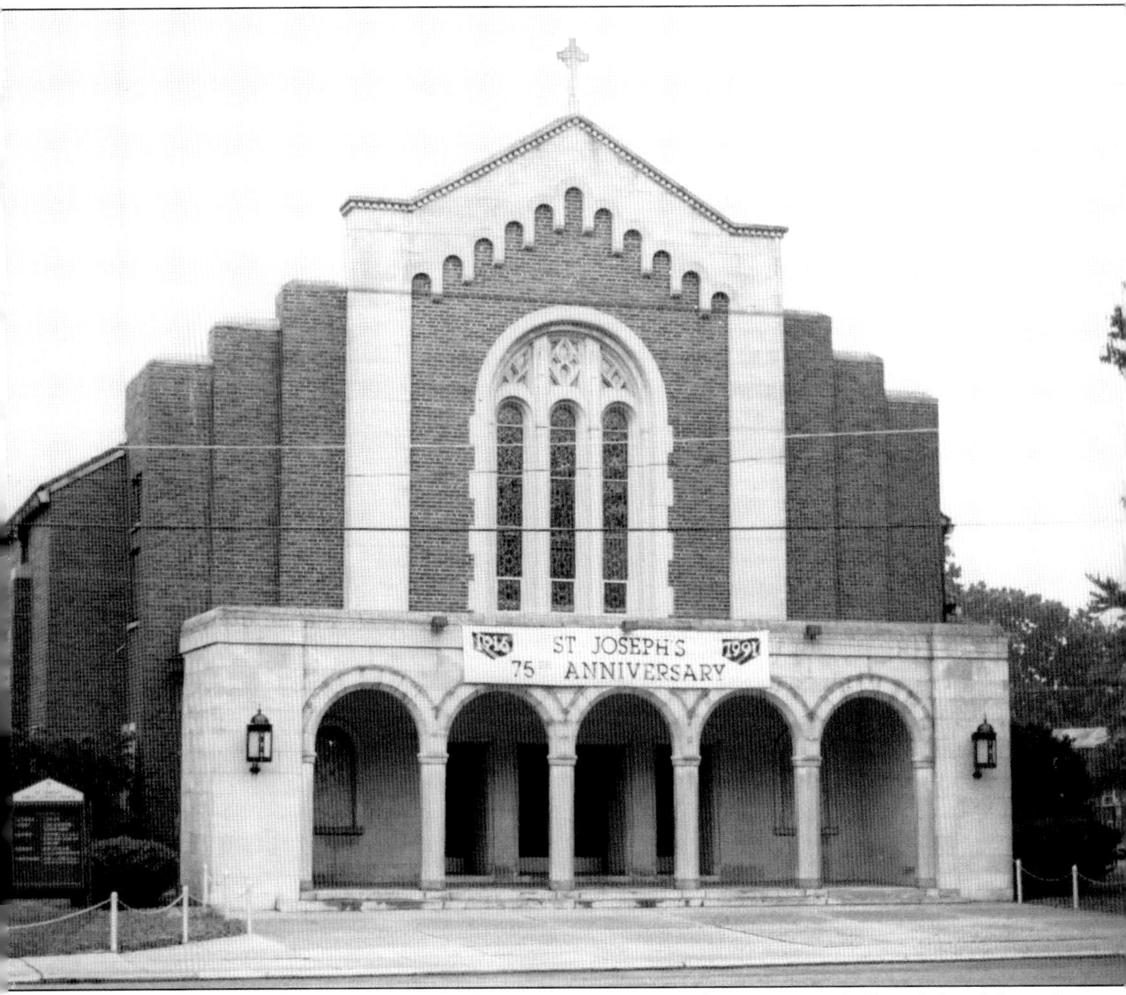

Saint Joseph Church celebrated its 75th anniversary in 1991, the same year Collingdale celebrated its 100th anniversary. It seems appropriate, as members of this parish have been actively involved in the community since the church was first established in December 1916. Many of the outreach programs were inspired by Fr. Otho Gromoll's example and his willingness to serve others. (Courtesy of Keith Lockhart.)

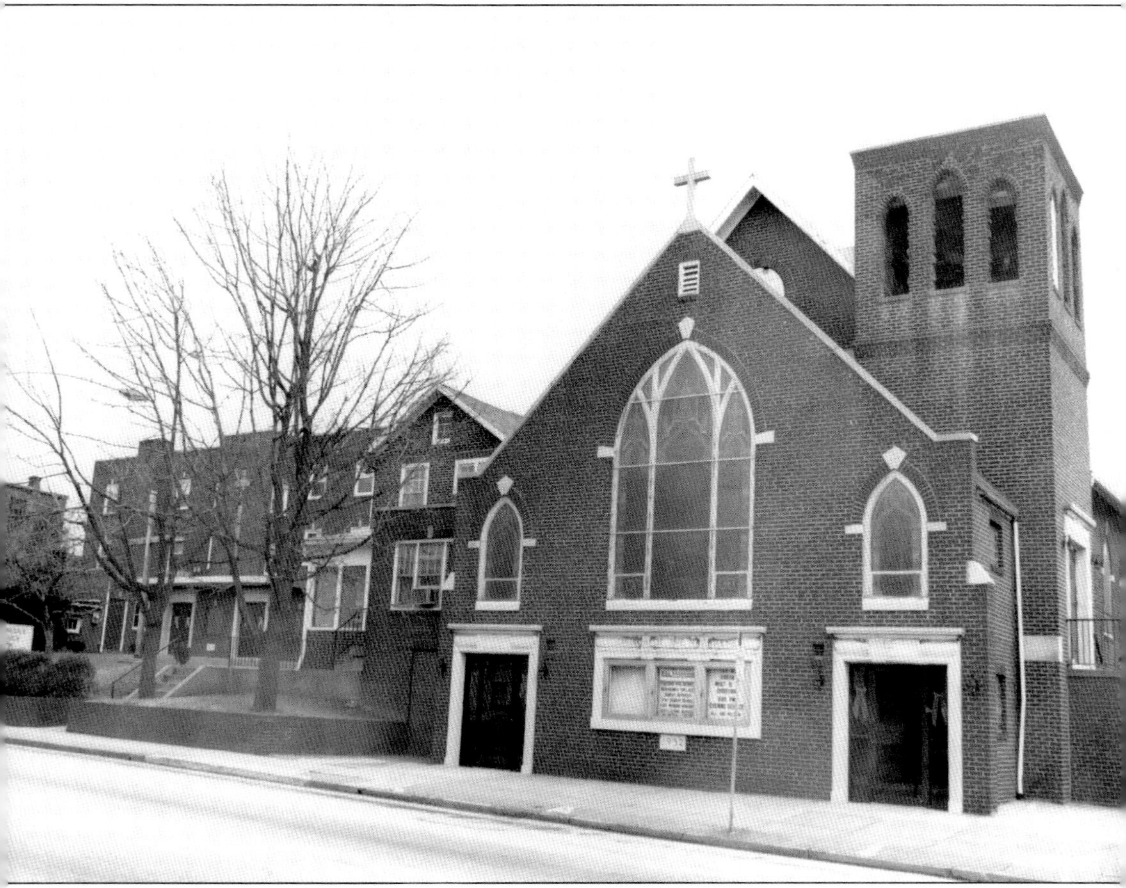

Church of the Nazarene, sometimes called Bethel Church of the Nazarene, was formed under the auspices of the Holiness Christian Association, also known as Heavenly Recruits, in 1906. It became its own entity in 1912, and the congregation worshipped in a frame house on Chester Pike until 1926. Its current location in Collingdale was established with a ground-breaking ceremony on October 18, 1925, and the building was dedicated on January 11, 1926. (Courtesy of Judy Wiedman and Keith Lockhart.)

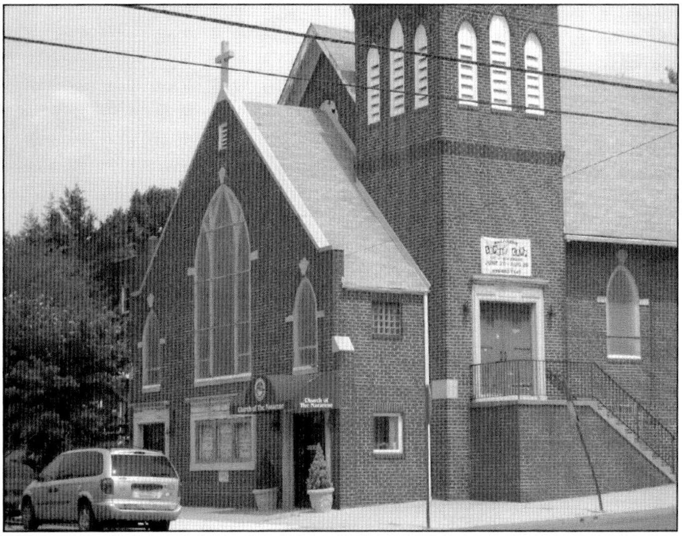

Because it started in Darby, Church of the Nazarene, pictured in May 2011, was often called Darby Pentecostal Church of the Nazarene in its early days. The church was established in Collingdale in April 1926. Additions to the building commenced in 1952, and the main sanctuary was renovated in 1960. Today, the church offers a soup kitchen and a community clothes closet for those in need. (Photograph by Elizabeth MacGuire.)

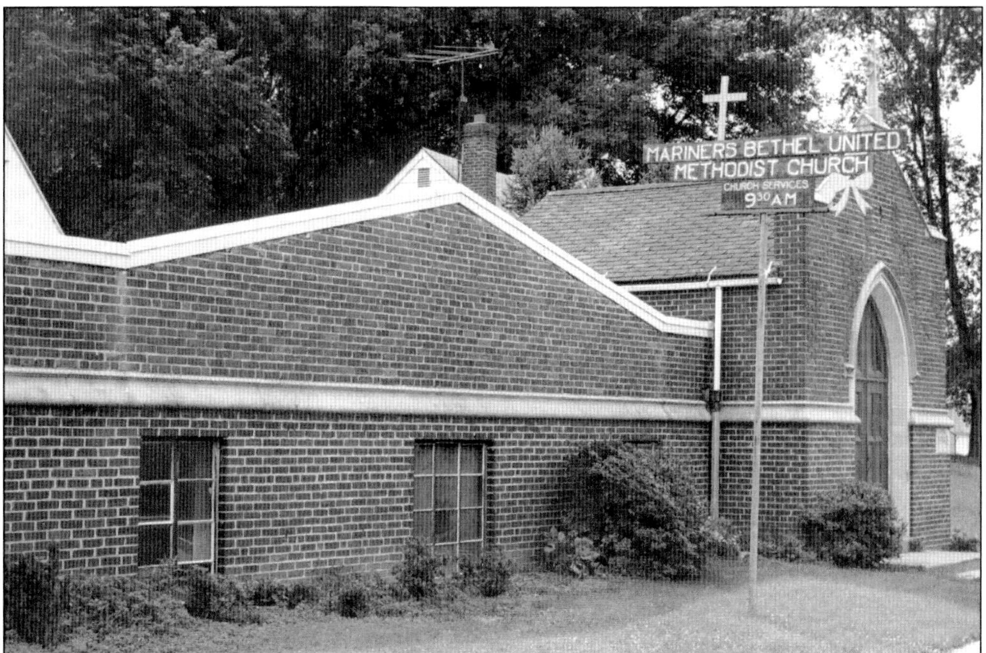

Central Methodist Church of Collingdale, formally organized at the home of James N. Dann in 1923, broke ground at its location on Clifton Avenue on November 2, 1924. In 1948, the church got involved with the Mariners' Bethel Church in Philadelphia, which was running into hard times and decided to sell its church. Proceeds from the sale were given to Central Methodist with the stipulation that the church be renamed Mariners' Bethel. (Courtesy of James Powers.)

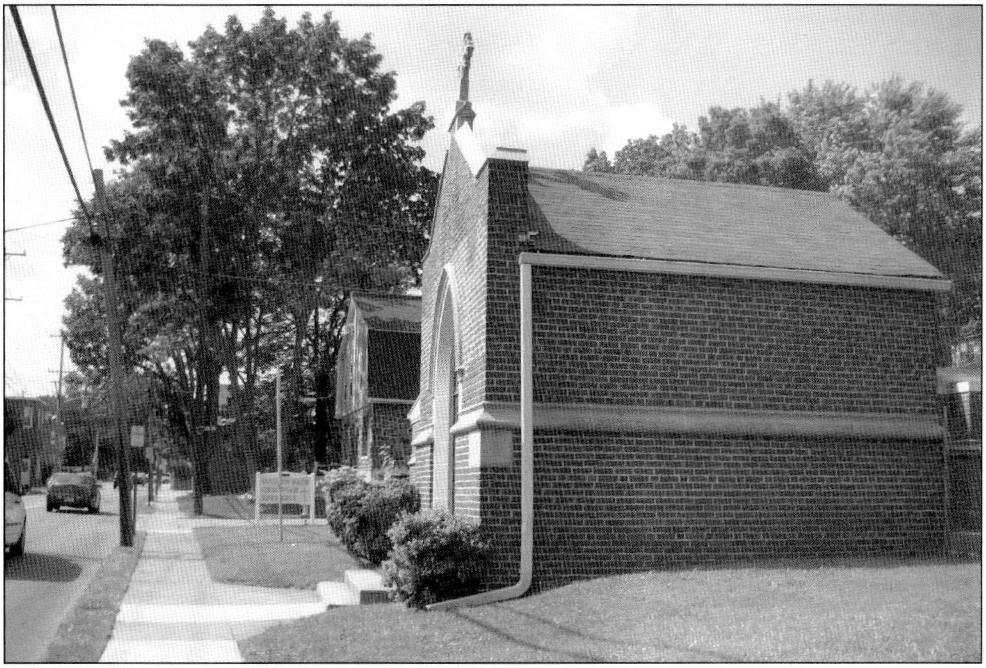

A ground-breaking ceremony was held for Mariners' Bethel church on April 25, 1948, and the cornerstone was laid on November 28, 1948. The first service, held on May 29, 1949, was bittersweet as Dr. John W. Tindall, who was an integral part of raising needed funds for the church, passed away a few weeks earlier. The church served the community until it closed in 2010. Fortunately, the building did not remain idle for long, as Golden Gate Assembly moved there in 2011. It is pictured here in May 2011. (Photograph by Elizabeth MacGuire.)

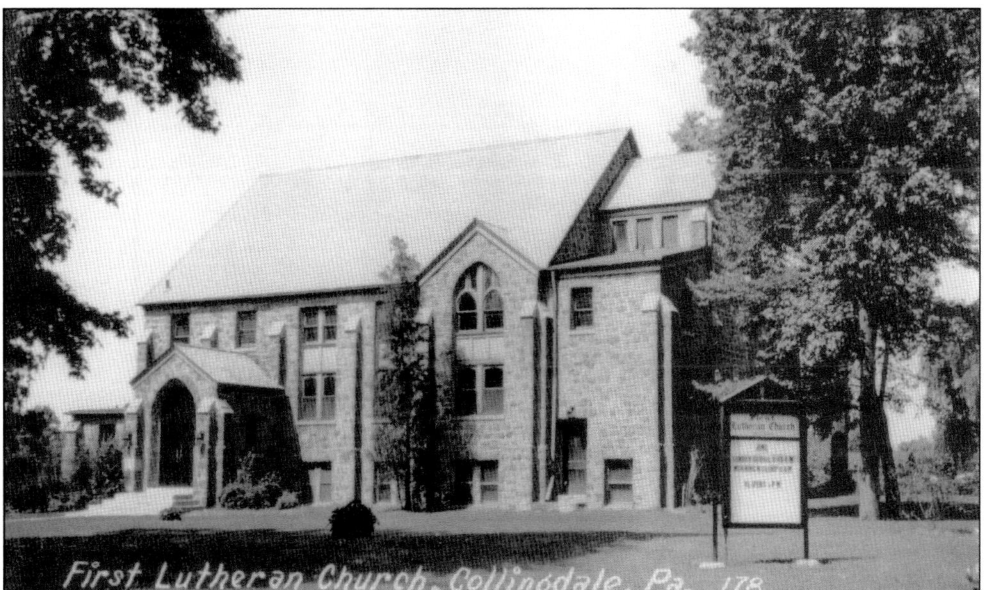

Rev. B.S. Dice was instrumental in starting services at the First Lutheran Church of Collingdale in September 1920. After it was incorporated on May 8, 1923, and dedicated on November 7, 1926, church members actively became involved in the community. (Courtesy of Keith Lockhart.)

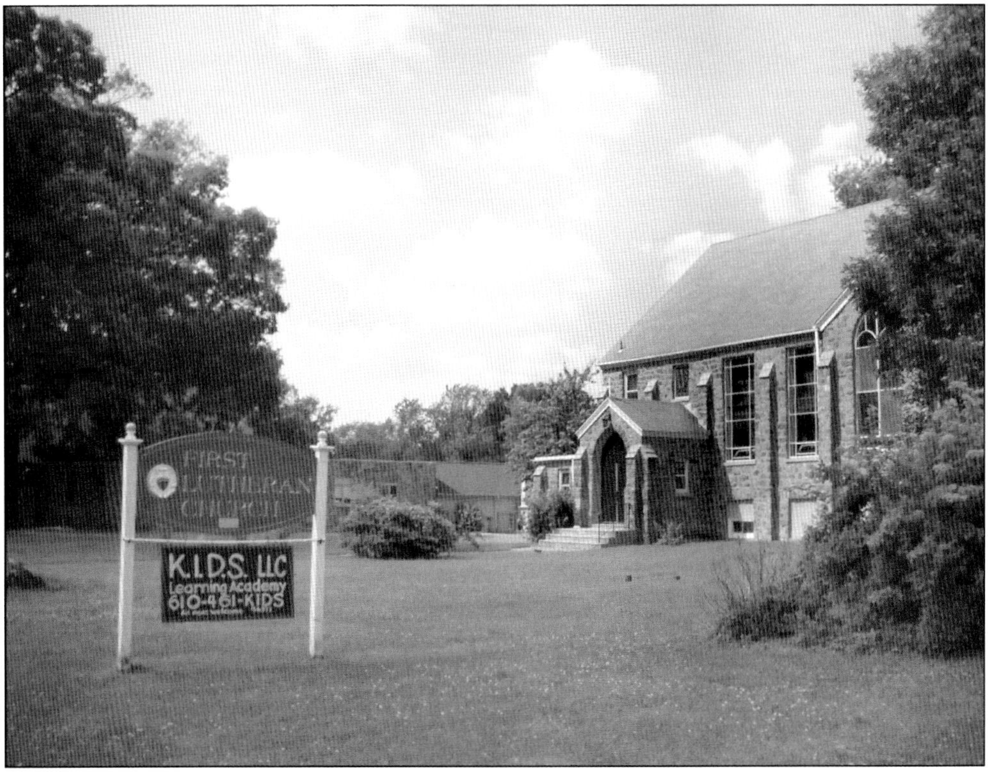

Christian Endeavor, started in 1927, was one of many organizations started by First Lutheran Church of Collingdale. During World War II, the basement served as a headquarters for the war effort in the community. Its primary mission was education, and to this end, the church established a day care center called Kids LLC, which also had after-school programs. Though the church closed on Easter Sunday 2011, the day care center remained open. (Photograph by Elizabeth MacGuire.)

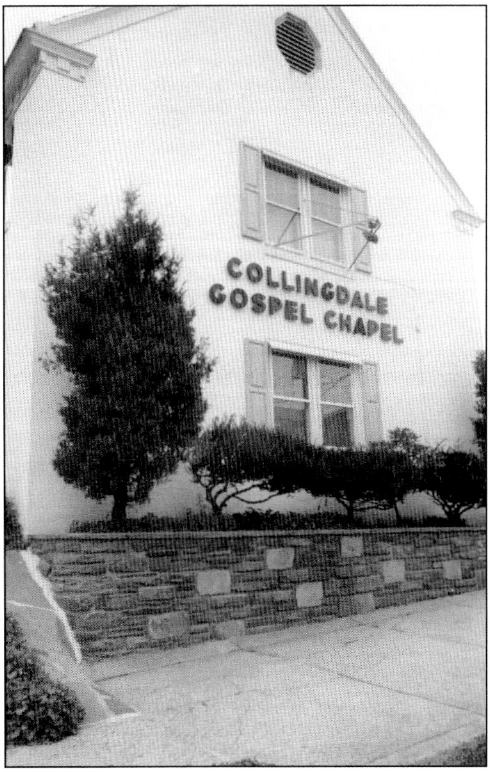

Collingdale Gospel Chapel formed after an Irish evangelist held services in Darby in 1914. No record exists as to where the congregation met at first. The only existing record about the church states that the current location on Hillside Avenue was purchased in 1920 and construction commenced in 1921. The church provided an alternative to the Catholic and Protestant denominations that existed in Collingdale, as its teachings were nondenominational. (Courtesy of James Powers.)

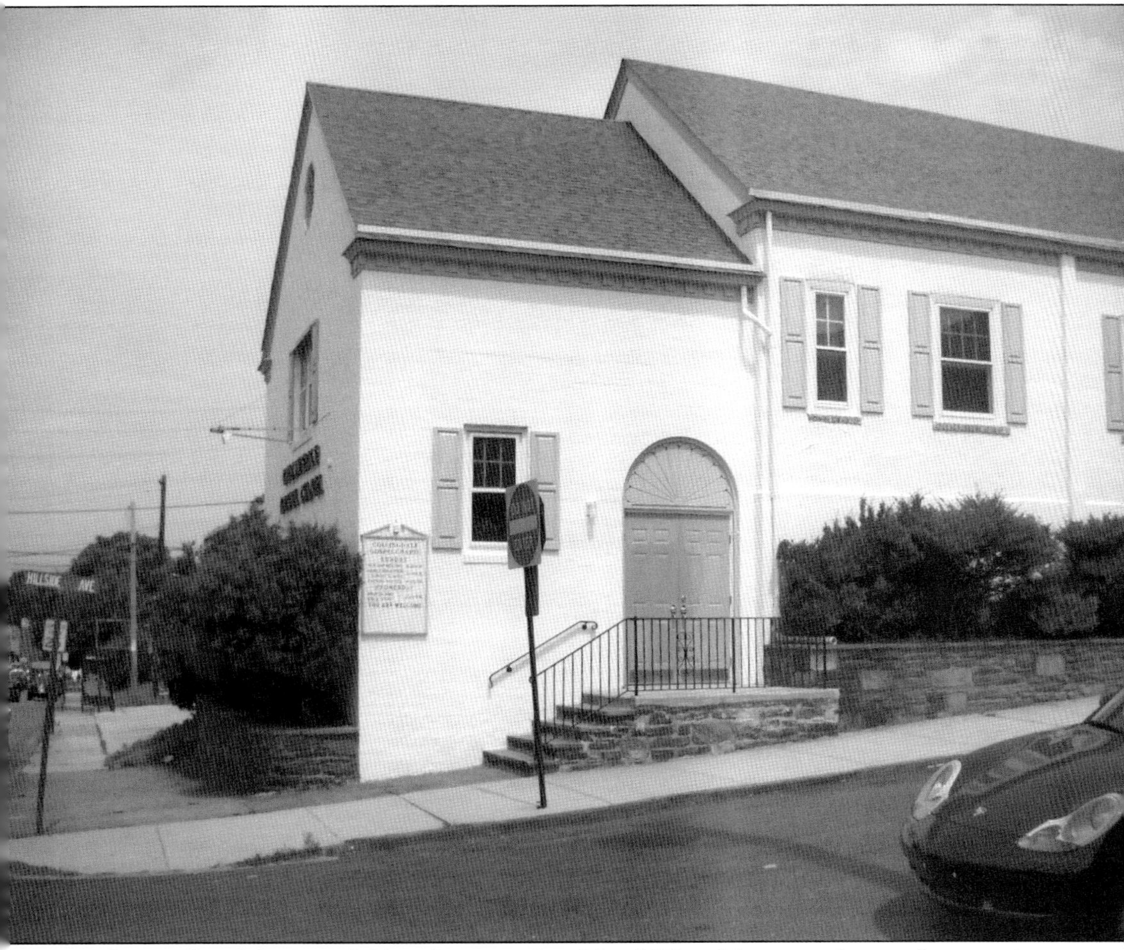

Today, Collingdale Gospel Chapel, pictured in May 2011, celebrates its history by providing various programs for youth and adults. Pioneer Girls is one of the programs Collingdale Gospel sponsored over the years. (Courtesy of Elizabeth MacGuire.)

Bibliography

50th Anniversary of Collingdale Borough. Collingdale, PA: Frank Hansen Printing, 1941.

75th Anniversary of Collingdale Borough. Collingdale, PA: Frank Hansen Printing, 1966.

100th Anniversary of Collingdale Borough. Collingdale, PA: Frank Hansen Printing, 1991.

Bird, Joe. "History and Recollections of Collingdale" *ColHums* Vols. I, II, III, IV: 2006.

Collingdale Fire Co. No. 1 Station 06 100th Anniversary 1906–2006.

St. Joseph's, Celebrating our 75th Anniversary: 1916–1991. Devon, PA: Cooke Publishing Company, 1991.

Wardell, Lindy Constance. *Mount Zion Methodist Meeting Established In 1808*. Darby, PA: Friends of Darby Methodist Meeting Cemetery, 2009.

Wiley, Samuel T. *Biographical and Historical Cyclopedia of Delaware County, Pennsylvania*. Richmond, ID, and New York: Gresham Publishing Company, 1894.

Index